Advances in Experimental Philosophy of Free Will and Responsibility

Advances in Experimental Philosophy

Series Editor:
James Beebe, Professor of Philosophy, University at Buffalo, USA

Editorial Board:
Joshua Knobe, Yale University, USA
Edouard Machery, University of Pittsburgh, USA
Thomas Nadelhoffer, College of Charleston, USA
Eddy Nahmias, Neuroscience Institute at Georgia State University, USA
Jennifer Nagel, University of Toronto, Canada
Joshua Alexander, Siena College, USA

Empirical and experimental philosophy is generating tremendous excitement, producing unexpected results that are challenging traditional philosophical methods. *Advances in Experimental Philosophy* responds to this trend, bringing together some of the most exciting voices in the field to understand the approach and measure its impact in contemporary philosophy. The result is a series that captures past and present developments and anticipates future research directions.

To provide in-depth examinations, each volume links experimental philosophy to a key philosophical area. They provide historical overviews alongside case studies, reviews of current problems and discussions of new directions. For upper-level undergraduates, postgraduates and professionals actively pursuing research in experimental philosophy these are essential resources.

Titles in the series include:
Advances in Experimental Epistemology, edited by James R. Beebe
Advances in Experimental Moral Psychology, edited by Hagop Sarkissian and Jennifer Cole Wright
Advances in Experimental Philosophy and Philosophical Methodology, edited by Jennifer Nado

Advances in Experimental Philosophy of Aesthetics, edited by Florian Cova and Sébastien Réhault

Advances in Experimental Philosophy of Language, edited by Jussi Haukioja

Advances in Experimental Philosophy of Logic and Mathematics, edited by Andrew Aberdein and Matthew Inglis

Advances in Experimental Philosophy of Mind, edited by Justin Sytsma

Advances in Religion, Cognitive Science, and Experimental Philosophy, edited by Helen De Cruz and Ryan Nichols

Experimental Metaphysics, edited by David Rose

Methodological Advances in Experimental Philosophy, edited by Eugen Fischer and Mark Curtis

Advances in Experimental Philosophy of Free Will and Responsibility, edited by Thomas Nadelhoffer and Andrew Monroe

Advances in Experimental Philosophy of Free Will and Responsibility

Edited by
Thomas Nadelhoffer and Andrew Monroe

BLOOMSBURY ACADEMIC
LONDON • NEW YORK • OXFORD • NEW DELHI • SYDNEY

BLOOMSBURY ACADEMIC
Bloomsbury Publishing Plc
50 Bedford Square, London, WC1B 3DP, UK
1385 Broadway, New York, NY 10018, USA
29 Earlsfort Terrace, Dublin 2, Ireland

BLOOMSBURY, BLOOMSBURY ACADEMIC and the Diana logo are trademarks of
Bloomsbury Publishing Plc

First published in Great Britain 2022
This paperback edition published 2023

Copyright © Thomas Nadelhoffer, Andrew Monroe and Contributors, 2022

Thomas Nadelhoffer and Andrew Monroe have asserted their right under the Copyright,
Designs and Patents Act, 1988, to be identified as Editors of this work.

Series design by Catherine Wood
Cover image © Dieter Leistner / Gallerystock

All rights reserved. No part of this publication may be reproduced or transmitted
in any form or by any means, electronic or mechanical, including photocopying,
recording, or any information storage or retrieval system, without
prior permission in writing from the publishers.

Bloomsbury Publishing Plc does not have any control over, or responsibility for, any
third-party websites referred to or in this book. All internet addresses given in this
book were correct at the time of going to press. The author and publisher regret
any inconvenience caused if addresses have changed or sites have ceased
to exist, but can accept no responsibility for any such changes.

A catalogue record for this book is available from the British Library.

A catalog record for this book is available from the Library of Congress.

ISBN: HB: 978-1-3501-8808-2
PB: 978-1-3501-8812-9
ePDF: 978-1-3501-8809-9
eBook: 978-1-3501-8810-5

Series: Advances in Experimental Philosophy

Typeset by Integra Software Services Pvt. Ltd.

To find out more about our authors and books visit www.bloomsbury.com
and sign up for our newsletters.

Contents

List of Figures and Tables	viii
Notes on Contributors	xi

	Experimental Philosophy of Free Will and Moral Responsibility: An Introduction *Thomas Nadelhoffer and Andrew Monroe*	1
1	Belief in Free Will Relates to Attributions of Intentionality and Judgments of Responsibility *Oliver Genschow and Marcel Brass*	13
2	The Blame Efficiency Hypothesis: An Evolutionary Framework to Resolve Rationalist and Intuitionist Theories of Moral Condemnation *Cory J Clark*	27
3	Mental State Control and Responsibility *Corey Cusimano and Geoffrey P. Goodwin*	45
4	"It Was All a Cruel Angel's Thesis from the Start": Folk Intuitions about Zygote Cases Do Not Support the Zygote Argument *Florian Cova*	65
5	Moral Responsibility without (Some Kinds of) Freedom *Walter Sinnott-Armstrong*	91
6	Folk Jurisprudence and Judgments about Free Will and Responsibility *Thomas Nadelhoffer and Andrew Monroe*	115
7	Moral Responsibility, Manipulation, and Experimental Philosophy *Alfred R. Mele*	131
8	Direct and Derivative Moral Responsibility: An Overlooked Distinction in Experimental Philosophy *Pascale Willemsen*	143
9	Victim Omissions: How Doing Nothing Affects Judgments of Cause and Blame *Laura Niemi and Paul Henne*	167
10	Free Will and Skilled Decision Theory *Adam Feltz, Braden Tanner, Gwen Hoang, Jenna Holt and Asif Muhammad*	185

Index	203

List of Figures and Tables

Figures

3.1 Mean attributions of blameworthiness for immoral mental states (Cusimano & Goodwin, 2019, Study 4; error bars represent standard errors). (A) Attributions of blameworthiness across four kinds of immoral attitudes, averaged over all mental states. (B) Attributions of blameworthiness in the "dying mother" scenario separated by mental state type. Examples of bad attitudes are in the right-most column   52

3.2 Attributions of control for mundane involuntary behaviors (e.g., sneezing), mental states (light gray bars), and prototypical voluntary behaviors (e.g., speaking)   55

3.3 The relationship between judgments of control, blameworthiness, and responsibility. (A) The relationship between control and blameworthiness in Cusimano and Goodwin (2019) Study 4. See Figure 1 for average control ratings. (B) The relationship between control and responsibility ratings in Cusimano and Goodwin (2019) Study 1, based on average control judgments for emotions, desires, beliefs, and evaluations. See Figure 2 for average control ratings for these mental states   57

4.1 Deep Self scores as mediators of the effect of manipulation (Manipulation vs. Control and Modified vs. Control) in Study 1   79

4.2 Deep Self scores as mediators of the effect of manipulation (Manipulation vs. Normal) in follow-up to Study 2   85

4.3 Boxplots of Aggregate Responsibility Scores (ARS) in function of CONDITION and OUTCOME VALENCE for all three studies   88

8.1 Participant's mean agreement with ability and blame questions in both conditions and vignettes. Error bars indicate 95% confidence intervals   153

8.2 Percentages of people indicating that the agents were to blame although they had no control or because they had control in the Original condition   155

8.3 Participants' mean agreement with ability and moral responsibility questions in both conditions and vignettes. Error bars indicate 95% confidence intervals   156

8.4 Percentages of people indicating that the agents were to blame although they had no control or because they had control in the Original condition   157

8.5 Participants' mean agreement with ability and moral responsibility questions in all three conditions. Error bars indicate 95% confidence intervals 160
9.1 Mean agreement with the causal *(A)* and blame *(B)* statements in Experiment 1. Error bars indicate 95 percent confidence intervals. Light grey points represent individual participant responses evenly jittered 175
9.2 Mean agreement with the causal *(A)* and blame *(B)* statements in Experiment 2. Error bars indicate 95 percent confidence intervals. Light grey points represent individual participant responses evenly jittered 177
9.3 Mean agreement with the causal *(A)* and blame *(B)* statements in Experiment 3. Error bars indicate 95 percent confidence intervals. Light grey points represent individual participant responses evenly jittered 178
9.4 Mean agreement with the causal *(A)* and blame *(B)* statements in Experiment 4. Error bars indicate 95 percent confidence intervals. Red diamonds represent means for each vignette. Light grey points represent individual participant responses evenly jittered 180
10.1 The Framework for Skilled Decision Making, taken from Cokely et al. (2018) 188
10.2 The hypothesized model for the understanding components of skilled decisions about free will 191
10.3 Path model representing the paths for the two groups. The first value represents the concrete standardized estimates, and the second value represents the abstract standardized estimate. $^\wedge p <.1$, $^{**} p <.01$ 195

Tables

4.1 Vignettes used by Sripada (2012) 68
4.2 Mean, Standard Deviation, and % of answers above the midpoint (= 0) for each condition in Pilot Study. Stars(*) present the results of Welch t-tests comparing the two cases (Modified, and Control) for each variable and each outcome valence. Interaction between Outcome Valence and Case was significant for: ARS, Resp, Blame/Praise, Desert, and Throughpass; but not significant for: Free Will, Deep Self, Bypass, and Control 73
4.3 Three different cases used in Study 1 (Bad Outcome version) 74
4.4 Mean, Standard Deviation and % of answers above the midpoint (= 0) for each condition in Study 1. Superscripts present the results of Tukey tests comparing the three cases (Manipulation, Indeterministic, and

Control) for each variable and each outcome valence. When superscripts are present, two conditions that do not share a common letter in superscript significantly differ from each other. When no superscript is present, this means that there was no difference between conditions. Interaction between Outcome Valence and Condition was significant for: ARS, Blame/Praise, and Desert; but not significant for: Resp., Free Will, Deep Self, Bypass, Control, and Throughpass 77

4.5 Inter-correlations between variables in Study 1 78

4.6 Mean and Standard Deviation for each condition in Study 2. Superscripts present the results of Tukey tests comparing the four cases for each variable and each outcome valence. When superscripts are present, two conditions that do not share a common letter in superscript significantly differ from each other. When no superscript is present, this means that there was no difference between conditions. There was no significant interaction effect 82

4.7 Inter-correlations between variables in Study 2 82

4.8 The two *Normal* cases used in Study 2 to collect additional data 83

4.9 Mean and Standard Deviation for each condition in follow-up to Study 2. Stars(*) present the results of Welch t-tests comparing the two cases (Manipulation and Normal) for each variable and each outcome valence 84

5.1 Responses to Q1 and Q3 about Bill in AS in Hannikainen et al. (2019) 95

5.2 Number (percentage) of affirmative answers to questions on each row 106

5.3 Number (percentage) of the participants in the second survey who initially said that the agent acted freely who later agreed with the statement on that row 107

7.1 Moral Responsibility and Desert Results 136

8.1 Modified vignettes used in the experiment. Underlined sections represent additions made to the original vignettes 151

9.1 Burglary vignette used in Experiment 1 and the dependent variables 173

10.1 Correlations for Comprehension, Bypassing, Free Will, and Numeracy separated by condition. Note: ^ $p<.1$, ** $p<.01$ 194

Notes on Contributors

Chapter 1:
Oliver Genschow is Junior Professor of Social Psychology and Social Cognition at the University of Cologne (Germany).

Marcel Brass holds an Einstein Strategic Professorship at Humboldt University of Berlin and a professorship at Ghent University.

Chapter 2:
Cory Clark is the Director of the Adversarial Collaboration Project at the University of Pennsylvania and a visiting scholar in the Psychology Department.

Chapter 3:
Corey Cusimano is a postdoctoral research associate at the University Center for Human Values at Princeton University.

Geoff Goodwin is Associate Professor in the Department of Psychology at the University of Pennsylvania.

Chapter 4:
Florian Cova is Assistant Professor in the Department of Philosophy at the University of Geneva.

Chapter 5:
Walter Sinnott-Armstrong is Chauncey Stillman Professor of Practical Ethics in the Department of Philosophy and the Kenan Institute for Ethics at Duke University.

Chapter 6:
Thomas Nadelhoffer is Associate Professor in the Department of Philosophy at the College of Charleston.

Andrew Monroe is a Senior Project Manager at Ivy Research Council (IRC) studying human decision-making. Prior to joining IRC, Dr. Monroe was Associate Professor in the Department of Psychology at Appalachian State University.

Chapter 7:
Alfred R. Mele is the William H. and Lucyle T. Werkmeister Professor of Philosophy at Florida State University.

Chapter 8:
Pascale Willemsen is a postdoctoral researcher at the University of Zurich.

Chapter 9:

Laura Niemi is Assistant Professor in the Department of Psychology in the Charles H. Dyson School of Applied Economics and Management in the SC Johnson College of Business at Cornell University.

Paul Henne is Assistant Professor in the Department of Philosophy at Lake Forest College.

Chapter 10:

Adam Feltz is Associate Professor in the Psychology Department at the University of Oklahoma and the Center for Applied Social Research.

Uyen Hoang is a graduate student in psychology at the University of Oklahoma.

Braden Tanner is a graduate student in psychology at the University of Oklahoma.

Jenna Holt is a graduate student in psychology at the University of Oklahoma.

Asif Muhammad is a graduate student in psychology at the University of Oklahoma.

Experimental Philosophy of Free Will and Moral Responsibility: An Introduction

Thomas Nadelhoffer and Andrew Monroe

There is a storied history in philosophy of looking to science to shed light on philosophical problems. Those working in experimental philosophy take this interdisciplinary approach one step further. Rather than merely appealing to the data collected by scientists, experimental philosophers also actively take part in the collection and analysis of data and then try to show that their findings are philosophically probative. One need not be a professional philosopher to be an experimental philosopher—as evidenced by the work of many of the esteemed contributors to this volume who are professional psychologists.[1] One need only play a hand both in running the studies and in using the findings to contribute to a philosophical debate. In this way, experimental philosophy has helpfully blurred the line between philosophy and science.[2]

The work at these interdisciplinary cross-roads has been both fruitful and illuminating. Since the beginning of the twenty-first century, we have seen an explosion of interest in this kind of experimental philosophical work. However, we believe that the earliest research in experimental philosophy—at least as we have construed it here—was done by F. C. Sharp and M. C. Otto in the early twentieth century (1910a; 1910b). We cite Sharp and Otto here both because their research has unfortunately been largely forgotten and also because they explore some of the central themes discussed in this volume. Their goal was to understand people's "popular attitudes" and the "moral judgments of common sense" in the context of legal punishment. More specifically, Sharp and Otto wanted to see whether most people support retributivism (i.e., the view that morally deserving offenders ought to be proportionately punished even if no other benefits will come from the punishment) and/or deterrence (i.e., the view that offenders ought to be punished only when doing so is likely to deter other would-be offenders). In this way, Sharp and Otto were explicitly trying to contribute to a philosophical debate using empirical methods.

Anticipating the kind of research commonly done a century later by experimental philosophers, Sharp and Otto used the vignette method. One of the vignettes they used was borrowed directly from the "disbanding island" scenario from Immanuel Kant's *The Metaphysical Elements of Justice* (1785). The key issue for Sharp and Otto was whether participants agreed with Kant that the inhabitants should execute the last murderer before they disbanded the island simply because he deserved it. Sharp and Otto also used another vignette that described a situation where the only justification of the punishment in question is deterrence. They found that participants tended not to embrace pure versions of either retributivism or deterrence theory but instead broadly supported punishments that serve both ends. Sharp and Otto used their findings to criticize F. H. Bradley's philosophical work on the "vulgar" notion of punishment, which he claimed was purely retributive in nature (1876; 1894).

Looking back on the rest of the twentieth century in the wake of Sharp and Otto's groundbreaking work, we find a dearth of empirical research on people's attitudes, beliefs, and judgments about the relationship between free will, moral responsibility, and punishment. Given that free will is one of the perennial problems in philosophy and also has broad popular appeal, it is surprising how little empirical work has been done in this area until fairly recently. Most of the earliest research on commonsense views about free will beliefs focused on the relationship between people's attitudes, beliefs, and judgments about free will, determinism, and punishment (e.g., Nettler, 1959; 1961; Stroessner & Green, 1990; Viney et al., 1982; 1984; 1988). Though this kind of research on beliefs about free will and related constructs was long overdue, the findings were often mixed and hard to interpret.

For instance, in one of the first studies on free will beliefs, Nettler (1959) found that believing in free will is correlated with cruelty, retribution, and revenge and that believing in determinism is correlated with people being less punitive and treating others with more dignity. In response, Viney and colleagues (1982) first reported findings that seemed to support the opposite conclusion—namely, that people who believe in free will were less rather than more punitive—before later finding "neither reliable correlations between punitiveness and beliefs in free will or determinism nor reliable correlations between rationales for punishment and beliefs in free will or determinism" (Viney et al., 1988, p. 20).

These sorts of conflicting results have unfortunately been one of the hallmarks of empirical work on beliefs about free will and responsibility. Nowhere is this truer than the research from experimental philosophy on whether most people believe that free will and responsibility are compatible with determinism—that is, "the thesis that there is at any instant exactly one physically possible future" (van Inwagen, 1983, p. 3). Philosophers have long argued about which theory of free will, if any, best captures how people ordinarily think about free and responsible agency. According to proponents of natural compatibilism, most people intuitively believe that free will and/or moral responsibility are incompatible with determinism (see, e.g., Cover & O'Leary-Hawthorne, 1996; Ekstrom, 2000; Kane, 1999; Nichols, 2015; O'Connor, 2000; Pereboom, 2001; Searle, 1984; Smilansky, 2003; Strawson, 1986). According to proponents of natural compatibilism, most people intuitively believe that free will and/or moral responsibility are compatible with determinism (see, e.g., Ayer, 1954; Dennett, 1984; Fischer & Ravizza, 1998; Lycan, 2003; Nahmias, 2014; Nowell-Smith, 1949; Stace, 1952; Wolf, 1990).

But this is ultimately an empirical issue. So, for the past 15+ years experimental philosophers have made a concerted effort to figure out which theory about the commonsense view of free will and responsibility fares best in the court of public opinion. Unfortunately, researchers once again find themselves at a stalemate. On the one hand, there are findings that support natural incompatibilism (e.g., Chan, Deutsch, & Nichols, 2016; Deery, Bedke, & Nichols, 2013; Feltz & Milan, 2013; Nadelhoffer, Yin, & Graves, 2020; Nadelhoffer, Rose, Buckwalter, & Nichols, 2020; Nichols, 2004; 2006a; 2006b; Nichols & Knobe, 2007; Rose & Nichols, 2013; Rose, Buckwalter, & Nichols, 2017; Roskies & Nichols, 2008; Sarkissian et al., 2010; Wisniewski, Deutschländer, & Haynes, 2019). On the other hand, there are findings that support natural compatibilism (e.g., Andow & Cova, 2016; Deery, Davis, & Carey, 2015; Feltz, 2013; Hainnikainen et al., 2019; Miller & Feltz, 2011; Monroe & Malle, 2010; Murray & Nahmias, 2014; Nahmias, Coates, & Kvaran, 2007; Nahmias, Morris, Nadelhoffer, & Turner, 2005; 2006; Nahmias & Murray, 2011; Nahmias, Shepard, & Reuter, 2014; Sripada, 2012; Turner & Nahmias, 2006; Turri, 2017; Woolfolk, Doris, & Darley, 2006).

There is an ongoing debate about how best to explain these conflicting findings (e.g., Bear & Knobe, 2016; Bourgeois-Gironde, Cova, Bertoux, & Dubois, 2012; Clark, Winegard, & Baumeister, 2019; Cokely & Feltz, 2010; Cova & Kitano, 2014; Feldman, Wong, & Baumeister, 2016; Feltz & Cokely, 2009; Feltz, Cokely, & Nadelhoffer, 2009; Feltz & Cokely, 2012; Feltz, Perez, & Harris, 2012; Feltz & Cova, 2014; Knobe, 2014; Lim & Chem, 2018; Mandelbaum & Ripley, 2012; May, 2015; Phillips & Knobe, 2009; Shepherd, 2012; 2015; Sinnott-Armstrong, 2008; Weigel, 2011). A common strategy that has been adopted by both sides is to develop error theories to explain away findings that conflict with one's own preferred view. Natural compatibilists argue that people tend to mistakenly assume that deterministic causal chains bypass deliberative processes that we ordinarily take to be implicated in the production of intentional action (Murray & Nahmias, 2014; Nahmias & Murray, 2011; cf. Björnsson, 2014; Björnsson & Pereboom, 2014; Rose & Nichols, 2013). On the other hand, natural incompatibilists argue that background indeterministic beliefs appear to intrude on how some participants understand the deterministic scenarios used as stimuli to elicit judgments about free will (Nadelhoffer et al., 2020; Rose et al., 2017). For instance, participants often mistakenly think that agents in deterministic scenarios can have the unconditional ability to do otherwise, which both incompatibilists and compatibilists agree requires indeterminism.

While the debate about natural incompatibilism and natural compatibilism continues (as reflected in several of the contributions to this volume), this is not the only issue worth exploring when it comes to the role that attitudes and beliefs about free will and moral responsibility play in our daily lives. Rather than focusing on whether philosophical theories map onto commonsense thinking, some researchers have simply tried to better understand the interpersonal and intrapersonal impact that our attitudes, beliefs, and judgments about free will and moral responsibility have. For instance, researchers have found that free will beliefs are associated with higher levels of autonomy and proactivity (Alquist, Ainsworth, & Baumeister, 2013), greater self-efficacy and less perceived helplessness (Baumeister & Brewer, 2012), better academic performance (Feldman, Chandrashekar, & Wong, 2016), increased satisfaction with decision-making and choices (Feldman, Baumeister, & Wong, 2014), endorsement of dispositional explanations of behavior over situational explanations (Genschow, Rigoni, & Brass, 2017), improved feelings of belonging, self-control, and meaningfulness (Moynihan, Igou, & van Tilberg, 2007), improved learning from negative emotions (Stillman & Baumeister, 2010), more positive ratings from work supervisors and higher job approval ratings (Stillman et al., 2010), and self-control, pursuing and accomplishing goals, and conscious thought and deliberation (Stillman, Baumeister, & Mele, 2011).

As for the relationship between free will beliefs and explicitly moral beliefs and behavior, researchers have reported that free will beliefs are associated with decreased aggression and increased helpfulness toward strangers (Baumeister, Masicampo, & DeWall, 2009), causal cognition (Genschow & Brass, 2017; Genschow, Rigoni, & Brass, 2019), moral attitudes (Paulhus & Carey, 2011), subjective well-being (Li, Wang, Zhao, Kong, & Li, 2017; Moynihan et al., 2017; Feldman & Chandrashekar, 2018), moralization and political ideology (Everett et al. 2021), attitudes toward authoritarianism (Carey & Paulhus, 2013; Costello, Bowes, & Lilienfeld, 2020; Nadelhoffer & Goya-Tocchetto, 2013), heightened moral judgments and attributions of blame and punishment (Carey & Paulhus, 2013; Clark, Luguri, Ditto, Knobe, Shariff, & Baumeister, 2014; Clark, Baumeister, & Ditto, 2017; Krueger, Hoffman, Walter, & Grafman, 2014; Martin, Rigoni, & Vohs, 2017; Shariff et al., 2014), and views about inequality (Mercier, Wiwad, Piff, Aknin, Robinson, & Shariff, 2020).[3]

In short, the gathering data highlight that what people think about free will and moral responsibility is both theoretically interesting and practically important. It is for precisely this reason that we decided to put together this volume. Our goal was to bring together some of the leading philosophers and psychologists doing experimental work on free will and/or moral responsibility. All we asked of contributors is that they write about free will, moral responsibility, or both. Since each chapter has an abstract, we are going to forgo providing brief synopses here. We nevertheless want to say a few words about the content of the volume.

In the first three chapters, the authors provide a detailed survey of the relevant extant research (including their own) in order to shed light on philosophical issues surrounding free will and responsibility. These three chapters cover a variety of interrelated issues. For instance, what is the relationship between attributions of free will, intentionality, and moral judgment (negative and positive)? What role do beliefs about free will and responsibility play in victim blaming? What can evolutionary theory, error management, and moral psychology tell us about the nature of punishment itself? Do people think that we have control over our beliefs, desires, emotions, and other mental states, and if so, does this explain why they tend to hold people responsible for these states and the behaviors they cause?

In the remaining chapters, the contributors present and discuss new findings in an effort to explore a constellation of closely related issues concerning free will and moral responsibility. For instance, do people attribute free will and responsibility to agents who have been manipulated (and if not, why not)? Do people's intuitions about free will and responsibility come apart as semi-compatibilists have suggested (problematizing the aforementioned debate about natural incompatibilism vs. natural compatibilism)? What role do beliefs about free will, control, choice, and moral responsibility play in lay persons' judgments about legal excuses and the *mens rea* elements of the criminal law? Can the distinction between direct versus derivative moral responsibility problematize the evidence commonly used to support natural compatibilism? What does the research on causal modeling and moral judgment tell us about how we think about the actions and inactions of victims? Finally, are those who are more skilled decision-makers (e.g., people who are more numerate) more likely to properly understand deterministic scenarios than those who are less skilled, and if so, what can that tell us about the extant findings on beliefs about free will and responsibility?

We believe that the contributors to this volume have done an exemplary job highlighting just how fruitful and stimulating interdisciplinary work can be. So, we would like to thank the contributors for their thought-provoking chapters. We would also like to thank the readers for their interest in the array of related issues discussed in this volume. We hope that our collective efforts inspire more philosophers and psychologists to work together under a single banner. Both fields will be the better for it as each discipline has something important to bring to the table when it comes to better understanding how people think about free will and moral responsibility.

Notes

1   While psychologists are the most common scientists to work under the banner of experimental philosophy, anthropologists, biologists, economists, neuroscientists, and many others can all engage in this kind of work.
2   Some researchers adopt a broader definition of experimental philosopher that includes both what we are calling experimental philosophy (narrowly construed) and what Nadelhoffer and Nahmias (2007) call empirically informed philosophy—that is, philosophers who appeal to empirical evidence but do collect any data themselves. There are virtues to both ways of carving out the field. However, while the broader definition is more inclusive, we believe it fails to capture the novelty of experimental philosophy. After all, if we lump together experimental philosophy and empirically informed philosophy, then philosophers have been doing experimental philosophy since Aristotle. Because we think this conception is overly inclusive, we have defined experimental philosophy more narrowly for the purposes of this volume.
3   It's worth noting that some of the high-profile findings on free will and moral behavior have failed to replicate. For instance, Vohs and Schooler (2008) reported that people exposed to deterministic primes were more likely to cheat. Yet a number of researchers have failed to conceptually or directly replicate these widely cited and influential findings—for example, Crone & Levy (2019), Monroe, Brady, & Malle (2017), Nadelhoffer, Shepard, Crone, Everett, Earp, and Levy (2020), and Schooler, Nadelhoffer, Nahmias, and Vohs (2014).

References

Alquist, J. L., Ainsworth, S. E., & Baumeister, R. F. (2013). Determined to conform: Disbelief in free will increases conformity. *Journal of Experimental Social Psychology*, 49, 80–6.

Andow, J., & Cova, F. (2016). Why incompatibilist intuitions are not mistaken: A reply to Feltz and Millan. *Philosophical Psychology*, 29(4), 550–66.

Ayer, A. J. (1954). Freedom and necessity. In A. J. Ayer (Ed.), *Philosophical Essays* (pp. 271–84). London: Macmillan.

Baumeister, R. F., & Brewer, L. E. (2012). Believing versus disbelieving in free will: Correlates and consequences. *Social and Personality Psychology Compass, 6*(10), 736–45.

Baumeister, R. F., Masicampo, E. J., & DeWall, C. N. (2009). Prosocial benefits of feeling free: Disbelief in free will increases aggression and reduces helpfulness. *Personality and Social Psychology Bulletin, 35*, 260–8.

Bear, A., & Knobe, J. (2016). What do people find incompatible with causal determinism? *Cognitive Science, 40*, 2025–49.

Björnsson, G. (2014). Incompatibilism and "bypassed agency." In A. Mele (Ed.), *Surrounding Free Will* (pp. 95–112). New York: Oxford University Press.

Björnsson, G., & Pereboom, D. (2014). Free will skepticism and bypassing. In W. Sinnott-Armstrong (Ed.), *Moral Psychology: Free Will and Moral Responsibility, Volume 4* (pp. 27–36). Cambridge, MA: MIT Press.

Bourgeois-Gironde, S., Cova, F., Bertoux, M., & Dobois, B. (2012). Judgments about moral responsibility and determinism in patients with behavioral variant of frontotemporal dementia: Still compatibilists. *Consciousness and Cognition, 21*, 851–64.

Bradley, F. H. (1876). *Ethical Studies*. London: Oxford University Press.

Bradley, F. H. (1894). Some remarks on punishment. *International Journal of Ethics, 4*, 269–84.

Carey, J. M., & Paulhus, D. L. (2013). Worldview implications of believing in free will and/or determinism: Politics, morality, and punitiveness. *Journal of Personality, 81*(2), 130–41.

Chan, H.-Y., Deutsch, M., & Nichols, S. (2016). Free will and experimental philosophy. In J. Sytsma & W. Buckwalter (Eds.), *A Companion to Experimental Philosophy* (pp. 158–72). Hoboken, NJ: John Wiley & Sons, Ltd.

Clark, C. J., Lugari, J. B., Ditto, P. H., Knobe, J., Shariff, A. F., & Baumeister, R. F. (2014). Free to punish: A motivated account of free will belief. *Journal of Personality and Social Psychology, 106*(4), 501–13.

Clark, C. J., Baumeister, R. F., & Ditto, P. H. (2017). Making punishment palatable: Belief in free will alleviates punitive distress. *Consciousness and Cognition, 51*, 193–211.

Clark, C. J., Winegard, B. M., & Baumeister, R. F. (2019). Forget the folk: Moral responsibility preservation motives and other conditions for compatibilism. *Frontiers in Psychology*, https://doi.org/10.3389/fpsyg.2019.00215

Cokely, E. T., & Feltz, A. (2010). Questioning the free will comprehension question. In S. Ohlsson & R. Catrambone (Eds.), *Proceedings of the 32nd Annual Conference of the Cognitive Science Society* (pp. 2440–5). Austin, TX: Cognitive Science Society.

Costello, H., Bowes, S. M., & Lilienfeld, S. O. (2020). "Escape from Freedom": Authoritarianism-related traits, political ideology, personality, and belief in free will/determinism. *Journal of Research in Personality, 86*, e103957. https://doi.org/10.1016/j.jrp.2020.103957

Cova, F., & Kitano, Y. (2014). Experimental philosophy and the compatibility of free will and determinism: A survey. *Annals of the Japan Association for Philosophy of Science, 22*, 17–37.

Cover, J. A., & O'Leary-Hawthorne J. (1996). Free agency and materialism. In J. Jordan & D. Howard-Snyder (Eds.), *Faith, Freedom and Rationality* (pp. 47–71). Lanham, MD: Roman and Littlefield.

Crone, D., & Levy, N. (2019). Are free will believers nicer people? Four studies suggest not. *Social Psychological and Personality Science, 10*(5), 1–8.

Deery, O., Bedke, M., & Nichols, S. (2013). Phenomenal abilities: Incompatibilism and the experience of agency. In D. Shoemaker (Ed.), *Oxford Studies in Agency and Responsibility* (pp. 126–50). New York: Oxford University Press.

Deery, O., Davis, T., & Carey, J. (2015). The free-will intuitions scale and the question of natural compatibilism. *Philosophical Psychology, 26*(8), 776–801.

Dennett, D. (1984). I could not have done otherwise: So what? *Journal of Philosophy, 81*(10), 553–65.

Ekstrom, L. (2000). *Free Will: A philosophical Study*. Boulder, CO: Westview Press.

Everett, J. A. C., Clark, C. J., Meindl, P., Luguri, J. B., Earp, B. D., Graham, J., Ditto, P. H., & Shariff, A. F. (2021). Political differences in free will belief are associated with differences in moralization. *Journal of Personality and Social Psychology, 120*(2), 461–83.

Feldman, G., Baumeister, R. F., & Wong, K. F. E. (2014). Free will is about choosing: The link between choice and the belief in free will. *The Journal of Experimental Social Psychology, 55*, 239–45.

Feldman, G., Chandrashekar, S. P., & Wong, K. F. E. (2016). The freedom to excel: Belief in free will predicts better academic performance. *Personality and Individual Differences, 90*, 377–83.

Feldman, G., Wong, K. F. E., & Baumeister, R. F. (2016). Bad is freer than good: Positive–negative asymmetry in attributions of free will. *Consciousness and Cognition, 42*, 26–40.

Feldman, G., & Chandrashekar, S. P. (2018). Laypersons' beliefs and intuitions about free will and determinism: New insights linking the social psychology and experimental philosophy paradigms. *Social Psychological and Personality Science, 9*(5), 539–49

Feltz, A., & Cokely, E. T. (2009). Do judgments about freedom and responsibility depend on who you are? Personality differences in intuitions about compatibilism and incompatibilism. *Consciousness and Cognition, 18*, 342–50.

Feltz, A., & Cokely, E. T. (2012). The Philosophical Personality Argument. *Philosophical Studies, 161*, 227–46.

Feltz, A. & Cova, F. (2014). Moral responsibility and free will: A meta-analysis. *Consciousness and Cognition, 30*, 234–46.

Feltz, A., & Millan, M. (2013). An error theory for compatibilist intuitions. *Philosophical Psychology, 28*, 529–55.

Feltz, A., Cokely, E.T., & Nadelhoffer, T. (2009). Natural compatibilism v. natural incompatibilism. *Mind & Language, 24*, 1–23.

Feltz, A., Perez, A., & Harris, M. (2012). Free will, causes, and decisions: Individual differences in written reports. *The Journal of Consciousness Studies, 19*, 166–89.

Fischer, J., & Ravizza, M. (1998). *Responsibility and Control*. New York: Cambridge University Press.

Genschow, O., Rigoni, D., & Brass, M. (2017). Belief in free will affects causal attributions when judging others' behavior. *Proceedings of the National Academy of Sciences, 114*, 10071–6.

Genschow, O., Rigoni, D., & Brass, M. (2019). The hand of God or the hand of Maradona? Believing in free will increases perceived intentionality of others' behavior. *Consciousness and Cognition, 70*, 80–7.

Hainnikainen, I. R., Machery, E., Rose, D., Stich, S., Olivola, C. Y., Sousa, P., et al. (2019). For whom does determinism undermine moral responsibility? Surveying the conditions for free will across cultures. *Frontiers in Psychology, 10*, e2028.

Kane, R. (1999). Responsibility, luck, and chance: Reflections on free will and indeterminism. *Journal of Philosophy, 96*, 217–40.

Kant, I. 1785. *The Metaphysical Elements of Justice*, J. Ladd (Tr.). Indianapolis: Bobbs-Merrill, 1965.

Knobe, J. (2014). Free will and the scientific vision. In E. Machery & E. O'neill (Eds.), *Current Controversies in Experimental Philosophy* (pp. 69–85). New York: Routledge.

Krueger, F., Hoffman, M., Walter, H., & Grafman, J. (2014). An fMRI investigation of the effects of belief in free will on third-party punishment. *Social Cognitive and Affective Neuroscience*, 9(8), 1143–9.

Li, C., Wang, S., Zhao, Y., Kong, F., & Li, J. (2017). The freedom to pursue happiness: Belief in free will predicts life satisfaction and positive affect among Chinese adolescents. *Frontiers in Psychology*, doi.org/10.3389/fpsyg.2016.02027

Lim, D., & Chen, J. (2018): Is compatibilism intuitive? *Philosophical Psychology*, 31(6), 878–97.

Lycan, W. (2003). Free will and the burden of proof. In A. O'Hear (Ed.), *Proceedings of the Royal Institute of Philosophy for 2001-02* (pp. 107–22). Cambridge, UK: Cambridge University Press.

Mandelbaum, E., & Ripley, D. (2012). Explaining the abstract/concrete paradoxes in moral psychology: The NBAR hypothesis. *Review of Philosophy and Psychology*, 3, 351–68.

Martin, N. D., Rigoni, D., & Vohs, K. D. (2017). Free will beliefs predict attitudes toward unethical behavior and criminal punishment. *PNAS*, 114(28), 7325–30.

May, J. (2015). On the very concept of free will. *Synthese*, 191(12), 2849–66.

Mercier, B., Wiwad, D., Piff, P., Aknin, L. B., Robinson, A. R., & Shariff, A. (2020). Does belief in free will increase support for economic inequality? *Collabra: Psychology*, 6(1), 25. https://doi.org/10.1525/collabra.303

Miller, J., & Feltz, A. (2011). Frankfurt and the folk: An empirical investigation. *Consciousness and Cognition*, 20, 401–14.

Monroe, A. E., & Malle, B. F. (2010). From uncaused will to conscious choice: The need to study, not speculate about people's folk concept of free will. *Review of Philosophy and Psychology*, 1, 211–24.

Monroe, A. E., Brady, G. L., & Malle, B. F. (2017). This isn't the free will worth looking for. *Social Psychological and Personality Science*, 8, 191–9.

Moynihan, A. B., Igou, E. R., & van Tilberg, W. A. P. (2007). Free, connected, and meaningful: Free will beliefs promote meaningfulness through belongingness. *Personality and Individual Differences*, 107, 54–65.

Moynihan, A. B., Igou, E. R., & Van Tilberg, V. A. P. (2017). "Free, connected, and meaningful" Free will beliefs promote meaningfulness through belongingness. *Personality and Individual Differences*, 107, 54–65.

Murray, D., & Nahmias, E. (2014). Explaining away incompatibilist intuitions. *Philosophy and Phenomenological Research*, 88, 434–67.

Nadelhoffer, T., & Goya-Tocchetto, D. (2013). The potential dark side of free will: Some preliminary findings. In G. Caruso (Ed.), *Exploring the Illusion of Free Will and Moral Responsibility* (pp. 121–40). Lanham, MD: Lexington Books.

Nadelhoffer, T., & Nahmias, E. (2007). The past and future of experimental philosophy. *Philosophical Explorations*, 10(2), 123–49.

Nadelhoffer, T., Rose, D., Buckwalter, W., & Nichols, S. (2020). Natural compatibilism, indeterminism, and intrusive metaphysics. *Cognitive Science*, 44(8), e12873.

Nadelhoffer, T., Shepard, J., Crone, D., Everett, J. A. C., Earp, B. D., & Levy, N. (2020). Does encouraging a belief in determinism increase cheating? Reconsidering the value of believing in free will. *Cognition*, 203, e10432. https://doi.org/10.1016/j.cognition.2020.104342

Nadelhoffer, T., Yin, S., & Graves, R. (2020). Folk intuitions and the conditional ability to do otherwise. *Philosophical Psychology*, *33*(7), 968–96.

Nahmias, E. (2006). Folk fears about freedom and responsibility: Determinism vs. reductionism. *Journal of Cognition and Culture*, 6, 215–37. https://doi.org/10.1163/156853706776931295

Nahmias, E. (2014). Is free will an illusion? Confronting challenges from the modern mind sciences. In W. Sinnott-Armstrong (Ed.), *Moral Psychology, Vol. 4: Freedom and Responsibility* (pp. 1–25). Cambridge, MA: MIT Press.

Nahmias, E., & Murray, D. (2011). Experimental philosophy on free will: An error theory for incompatibilist intuitions. In J. Aguilar, A. Buckareff, & K. Frankish (Eds.), *New Waves in Philosophy of Action* (pp. 189–216). New York: Palgrave Macmillan.

Nahmias, E., Morris, S., Nadelhoffer, T., & Turner, J. (2005). Surveying free will: Folk intuitions about free will and moral responsibility. *Philosophical Psychology*, 18, 561–84.

Nahmias, E., Morris, S., Nadelhoffer, T., & Turner, J. (2006). Is incompatibilism intuitive? *Philosophy and Phenomenological Research*, 73, 28–53.

Nahmias, E., Coates, J., & Kvaran, T. (2007). Free will, moral responsibility, and mechanism: Experiments on folk intuitions. *Midwest Studies in Philosophy*, 31, 214–42.

Nahmias, E., Shepard, J., & Reuter, S. (2014). It's OK if "my brain made me do it": People's intuitions about free will and neuroscientific prediction. *Cognition*, *133*, 502–16.

Nettler, G. (1959). Cruelty, dignity, and determinism. *American Sociological Review*, 24, 375–84.

Nettler, G. (1961). Good men, bad men, and the perception of reality. *Sociometry*, 3, 279–94.

Nichols, S. (2004). The folk psychology of free will: fits and starts. *Mind and Language*, 19, 473–502.

Nichols, S. (2006a). Folk intuitions on free will. *Journal of Cognition and Culture*, 6, 57–86.

Nichols, S. (2006b). Free will and the folk: Response to commentators. *Journal of Cognition and Culture*, 6, 305–20.

Nichols, S. (2012). The indeterminist intuition. *The Monist*, 95, 290–307.

Nichols, S. (2015). *Bound*. Oxford: Oxford University Press.

Nichols, S., & Knobe, J. (2007). Moral responsibility and determinism: The Cognitive science of folk intuition. *Noûs*, *41*, 663–85.

Nowell-Smith, P. H. (1949). Free will and moral responsibility. *Mind*, *57*, 45–65.

O'Connor, T. (2000). *Persons and Causes: The Metaphysics of Free Will*. New York: Oxford University Press.

Paulhus, D. L., & Carey, J. M. (2011). The FAD+: Measuring lay beliefs regarding free will and related constructs. *Journal of Personality Assessment*, 93, 96–104.

Pereboom, D. (2001). *Living without Free Will*. Cambridge, UK: Cambridge University Press.

Phillips, J., & Knobe, J. (2009). Moral judgments and intuitions about freedom. *Psychological Inquiry*, *20*(1), 30–6.

Rose, D., & Nichols, S. (2013). The lesson of bypassing. *Review of Philosophy and Psychology*, 4, 599–619.

Rose, D., Buckwalter, W., & Nichols. (2017). Neuroscientific prediction and the intrusion of intuitive metaphysics. *Cognitive Science*, *41*, 482–502.

Roskies, A., & Nichols, S. (2008). Bringing moral responsibility down to Earth. *The Journal of Philosophy*, *105*, 371–88.

Sarkissian, H., Chatterjee, A., De Brigard, F., Knobe, J., Nichols, S., & Sirker, S. (2010). Is belief in free will a cultural universal? *Mind & Language, 35*, 346-58.

Searle, J. (1984). *Minds, Brains, and Science.* Cambridge, MA: Harvard University Press.

Schooler, J., Nadelhoffer, T., Nahmias, E., & Vohs, K. (2014). Measuring and manipulating beliefs and behaviors associated with free will: The good, the bad, and the ugly. In A. Mele (Ed.), *Surrounding Free Will* (pp. 72-94). New York: Oxford University Press.

Shariff, A. F., Greene, J. D., Karremans, J. C., Luguri, J. B., Clark, C. J., Schooler, J. W., et al. (2014). Free will and punishment: A mechanistic view of human nature reduces retribution. *Psychological Science, 25*, 1563-70.

Sharp, F. C., & Otto, M. C. (1910a). A study of the popular attitude towards retributive punishment. *International Journal of Ethics, 20*(3), 341-57.

Sharp, F. C., & Otto, M. C. (1910b). Retribution and deterrence in the moral judgments of common sense. *International Journal of Ethics, 20*(4), 438-53.

Shepherd, J. (2012). Free will and consciousness: Experimental studies. *Consciousness and Cognition, 21*(2), 915-27.

Shepherd, J. (2015). Consciousness, free will, and moral responsibility: Taking the folk seriously. *Philosophical Psychology, 28*(7), 929-46.

Sinnott-Armstrong, W. (2008). Abstract + concrete = paradox. In J. Knobe & S. Nichols (Eds.), *Experimental Philosophy* (pp. 209-30). New York: Oxford University Press.

Smilansky, S. (2003). Compatibilism: The argument from shallowness. *Philosophical Studies, 115*(3), 257-82.

Sripada, C. S. (2012). What makes a manipulated agent unfree? *Philosophy and Phenomenological Research, 85*(3), 563-93.

Stace, W. T. (1952). *Religion and the Modern Mind.* New York: Lippincott.

Stillman, T. F., & Baumeister, R. F. (2010). Guilty, free, and wise: Determinism and psychopathy diminish learning from negative emotions. *Journal of Experimental Social Psychology, 46*, 951-60.

Stillman, T. F., Baumeister, R. F., Vohs, K. D., Lambert, N. M., Fincham, F. D., & Brewer, L. E. (2010). Personal philosophy and personnel achievement: Belief in free will predicts better job performance. *Social Psychological and Personality Science, 1*, 43-50.

Stillman, T., Baumeister, R., & Mele, A. (2011). Free will in everyday life: Autobiographical accounts of free and unfree action. *Philosophical Psychology, 24*, 381-94.

Strawson, G. (1986). *Freedom and Belief.* Oxford: Oxford University Press.

Stroessner, S. J., & Green, C. W. (1990). Effects of belief in free will or scientific determinism on attitudes toward punishment and locus of control. *Journal of Social Psychology, 130*, 789-99.

Turner, J., & Nahmias, E. (2006). Are the folk agent-causationists? *Mind & Language, 21*(5), 597-609.

Turri, J. (2017). Compatibilism can be natural. *Consciousness and Cognition, 51*, 68-81.

van Inwagen, P. (1983). *An Essay on Free Will.* Oxford: Oxford University Press.

Viney, W., Waldman, D., & Barchilon, J. (1982). Attitudes towards punishment in relation to beliefs in free will and determinism. *Human Relations, 35*, 939-50.

Viney, W., McIntyre, R., & Viney, D. (1984). Validity of a scale designed to measure beliefs in free will and determinism. *Psychological Reports, 54*, 867-72.

Viney, W., Parker-Martin, P., & Dotten, S. (1988). Beliefs in free will and determinism and lack of relation to punishment rational and magnitude. *Journal of General Psychology, 115*, 15-23.

Vohs, K. D., & Schooler, J. W. (2008). The value of believing in free will: Encouraging a belief in determinism increases cheating. *Psychological Science, 19*, 49-54.

Weigel, C. (2011). Distance, anger, freedom: An account of the role of abstraction in compatibilist and incompatibilist intuitions. *Philosophical Psychology*, *24*(6), 803–23.

Wisniewski, D., Deutschländer, R., & Haynes, J-D. (2019). Free will beliefs are better predicted by dualism than determinism beliefs across different cultures. *PLoS ONE, 14*, e0221617.

Wolf, S. (1990). *Freedom within Reason*. New York: Oxford University Press.

Woolfolk, R. L., Doris, J. M., & Darley, J. M. (2006). Identification, situational constraint, and social cognition: Studies in the attribution of moral responsibility. *Cognition*, *100*, 283–301.

1

Belief in Free Will Relates to Attributions of Intentionality and Judgments of Responsibility

Oliver Genschow and Marcel Brass

Introduction

Free will is a cornerstone of our society and relates to nearly everything we care about. The most prominent example in this respect may be our legal system in which punishment strongly depends on the degree to which a person acted "freely" (e.g., Newman & Weitzer, 1956). Thus, not surprisingly, across cultures (Sarkissian et al., 2010) and ages (Nichols, 2004), most people believe that they have free will (see also Baumeister et al., 2009; Nahmias et al., 2005). At the same time, there is a long-standing philosophical debate about whether free will actually exists (e.g., Dennett, 2015; Van Inwagen, 1983). In the last few decades, prominent voices in cognitive neuroscience and psychology have entered this debate by claiming that free will is nothing more than an illusion (e.g., Crick, 1994; Harris, 2012; Wegner, 2002). One of the most often mentioned support for this claim comes from a seminal experiment conducted by Libet and colleagues (1983). In this experiment, the researchers measured neural activity while participants had to make voluntary finger movements. After each movement, participants indicated on a clock the time at which they formed the intention to act. The results indicated that the readiness potential—an electrophysiological marker of action preparation—preceded the conscious intention to act by a few hundred milliseconds. In the literature, these and similar findings (Libet et al., 1983; Libet et al., 1993) are often used as an argument for the claim that conscious free will is an illusion. Although this argument has been criticized (Bode et al., 2014; Brass et al., 2019; Saigle et al., 2018; Schurger et al., 2012), anti-free will viewpoints have become more and more popular not only within academia (e.g., Greene & Cohen, 2004), but also in the media (e.g., Chivers 2010; Griffin, 2016; Wolfe, 1997). This raises the fundamental question: what would happen if people start to be convinced that free will is an illusion?

In philosophy, there has been a debate about whether a world without free will would lead to negative or positive societal consequences. Some philosophers have put forward the notion that anti-free will viewpoints should be kept away from the public, because people would no longer try controlling their behavior and start acting immorally (e.g., Smilansky, 2000, 2002). Other philosophers argue that disbelieving in free will may lead to overall positive effects, as people would abandon inadequate retribution-based morality and illusory beliefs in a just world (e.g., Caruso, 2014; Greene & Cohen, 2004; Nadelhoffer, 2011; Pereboom, 2006). To test potential societal effects, psychologists have experimentally manipulated free will beliefs and have investigated whether exposing participants to anti-free will messages influences their belief in free will and subsequently social attitudes, judgments, and behaviors (for reviews, see Ewusi-Boisvert & Racine, 2018; Genschow et al., 2021). In this chapter we will briefly summarize how free will beliefs have been conceptualized. Then, we will address the question, to which degree such beliefs can be experimentally manipulated. Finally, we will present recent research on how interindividual differences in free will belief are related to attributions of intentionality and judgments of responsibility, and thereby account for social judgments, attitudes, as well as behaviors.

Belief in Free Will

Definitions regarding the concept of free will are rather diverse and became quite complex (Carey & Paulhus, 2013). Recently, scholars proposed bottom-up approaches to analyze laypeople's conceptions of belief in free will (e.g., Nichols, 2006). Such analyses indicate that free will beliefs are metacognitive judgments about the extent to which individuals intentionally guide their own thoughts and actions (Frith, 2012). Specifically, belief in free will relates to the conviction that people are responsible for their actions (Carey & Paulhus, 2013), because they can decide and control their own behavior (Paulhus & Carey, 2011).

Associated with the belief in free will is the belief in determinism. From a philosophical point of view, determinism refers to the idea that given the past and the laws of nature, there is only one possible future at any moment in time (e.g., Van Inwagen, 1983). To which degree belief in determinism and belief in free will are separate constructs or the endpoints of the same continuum is part of a debate in philosophy and psychology. On the one hand, incompatibilists see free will as the exact opposite of determinism. This view implies that the more a person believes in determinism, the less (s)he believes in free will (e.g., Rakos et al., 2008; Viney et al., 1982). On the other hand, compatibilists view free will and determinism as independent constructs. From this perspective, belief in free will and determinism are completely compatible. Interestingly, past research indicates that among the general public, a compatibilistic view is more widespread than philosophers and psychologists may have traditionally assumed (e.g., Monroe & Malle, 2010; Murray & Nahmias, 2014; Nadelhoffer et al., 2014; Nahmias et al., 2006; Nichols, 2004, 2006; Nichols & Knobe, 2007; Rose & Nichols, 2013; Shepard & Reuter, 2012; Shepherd, 2012).

To measure belief in free will and related beliefs, researchers have constructed and validated different scales. Among the most often-used scales are the Free Will and Determinism Scale (FWD; Rakos et al., 2008), the Free Will and Determinism Scale (FAD; Paulhus & Carey, 2011), and the Free Will Inventory (FWI; Nadelhoffer et al., 2014). While the FWI and the FAD measure belief in free will and determinism as separate constructs and thus pursue a compatibilistic approach, the FWD considers belief in free will and determinism as the endpoints of the same construct and thereby assumes an incompatibilistic structure underlying free will belief. The FWI measures in addition to the belief in free will and belief in determinism also the belief in dualism, which relates to the idea that people have non-physical souls that survive after their bodies die. Interestingly, past research has indicated that belief in free will positively correlates with belief in dualism (Genschow & Vehlow, 2021; Nadelhoffer et al., 2014; Wisniewski et al., 2019).

Psychological Research on Manipulating Belief in Free Will

To investigate whether exposing people to anti-free will viewpoints has societal consequences, psychologists developed experimental manipulations with the aim to decrease participants' belief in free will and to increase their belief in determinism (for reviews, see Ewusi-Boisvert & Racine, 2018; Genschow et al., 2021). In a typical experiment, researchers present two groups of participants with different messages. While participants in the anti-free will group read a text questioning the existence of free will, participants in the control group read a text which is not related to free will.

When applying such and similar experimental manipulations, researchers found shifts in participants' social attitudes, judgments, and behaviors. For example, when reading anti-free will messages, participants behaved more antisocially. That is, they cheated more often (Vohs & Schooler, 2008), expressed more racism (Zhao et al., 2014), as well as behaved more aggressively (Baumeister et al., 2009) and less prosocially toward others (Protzko et al., 2015). Yet other researchers found that reading anti-free will viewpoints leads to reduced retributive punishment (Shariff et al., 2014), an increase in conformity (Alquist et al., 2013), and feelings of alienation (Seto & Hicks, 2016). Moreover, manipulating participants' belief in free will also influences causal attributions of other people's actions (Genschow et al., 2017), perceived meaningfulness of life (Crescioni et al., 2016; Moynihan et al., 2019), perceived gratitude (MacKenzie et al., 2014), counterfactual thinking (Alquist et al., 2015), and risk-taking behavior (Schrag et al., 2016). Finally, a last line of research investigated neurocognitive processes underlying the influence of anti-free will manipulations. Such research indicates that reading messages claiming that free will does not exist affects intentional action preparation (Rigoni et al., 2011), deliberate motor inhibition (Lynn et al., 2013; Rigoni et al., 2012), and the processing of performance errors (Rigoni et al., 2013; Rigoni et al., 2015).

While the above-reviewed literature suggests that merely exposing individuals once to short anti-free will viewpoints has meaningful downstream consequences, recent research casts doubt on the validity of these manipulations as several landmark findings could not be successfully replicated (Crone & Levy, 2019; Eben et al., 2020; Genschow et al., 2020; Giner-Sorolla et al., 2016; Monroe et al., 2017; Nadelhoffer et al., 2020; Open Science Collaboration, 2015; Schooler et al., 2014; Shariff & Vohs, 2014; Zwaan, 2014). For example, Monroe et al. (2017) could not find evidence for the idea that experimentally reducing participants' belief in free will influences moral behavior, judgments of blame, and punishment decisions. Relatedly, research from Nadelhoffer et al. (2020) showed that successfully reducing free will beliefs is more difficult than previously suggested and that the assumed link between manipulated free will beliefs and immoral behavior, such as cheating, is similarly tenuous (for similar findings, see Crone & Levy, 2019; Giner-Sorolla et al., 2016; Zwaan, 2014).

Research from our own lab (Genschow et al., 2020) suggests that exposing professional judges with anti-free will viewpoints does not influence their recommended sentences for criminal offenders. In an experiment, we first implemented a standard procedure to manipulate judges' belief in free will (Vohs & Schooler, 2008). That is, all judges read a text from Francis Crick's book *The Astonishing Hypothesis* (Crick, 1994). While judges in the experimental group read a text passage in which Francis Crick argues against the plausibility of free will, the judges in the control group read a text in which Francis Crick discussed research on consciousness. Afterward, all judges indicated their belief in free will by filling in the FWI scale (Nadelhoffer et al., 2014). At the end, we presented the judges with ten descriptions in which a person behaved criminally (e.g., strangling somebody to death, contract killing, killing somebody in a car accident, shooting somebody, stabbing somebody to death). For each criminal behavior, the judges had to recommend the length (in years and months) of the prison sentence that the involved offender should serve. The results indicated that although the judges in the anti-free will group reported lower levels of free will belief, they did not recommend lighter sentences than the judges in the control group.

In principle, different reasons could account for the difficulties in finding meaningful downstream consequences of experimental free will belief manipulations. First, it could be that the recently published replications are false negatives meaning that these investigations were not able to detect effects that actually exist. Second, it might be that the applied manipulations do not influence individuals' belief in free will and therefore cannot lead to any downstream consequence. Third, it is reasonable to assume that the applied experimental manipulations successfully affect beliefs related to free will, but this effect does not transfer to other attitudes, judgments, and behaviors. To investigate these different reasons, we recently conducted a large-scale meta-analyses involving more than 140 experiments (most of them unpublished) in which more than 25,000 participants took part (Genschow et al., 2021). The results of the meta-analysis support the third explanation: while exposing participants to anti-free will messages does reliably reduce their belief in free will and increase their belief in determinism, we did not find support for the idea that these manipulations have any meaningful downstream consequences. Importantly, we found that the effects of the anti-free will manipulations have rather weak effects on the belief in free will and are rather unspecific in the sense that they influence not only the belief in free will, but also other beliefs such as the belief in dualism, for instance. Given that any downstream effect of anti-free will manipulations is likely smaller than the effect on the beliefs they purport to change (i.e., belief in free will), it makes finding evidence for attitudes, judgments, and behaviors that are only marginally related to free will particularly challenging.

Taken together, recent research indicates that merely exposing people in laboratory experiments to brief anti-free will viewpoints is not sufficient to fundamentally change social attitudes, judgments, and behaviors. This does not, however, mean that free will belief manipulations could not work in principle. It might well be that the development of stronger manipulations will affect free will beliefs and its downstream consequences more fundamentally. In the meantime, given that previously experimental manipulations are not strong and specific enough to meaningfully influence fundamental beliefs of free will, an interindividual difference approach that capitalizes on "natural" variation in free will beliefs might be a more promising avenue to test the relation of free will beliefs to social attitudes, judgments, and behaviors. Indeed, several investigations from our own and other laboratories reveal that this approach might be more promising, as we will outline below.

The Intention-Hypothesis

Perceiving intentions in others' behavior is pervasive in our social life and is the basis for the way we interact with each other. For example, research on nonverbal behavior has shown that perceiving the intentionality of a certain action in others can shape the way individuals respond to others' behaviors (Genschow & Brass, 2015; Genschow & Groß-Bölting, 2021). Moreover, in the legal system punishing decisions strongly depends on how intentionally a person behaved (e.g., Newman & Weitzer, 1956). Likewise, in sports, referees' disciplinary punishments often depend on how intentional a player's behavior is perceived (e.g., Federation Internationale de Football Association, 2015).

Several investigations in the domain of free will beliefs suggest that an individual's belief in free will might be related to perceiving intentions. For instance, research from Nahmias et al. (2005) indicates that the more individuals believe in free will, the more they think that other individuals are responsible for their behavior. Likewise, research in cognitive psychology suggests that believing in free will is connected with perceiving intentional control of one's own actions (Aarts & van den Bos, 2011; Lynn et al., 2014; Rigoni et al., 2012). Based on this research we formulated the intention-hypothesis (Genschow et al., 2017), according to which belief in free will is associated with perceiving one's own and others' behavior as intentionally driven. To test this hypothesis, we conducted several studies.

In a first series of studies (Genschow et al., 2019) we tested whether believing in free will is positively correlated with perceived intentions in concrete and more abstract behaviors. In the first study, we presented participants with ten different video clips of soccer players committing handball. Referees' punishment decisions for such a misbehavior largely depend on the degree to which a player touched the ball with the hand or arm intentionally (Federation Internationale de Football Association, 2015). After each video clip, participants indicated the degree to which they perceived the player touching the ball with the hand or arm intentionally. At the end of the study, we measured participants' belief in free will with the Free Will Inventory (FWI; Nadelhoffer et al., 2014). Supporting the intention-hypothesis, the results demonstrated that the stronger a person believed in free will, the more intentionality (s)he perceived in the player's behavior. In another study, we went one step further and tested whether the link between belief in free will and perceived intentions holds for the perception of very abstract behaviors. To this end we presented participants with different video clips of geometrical shapes moving around (Castelli et al., 2000). After each video clip, we asked participants to indicate the degree to which they perceived the shapes moving around intentionally or randomly. The results mirrored the findings observed in the previous study: the stronger a participant believed in free will, the more intentions (s)he perceived in the abstract shapes. Additional analyses revealed that belief in free will even predicted perceived intentions when controlling for other related beliefs such as the belief in dualism and the belief in determinism.

Given that belief in free will is related to perceiving intentions in other persons' behavior, an intriguing question is to which degree belief in free will contributes to fundamental biases in person perception. One of the most pervasive biases in person perception is the correspondence bias (Gilbert & Malone, 1995), according to which individuals have the tendency to attribute other person's behavior more strongly to internal (e.g., personality) than to external (e.g., situation) forces. In line with the intention-hypothesis we predicted that belief in free will is positively related with the correspondence bias. To test this prediction, we conducted several studies (Genschow et al., 2017). In one study, we presented participants with different vignettes in which a behavior of a target person was described. Depending on the vignette, the behavior was either moral (e.g., volunteer work for poor people) or immoral (e.g., lying). After each vignette, participants evaluated different reasons for the target person's behavior by indicating their agreement on different items on a rating scale. One half of the items involved internal reasons and the other half external reasons for the behavior. The results indicated that participants attributed the target person's behavior more strongly to internal than to external forces. This typical correspondence bias was the larger, the more strongly participants believed in free will. Interestingly, the relation between belief in free will and the correspondence bias held irrespective of whether participants evaluated immoral or moral behavior.

In a further study we replicated this finding and assessed in addition to belief in free will, their locus of control. While persons with an internal locus of control believe that they can influence outcomes through ability, effort, or skills, persons with an external locus of control believe that factors outside of their control determine outcomes (Rotter, 1966). Hence, it might well be that people believing in free will also have a relative strong internal locus of control, and that it is their internal locus of control (instead of their belief in free will) that accounts for the relation between belief in free will and the correspondence bias. However, our results do not support this alternative explanation: although locus of control was related with belief in free will as well as with the correspondence bias, when statistically controlling for locus of control, free will beliefs were still a significant predictor of the correspondence bias.

A bias that concerns the self, but is strongly related to the correspondence bias, is the self-serving bias (Miller & Ross, 1975). According to the self-serving bias, people have the tendency to attribute personal success more strongly to internal factors (e.g., one's own ability or effort) as compared with external factors (e.g., task difficulty or bad luck) and vice versa for personal failures. The correspondence bias is known to buffer against attacks on the self-concept as people take responsibility for their positive, but not negative behaviors (e.g., Greenberg, 1991; Greenberg et al., 1982; Sedikides & Strube, 1997). Thus, not surprisingly, the engagement in the self-serving bias positively relates to individuals' psychological health (Mezulis et al., 2004). To investigate the relation between belief in free will and the self-serving bias we conducted six high-powered studies (Genschow & Lange, 2021). Depending on the study, participants either imagined or engaged in a behavior in which they experienced success or failure. After each behavior, participants indicated the degree to which they felt that the outcome of the behavior was due to internal or external factors. Although we found support for the self-serving bias across all studies, belief in free will did not correlate with the self-serving bias. However, in line with the prediction put forward by the intention-hypothesis, the results showed that the stronger participants believed in free will, the more they attributed success as well as failure to internal, as compared with external factors.

In sum, our research suggests that belief in free will is related to the attribution of intentions. However, this research does not address the question whether the relationship between free will beliefs and intention attribution is primarily driven by a positive relationship of free will beliefs to internal factors or a negative relationship to external factors. To address this question, we tested these different relationships in post-hoc analyses across all our studies on the self-serving bias and the correspondence bias. These analyses indicate that people's belief in free will is more strongly positively correlated with internal attributions than it is negatively correlated with external attributions (Genschow & Lange, 2021). This furthermore supports our prediction that belief in free will relates to attributing intentions in others.

Consequences of the Link between Free Will Beliefs and Perceived Intentions

The above-reviewed literature indicates that free will is central for attributing responsibility—irrespective of whether the attributions concern behaviors of the self or of others and irrespective of whether the valence of the behavior is positive or negative. However, it remains open to which degree the link between belief in free will and perceived intentions relates to societal relevant behaviors, attitudes, and judgments. Recent research indicates that perceiving intentions in others contributes to punishment, victim blaming, and rewarding behavior.

Punishment

In many legal systems, punishment depends on the degree to which a person is responsible for his or her behavior (e.g., Newman & Weitzer, 1956). Therefore, given that free will belief is related to perceiving intentions and responsibility in others' behavior, a straightforward prediction is that higher endorsements in free will beliefs relate to harsher punishment of criminal behavior. First support for this prediction comes from experiments conducted by Shariff and colleagues (2014). In these experiments, the researchers experimentally reduced participants' belief in free will and then subsequently let them recommend prison sentences for criminal offenders. While Shariff et al. found that a decreased belief in free will reduces recommended sentences, other researchers were not able to replicate this finding (Genschow et al., 2021; Genschow et al., 2020; Monroe et al., 2017). However, as discussed previously in this chapter, this lack of evidence does not necessarily mean that belief in free will on an interpersonal level is not related to punishing behavior. Indeed, when analyzing data from the World Values Survey that included residents of forty-six countries ($n = 65,111$ persons), Martin et al. (2017) found that free will beliefs positively relate to intolerance of unethical behavior and support for severe criminal punishment.

In line with the findings from Martin and colleagues (2017), we demonstrated that the belief in free will is positively correlated with the intention to punish others for their wrongdoings (Genschow et al., 2017). For example, in one study, we presented participants with the same vignettes that we used to measure the correspondence bias (cf. above). After participants indicated the degree to which they attributed internal versus external reasons to the target person's immoral behavior, we asked them to indicate how strongly they would punish the target person for their behavior. Replicating Martin and colleagues' finding, we found that participants' belief in free will was positively correlated with their punishing intentions. Moreover, additional analyses indicated that participants' correspondence bias mediated the influence of free will beliefs on punishing intentions indicating that perceiving intentions in others accounts for the link between belief in free will and punishment.

Victim Blaming

As we have seen in this chapter, people with a higher endorsement of free will belief attribute more intentionality to wrongdoers' behavior and, as a consequence, are willing to punish them more harshly. As previous research has mainly focused on offenders, it neglected the question of how belief in free will influences the perception of the victims. Past research indicates that victims do not only suffer from the psychological and physical consequences that stem from the victimizing event, but also from other people's deprecating responses (e.g., Janoff-Bulman & Frieze, 1983; Lerner, 1970; Ryan, 1976). Indeed, research against the backdrop of the so-called phenomenon of victim blaming indicates that victims are often made responsible for their bad luck, even when severe events did not arise through their own fault (Lerner, 1980; Lerner & Miller, 1978). In other words, victim blaming can be defined as an overestimation of internal, as compared to external, causes when making judgments about victims. As such an attribution pattern is very similar to the correspondence bias, we predicted that people's belief in free will relates to their tendency to blame victims. To test this hypothesis, we ran three studies (Genschow & Vehlow, 2021). In all studies we presented participants with four vignettes in which a person was victimized (e.g., knocked out by a burglar). After each vignette, participants filled in the Victim Blaming Scale (van Prooijen & van den Bos, 2009) as a measure of victim blaming. Across all experiments, the results support our hypothesis as participants' belief in free will was positively correlated with victim blaming.

In a seminal study, Carey and Paulhus (2013) found that belief in free will is related to belief in a just world, religiosity, and a conservative worldview. Interestingly, research on victim blaming shows that the very same factors also influence people's tendency to blame victims. That is, people who hold a fundamentalistic religious worldview

(Sheldon & Parent, 2002), believe in a just world (e.g., Strömwall et al., 2013; Van den Bos & Maas, 2009), and hold a conservative attitude (Lambert & Raichle, 2000; Williams, 1984) are more likely to blame victims. In a high-powered study with more than 600 participants (Genschow & Vehlow, 2021; Study 3), we assessed in addition to victim blaming and free will beliefs, also other related beliefs (i.e., dualism and determinism), belief in a just world, religious worldviews, and political ideology (i.e., conservatism vs. liberalism). The results demonstrate that even when statistically controlling for all these other factors, participants' belief in free will still predicted victim blaming.

Rewarding Behavior

So far, our previous research has mainly focused on how free will beliefs contribute to immoral or criminal behavior. However, as we have seen in this chapter, individuals' beliefs in free will do not only shape attributions of negative, but also those of positive behavior. Thus, one could predict that belief in free will relates to rewarding others for their moral behavior in the same way as it does to punishing others for their immoral behavior. To test this hypothesis, we once again presented participants with the vignettes to assess the correspondence bias. After each vignette, we measured the correspondence bias and let participants indicate to which degree they intended to punish the target person's immoral behavior and to reward their moral behavior (Genschow et al., 2017). The results demonstrated that participants' belief in free will is positively correlated with their intention to punish as well as to reward others. Moreover, participants' correspondence bias mediated this relationship indicating that ascribed intentionality is crucial not only for punishing others for their immoral behavior, but also for rewarding them for moral behavior.

Summary and Outlook

Although experimental manipulations on free will beliefs may not affect social attitudes, judgments, and behaviors as previously assumed, our investigations demonstrate that belief in free will measured as interindividual difference is related to various societal relevant behaviors including punishment, victim blaming, and rewarding behavior. A main reason of this relation is people's tendency to perceive others' behavior as internally generated and intentionally driven. It might well be that the link between belief in free will and perceiving behavior as intentionally driven also relates to other pro- and antisocial behaviors. For instance, it is reasonable to predict that since belief in free will is related to perceiving responsibility for one's own actions, free will beliefs reduce antisocial behavior such as prejudice and increase moral behavior such as helping or donating behavior. Future research may aim to investigate this relation more directly. Moreover, in future research we would like to test whether free will beliefs are positively related to emotions that are influenced by internal attributions. For example, a straightforward prediction is that people believing in free will experience more pride, embarrassment, shame, or guilt, because these emotions strongly depend on attributing one's own success and failure to internal factors (Tracy & Robins, 2004).

References

Aarts, H., & van den Bos, K. (2011). On the foundations of beliefs in free will: Intentional binding and unconscious priming in self-agency. *Psychological Science, 22*(4), 532–7.

Alquist, J. L., Ainsworth, S. E., & Baumeister, R. F. (2013). Determined to conform: Disbelief in free will increases conformity. *Journal of Experimental Social Psychology, 49,* 80–6.

Alquist, J. L., Ainsworth, S. E., Baumeister, R. F., Daly, M., & Stillman, T. F. (2015). The making of might-have-beens: Effects of free will belief on counterfactual thinking. *Personality and Social Psychology Bulletin, 41,* 268–83.

Association, F. I. d. F. (2015). *Laws of the Game 2015/2016.* Zürich, Switzerland: Federation Internationale de Football Association.

Baumeister, R. F., Masicampo, E., & DeWall, C. N. (2009). Prosocial benefits of feeling free: Disbelief in free will increases aggression and reduces helpfulness. *Personality and Social Psychology Bulletin, 35,* 260–8.

Bode, S., Murawski, C., Soon, C. S., Bode, P., Stahl, J., & Smith, P. L. (2014). Demystifying "free will": The role of contextual information and evidence accumulation for predictive brain activity. *Neuroscience & Biobehavioral Reviews, 47,* 636–45.

Brass, M., Furstenberg, A., & Mele, A. R. (2019). Why neuroscience does not disprove free will. *Neuroscience & Biobehavioral Reviews, 102,* 251–63.

Carey, J. M., & Paulhus, D. L. (2013). Worldview implications of believing in free will and/or determinism: Politics, morality, and punitiveness. *Journal of Personality, 81,* 130–41.

Caruso, G. D. (2014). (Un) just deserts: The dark side of moral responsibility. *Southwest Philosophy Review, 30,* 27–38.

Castelli, F., Happé, F., Frith, U., & Frith, C. (2000). Movement and mind: A functional imaging study of perception and interpretation of complex intentional movement patterns. *Neuroimage, 12,* 314–25.

Chivers, T. (2010). Neuroscience, free will and determinism: "I'm just a machine." *The Telegraph.* http://www.telegraph.co.uk/news/science/8058541/Neuroscience-free-will-and-determinism-Im-just-a-machine.html.

Crescioni, A. W., Baumeister, R. F., Ainsworth, S. E., Ent, M., & Lambert, N. M. (2016). Subjective correlates and consequences of belief in free will. *Philosophical Psychology, 29,* 41–63.

Crick, F. (1994). *The astonishing hypothesis: The science search for the soul.* New York: Touchstone.

Crone, D. L., & Levy, N. L. (2019). Are free will believers nicer people? (Four studies suggest not). *Social Psychological and Personality Science, 10,* 612–19.

Dennett, D. C. (2015). *Elbow Room: The Varieties of Free Will Worth Wanting.* Cambridge, MA: MIT Press.

Eben, C., Zhang, C., Cracco, E., Brass, M., Billieux, J., & Verbruggen, F. (2020). Are post-error adjustments influenced by beliefs in free will? A failure to directly replicate Rigoni, Wilquin, Brass and Burle, 2013. *Royal Society Open Science, 7*(11), 200664. DOI:10.1098/rsos.200664.

Ewusi-Boisvert, E., & Racine, E. (2018). A critical review of methodologies and results in recent research on belief in free will. *Neuroethics, 11*(1), 97–110.

Frith, C. D. (2012). The role of metacognition in human social interactions. *Phil. Trans. R. Soc. B, 367,* 2213–23.

Genschow, O., & Brass, M. (2015). The predictive chameleon: Evidence for anticipated action. *Journal of Experimental Psychology: Human Perception and Performance, 41*, 265–8.

Genschow, O., & Groß-Bölting, J. (2021). The role of attention in anticipated action effects. *Journal of Experimental Psychology: Human Perception and Performance, 47*, 323–330.

Genschow, O., & Lange, J. (2021). Belief in free will affects internal attribution in self-perception. *Manuscript in Preparation*.

Genschow, O., & Vehlow, B. (2021). Free to blame? The role of free will belief in victim blaming. *Consciousness and Cognition, 88*, 103074.

Genschow, O., Rigoni, D., & Brass, M. (2017). Belief in free will affects causal attributions when judging others' behavior. *Proceedings of the National Academy of Sciences, 114*, 10071–6.

Genschow, O., Rigoni, D., & Brass, M. (2019). The hand of god or the hand of Maradona? Believing in free will increases perceived intentionality of others' behavior. *Consciousness and Cognition, 70*, 80–7.

Genschow, O., Hawickhorst, H., Rigoni, D., Aschermann, E., & Brass, M. (2020). Professional judges' disbelief in free will and punishment. *Social Psychological and Personality Science, 12*, 357–62.

Genschow, O., Cracco, E., Schneider, J., Protzko, J., Wisniewski, D., Brass, M., & Schooler, J. (2021). Manipulating belief in free will and its downstream consequences: A meta-analysis *Psyarxiv*. doi:10.31234/osf.io/quwgr

Gilbert, D. T., & Malone, P. S. (1995). The correspondence bias. *Psychological Bulletin, 117*, 21–38.

Giner-Sorolla, R., Embley, J., & Johnson, L. (2016). Replication of Vohs & Schooler (2008, PS, Study 1). Retrieved from osf.io/i29mh.

Greenberg, J. (1991). Motivation to inflate performance ratings: Perceptual bias or response bias? *Motivation and Emotion, 15*, 81–97.

Greenberg, J., Pyszczynski, T., & Solomon, S. (1982). The self-serving attributional bias: Beyond self-presentation. *Journal of Experimental Social Psychology, 18*, 56–67.

Greene, J., & Cohen, J. (2004). For the law, neuroscience changes nothing and everything. *Philos Trans R Soc Lond B Biol Sci, 359*, 1775–85.

Griffin, A. (2016). Free will could all be an illusion, scientists suggest after study shows choice may just be brain tricking itself. *Independent*. http://www.independent.co.uk/news/science/free-will-could-all-be-an-illusion-scientists-suggest-after-study-that-shows-choice-could-just-be-a7008181.html.

Harris, S. (2012). *Free Will*. New York: Simon and Schuster.

Janoff-Bulman, R., & Frieze, I. H. (1983). A theoretical perspective for understanding reactions to victimization. *Journal of Social Issues, 39*, 1–17.

Lambert, A. J., & Raichle, K. (2000). The role of political ideology in mediating judgments of blame in rape victims and their assailants: A test of the just world, personal responsibility, and legitimization hypotheses. *Personality and Social Psychology Bulletin, 26*, 853–63.

Lerner, M. J. (1970). The desire for justice and reactions to victims. In J. Macaulay & L. Berkowitz (Eds.), *Altruism and Helping Behavior* (pp. 205–29). New York: Academic Press.

Lerner, M. J. (1980). *The Belief in a Just World: A Fundamental Delusion*. New York: Plenum Press.

Lerner, M. J., & Miller, D. T. (1978). Just world research and the attribution process: Looking back and ahead. *Psychological Bulletin, 85*, 1030–51.

Libet, B., Gleason, C. A., Wright, E. W., & Pearl, D. K. (1983). Time of conscious intention to act in relation to onset of cerebral activity (readiness-potential) the unconscious initiation of a freely voluntary act. *Brain, 106*, 623–42.

Libet, B., Wright, E. W., & Gleason, C. A. (1993). Readiness-potentials preceding unrestricted 'spontaneous' vs. pre-planned voluntary acts. In *Neurophysiology of Consciousness* (pp. 229–42). Boston: Springer.

Lynn, M., Van Dessel, P., & Brass, M. (2013). The influence of high-level beliefs on self-regulatory engagement: evidence from thermal pain stimulation. *Frontiers in Psychology, 4*.

Lynn, M. T., Muhle-Karbe, P. S., Aarts, H., Brass, M. (2014). Priming determinist beliefs diminishes implicit (but not explicit) components of self-agency. *Frontiers in Psychology, 17*, https://doi.org/10.3389/fpsyg.2014.01483.

MacKenzie, M. J., Vohs, K. D., & Baumeister, R. F. (2014). You didn't have to do that: Belief in free will promotes gratitude. *Personality and Social Psychology Bulletin, 40*, 1423–34.

Martin, N. D., Rigoni, D., & Vohs, K. D. (2017). Free will beliefs predict attitudes toward unethical behavior and criminal punishment: A global analysis. *Proceedings of the National Academy of Sciences, 114*, 7325–30.

Mezulis, A. H., Abramson, L. Y., Hyde, J. S., & Hankin, B. L. (2004). Is there a universal positivity bias in attributions? A meta-analytic review of individual, developmental, and cultural differences in the self-serving attributional bias. *Psychological Bulletin, 130*, 711–47.

Miller, D. T., & Ross, M. (1975). Self-serving biases in the attribution of causality: Fact or fiction? *Psychological Bulletin, 82*, 213–25.

Monroe, A. E., & Malle, B. F. (2010). From uncaused will to conscious choice: The need to study, not speculate about people's folk concept of free will. *Review of Philosophy and Psychology, 1*, 211–24.

Monroe, A. E., Brady, G., & Malle, B. F. (2017). This isn't the free will worth looking for general free will beliefs do not influence moral judgments, agent-specific choice ascriptions do. *Social Psychological and Personality Science, 8*(2), 191–9.

Moynihan, A. B., Igou, E. R., & Van Tilburg, W. A. (2019). Lost in the crowd: Conformity as escape following disbelief in free will. *European Journal of Social Psychology, 49*, 503–20.

Murray, D., & Nahmias, E. (2014). Explaining away incompatibilist intuitions. *Philosophy and Phenomenological Research, 88*, 434–67.

Nadelhoffer, T. (2011). The threat of shrinking agency and free will disillusionism. In L. Nadel & W. Sinnott-Armstrong (Eds.), *Conscious Will and Responsibility* (pp. 173–188). New York: Oxford University Press.

Nadelhoffer, T., Shepard, J., Crone, D. L., Everett, J. A., Earp, B. D., & Levy, N. (2020). Does encouraging a belief in determinism increase cheating? Reconsidering the value of believing in free will. *Cognition, 203*, 104342.

Nadelhoffer, T., Shepard, J., Nahmias, E., Sripada, C., & Ross, L. T. (2014). The free will inventory: Measuring beliefs about agency and responsibility. *Consciousness and Cognition, 25*, 27–41.

Nahmias, E., Morris, S., Nadelhoffer, T., & Turner, J. (2005). Surveying freedom: Folk intuitions about free will and moral responsibility. *Philosophical Psychology, 18*, 561–584.

Nahmias, E., Morris, S. G., Nadelhoffer, T., & Turner, J. (2006). Is incompatibilism intuitive? *Philosophy and Phenomenological Research, 73*, 28–53.

Newman, L., & Weitzer, L. (1956). Duress, free will and the criminal law. *Southern California Law Review, 30*, 313–34.

Nichols, S. (2004). The folk psychology of free will: Fits and starts. *Mind & Language, 19*, 473–502.
Nichols, S. (2006). Folk intuitions on free will. *Journal of Cognition and Culture, 6*, 57–86.
Nichols, S., & Knobe, J. (2007). Moral responsibility and determinism: The cognitive science of folk intuitions. *Nous, 41*, 663–85.
Open Science Collaboration. (2015). Estimating the reproducibility of psychological science. *Science, 349*, aac4716.
Paulhus, D. L., & Carey, J. M. (2011). The FAD-Plus: Measuring lay beliefs regarding free will and related constructs. *Journal of Personality Assessment, 93*, 96–104.
Pereboom, D. (2006). *Living without Free Will*. New York: Cambridge University Press.
Protzko, J., Ouimette, B., & Schooler, J. (2015). Believing there is no free will corrupts intuitive cooperation. Available at SSRN 2490855.
Rakos, R. F., Laurene, K. R., Skala, S., & Slane, S. (2008). Belief in free will: Measurement and conceptualization innovations. *Behavior and Social Issues, 17*, 20–40.
Rigoni, D., Kühn, S., Sartori, G., & Brass, M. (2011). Inducing disbelief in free will alters brain correlates of preconscious motor preparation the brain minds whether we believe in free will or not. *Psychological Science, 22*, 613–18.
Rigoni, D., Kühn, S., Gaudino, G., Sartori, G., & Brass, M. (2012). Reducing self-control by weakening belief in free will. *Consciousness and cognition, 21*, 1482–90.
Rigoni, D., Wilquin, H., Brass, M., & Burle, B. (2013). When errors do not matter: Weakening belief in intentional control impairs cognitive reaction to errors. *Cognition, 127*, 264–69.
Rigoni, D., Pourtois, G., & Brass, M. (2015). "Why should I care?"Challenging free will attenuates neural reaction to errors. *Social Cognitive and Affective Neuroscience, 10*, 262–8.
Rose, D., & Nichols, S. (2013). The lesson of bypassing. *Review of philosophy and psychology, 4*, 599–619.
Rotter, J. B. (1966). Generalized expectancies for internal versus external control of reinforcement. *Psychological Monographs: General and Applied, 80*, 1–28.
Ryan, W. (1976). *Blaming the Victim*. New York: Pantheon Books.
Saigle, V., Dubljević, V., & Racine, E. (2018). The impact of a landmark neuroscience study on free will: A qualitative analysis of articles using Libet and colleagues' methods. *AJOB Neuroscience, 9*, 29–41.
Sarkissian, H., Chatterjee, A., De Brigard, F., Knobe, J., Nichols, S., & Sirker, S. (2010). Is belief in free will a cultural universal? *Mind & Language, 25*, 346–58.
Schooler, J., Nadelhoffer, T., Nahmias, E., & Vohs, K. D. (2014). Measuring and manipulating beliefs and behaviors associated with free will. In A. R. Mele (Ed.), *Surrounding Free Will: Philosophy, Psychology, Neuroscience* (pp. 72–94). Oxford: Oxford University Press.
Schrag, Y., Tremea, A., Lagger, C., Ohana, N., & Mohr, C. (2016). Pro free will priming enhances "risk-taking" behavior in the iowa gambling task, but not in the balloon analogue risk task: Two independent priming studies. *PloS One, 11*, e0152297.
Schurger, A., Sitt, J. D., & Dehaene, S. (2012). An accumulator model for spontaneous neural activity prior to self-initiated movement. *Proceedings of the National Academy of Sciences, 109*, E2904–E2913.
Sedikides, C., & Strube, M. J. (1997). Self evaluation: To thine own self be good, to thine own self be sure, to thine own self be true, and to thine own self be better. In M. P. Zanna (Ed.), *Advances in Experimental Social Psychology* (Vol. 29, pp. 209–269). San Diego, CA: Academic Press.

Seto, E., & Hicks, J. A. (2016). Disassociating the agent from the self: Undermining belief in free will diminishes true self-knowledge. *Social Psychological and Personality Science, 7,* 726–34.

Shariff, A. F., & Vohs, K. D. (2014). The world without free will. *Scientific American, 310,* 76–9.

Shariff, A. F., Greene, J. D., Karremans, J. C., Luguri, J. B., Clark, C. J., Schooler, J. W., … Vohs, K. D. (2014). Free will and punishment: A mechanistic view of human nature reduces retribution. *Psychological Science, 25,* 1563–70.

Sheldon, J. P., & Parent, S. L. (2002). Clergy's attitudes and attributions of blame toward female rape victims. *Violence Against Women, 8,* 233–56.

Shepherd, J. (2012). Free will and consciousness: Experimental studies. *Consciousness and cognition, 21,* 915–27.

Shepard, J., & Reuter, S. (2012). Neuroscience, choice, and the free will debate. *AJOB Neuroscience, 3,* 7–11.

Smilansky, S. (2000). *Free Will and Illusion.* New York: Oxford University Press.

Smilansky, S. (2002). Free will, fundamental dualism, and the centrality of illusion. In R. Kane (Ed.), *The Oxford Handbook of Free Will.* New York: Oxford University Press.

Strömwall, L. A., Alfredsson, H., & Landström, S. (2013). Blame attributions and rape: Effects of belief in a just world and relationship level. *Legal and Criminological Psychology, 18,* 254–61.

Tracy, J. L., & Robins, R. W. (2004). " Putting the self into self-conscious emotions: A theoretical model." *Psychological Inquiry, 15,* 103–25.

Van Den Bos, K., & Maas, M. (2009). On the psychology of the belief in a just world: Exploring experiential and rationalistic paths to victim blaming. *Personality and Social Psychology Bulletin, 35,* 1567–78.

Van Inwagen, P. (1983). *An Essay on Free Will.* London: MIT Press.

Van Prooijen, J.-W., & Van Den Bos, K. (2009). We blame innocent victims more than I do: Self-construal level moderates responses to just-world threats. *Personality and Social Psychology Bulletin, 35,* 1528–39.

Viney, W., Waldman, D. A., & Barchilon, J. (1982). Attitudes toward punishment in relation to beliefs in free will and determinism. *Human Relations, 35,* 939–49.

Vohs, K. D., & Schooler, J. W. (2008). The value of believing in free will encouraging a belief in determinism increases cheating. *Psychological Science, 19,* 49–54.

Wegner, D. (2002). *The Illusion of Free Will.* Cambridge, MA: MIT Press.

Williams, S. (1984). Left-right ideological differences in blaming victims. *Political Psychology,* 573–81.

Wisniewski, D., Deutschländer, R., & Haynes, J.-D. (2019). Free will beliefs are better predicted by dualism than determinism beliefs across different cultures. *PloS One, 14,* e0221617.

Wolfe, T. (1997). Sorry, but your soul just died. *Forbes.* http://90.146.148.118/en/archiv_files/19971/E11997_19236.pdf.

Zhao, X., Liu, L., Zhang, X.-x., Shi, J.-x., & Huang, Z.-w. (2014). The effect of belief in free will on prejudice. *PloS One, 9,* e91572.

Zwaan, R. A. (2014). The value of believing in free will: A replication attempt. *Zeistgeist: Psychological Experimentation, Cognition, Language, and Academia.* https://rolfzwaan.blogspot.com/2013/03/the-value-of-believing-in-free-will.html (accessed November 30, 2019).

2

The Blame Efficiency Hypothesis: An Evolutionary Framework to Resolve Rationalist and Intuitionist Theories of Moral Condemnation

Cory J Clark

The history of punishment in human societies reveals a species as creative as it is brutal. Thousands of years ago in Ancient Rome, parricide may have been punished with *poena cullei* (penalty of the sack), or the practice of sewing up the offender in a leather sack along with a dog, a viper, a monkey, and a rooster and tossing the sack into the river (Bauman, 2002). Only hundreds of years ago in Europe, a method of execution involved trapping rats on the stomachs of prisoners and heating the rats' cages until they chewed their way through the prisoner to escape the heat (Motley, 1883). Many executions were public, and at least by modern standards, punishments often far outweighed the crimes. For example, under Hammurabi's Code, execution by drowning was considered an appropriate penalty for a tavern owner who cheated customers by watering down alcoholic drinks (Roth, 2014). Sometimes history reveals human nature better than any textbook filled with psychological studies ever could: Humans can be bitterly punitive, vengeful, and remorseless.

In the late 1800s, philosophical psychologist, Friedrich Nietzsche had the profound insight that notions of free will and human responsibility reflected these punitive instincts.

> Today we no longer have any pity for the concept of 'free will': we know only too well what it really is—the foulest of all theologians' artifices, aimed at making mankind 'responsible' in their sense ... Wherever responsibilities are sought, it is usually the instinct of wanting to judge and punish which is at work.
> (Nietzsche, 1889/1954, pp. 499)

One interpretation of this statement is that desires to blame and punish others influence beliefs in free will and attributions of responsibility to others. This suggestion is consistent with intuitionist theories of moral judgment (e.g., Haidt, 2001) and, as will be discussed in greater detail below, has been supported by research in social psychology and experimental philosophy (e.g., Alicke, 1992; Clark et al., 2014; Knobe, 2003; Reeder & Spores, 1983). In the present chapter, I review and expand on this work and incorporate insights from evolutionary psychology to forward the Blame

Efficiency Hypothesis, or the idea that people morally blame and judge others whose behavior is likely to be altered by blame and judgment. Under this perspective, the behavioral and psychological characteristics that people deem relevant to free will, moral responsibility, and blame deservingness (such as intentionality, age, apparent consciousness, cognitive or psychological impairment) are indicators of the extent to which moral blame and judgment would actually deter future bad behavior. If correct, we can expect people to ascribe free will, moral responsibility, and blameworthiness to actors who have the cognitive sophistication and social concern to *care* about their moral reputations, and to blame and judge actions that actors could possibly avoid in the future. For example, besmirching even the most obnoxious groundhog would be a waste of one's time because groundhogs do not care about their moral reputations (so far as I know anyway), whereas publicly criticizing an average twenty-year-old for behavior X might reduce recurrences of behavior X in both that twenty-year-old and similar others.

These considerations may also be subject to error management principles such that people will be *more* likely to assume a person has the requisite characteristics for responsibility in cases of harmful rather than helpful or neutral behavior. It would be more costly to erroneously not blame a harmdoer who could have been deterred by blame than to erroneously blame a harmdoer who could not have been deterred by blame, and so people should err on the side of thinking a harmdoer is morally responsible in ambiguous cases. In contrast, it is less clear that one sort of error (a false negative or false positive) would be more costly when determining whether a person is responsible for bringing about a neutral or helpful action, and so such cases should not motivate attributions of free will and responsibility in the same way harmful actions do. Overall then, the Blame Efficiency Hypothesis predicts that people (1) reserve attributions of moral responsibility (e.g., free will, causal control, intentionality, general responsibility) for actors and actions that would be deterred by moral judgment (i.e., actors who care about their moral reputations and actions such actors could avoid in the future), and (2) err on the side of assuming harmdoers are morally responsible in ambiguous situations.

The Crime Should Fit the Punishment

The notion that people should only be held responsible or blamed for actions within their control appears as a philosophical assumption (Kant, 1781/2005, 1785/1998), that is reflected also in legal systems (e.g., Appelbaum, 2006; Sayre, 1932), causal attribution models (Heider, 1958; Jones & Davis, 1965; Kelley, 1973), and normative models of responsibility and blame attribution (Alicke, 2000; Fincham & Jaspars, 1980; Shaver, 1985; Weiner, 1995). Blame often implies that a person should not have done what they did, which assumes that a person *could* not have done what they did. The implied causal order is that one should first assess the degree to which a harmful action was intentionally and deliberately performed by an agent (Schein & Gray, 2018), and *then* the appropriate amount of corresponding blame should be applied (Malle et al., 2014). If Jessica killed Emily because Jessica's car spun out of control on an icy road while Emily jogged on the sidewalk, we would assess that Jessica did not deliberately kill Emily and perhaps deserves no blame at all. In contrast, if Jessica intentionally swerved her car into Emily because Emily owned a rival pizzeria that was outperforming Jessica's, we would blame Jessica a great deal and likely desire a lengthy prison sentence for her.

Motivated Attributions of Responsibility. Over the past couple of decades, however, scholars have noticed that sometimes the causal order appears to occur in the opposite direction: when people are experiencing desires to blame and punish others, they attribute more intentionality, choice, freedom, and causal control to the person they wish to blame or punish (than when they have little or no desire to blame or punish). For example, people attributed more causal control to a speeding driver in a car accident when he was speeding home to hide a vial of cocaine than when he was speeding home to hide an anniversary present (Alicke, 1992), suggesting that perceptions of immorality increased perceptions of causal control. Similarly, people attributed more intentionality and causality to actors whose behavior produced harmful consequences than actors whose *identical* behaviors produced helpful consequences (e.g., Knobe, 2003, 2006; Knobe & Fraser, 2008; Leslie et al., 2006). In general, people seem to attribute more responsibility (and related attributes such as control and freedom) to harmful actions and actions with harmful outcomes than to closely matched helpful actions and actions with helpful outcomes (e.g., Clark et al., 2018; Reeder & Spores, 1983), neutral actions and actions with neutral outcomes (e.g., Cushman et al., 2008), and less harmful actions and actions with less harmful outcomes (e.g., Everett et al., 2020; Walster, 1966).

Most relevant to Nietzsche's assertion, research has found that people attribute more free will to morally bad actors than to comparable morally neutral (e.g., Clark et al., 2014) and morally good (Clark et al., 2018) actors. And people report stronger *beliefs* in free will and are more critical of science that threatens the existence of free will when they are experiencing desires to punish (Clark et al., 2021). For example, in one study, students in a social psychology course received an email from their professor shortly after a midterm exam informing them that one of their classmates had cheated, or in the control condition, students were simply told there would be an activity in the next class. All students were then asked to follow a link to an online survey which contained a short measure of free will belief and two questions about how severely students should be punished for cheating on exams. Those who believed one of their classmates had cheated recommended harsher punishments for cheaters and reported higher beliefs in free will than those who thought they were completing the survey for purposes of a class activity. These findings suggest the possibility that just as people are inclined to attribute more responsibility to harmful actions than to other sorts of actions, they become more attached to concepts of responsibility (i.e., free will) *in general* when they are exposed to harmful actions. Overall, the theoretical contribution of this and similar research is that the moral valence of an action, and specifically the moral *badness* of an action, contributes to judgments of responsibility above and beyond other kinds of more rational or normatively endorsed considerations.

Moral Intuitionism. According to moral intuitionist theories, many moral judgments arise from intuitive feelings and gut-level emotions rather than from careful, rational considerations (Haidt, 2001, 2012). Whereas a more rational process might be to evaluate carefully the specific circumstances of a harmful behavior, including how much control an actor hard, before deciding an appropriate level of punishment (à la "the punishment should fit the crime"), people might experience intuitive desires to blame and punish those who cause harm, and then decide the actor must have had control (à la "the crime should fit the punishment"). Although people prefer to think that their reasoning flows from evidence to conclusions, a large body of research suggests that sometimes the process flows the other way as well, such that we reason in order to obtain and justify preferred conclusions (e.g., Baumeister & Newman, 1994; Clark et al., 2015; Ditto et al., 2009; Ditto et al., 2019a; Ditto et al., 2019b; Ditto & Lopez, 1992; Haidt, 2001, 2012; Kunda, 1990; Liu & Ditto, 2013; Mercier & Sperber, 2011; Winegard & Clark, 2020). As an analogy, sometimes people reason more like lawyers, searching for evidence to support their preferred conclusion, rather than like scientists, carefully evaluating the evidence *before* coming to a conclusion. In the context of attributions of responsibility, exposure to harmful actions seems to trigger intuitive desires to blame or punish, and so people slightly ramp up their assessments of moral responsibility (e.g., Clark et al., 2014).

Some scholars have argued that motivated attribution effects can be explained away by other more rational processes. One argument involves the perceived counternormativity of harmful versus other kinds of actions: harmful actions tend to be more counternormative, and so people make stronger inferences about the agents who perform harmful actions, and thus attribute more responsibility (Monroe & Ysidron, 2020). For example, one discovery that has puzzled scholars for years, dubbed the side-effect effect or Knobe effect, finds that people will attribute more intentionality to a board chairman who *harms* the environment as a side-effect of his business plan than to a board chairman who *helps* the environment as a side-effect of his business plan, asserting that the harmful side-effect was intended but the helpful one was not (Knobe, 2003). Although one might interpret these findings as demonstrating motivated attributions of intentionality for harmful behaviors, there are more rational explanations: whereas almost nobody would abort a promising business plan to avoid causing positive environmental consequences, many might abort that exact same promising business plan to avoid causing harmful environmental consequences. And so, when evaluating the latter case, people know a bit more about the kind of person following through with the plan—that perhaps he is a bit selfish or callous—than when evaluating the former, and so attribute more intentionality to him.

Although people certainly take numerous situational variables into consideration when making moral assessments, I am not (at least yet) convinced that such an alternate explanation can fully account for many findings in the literature that demonstrate motivated attribution effects. For example, recent work has found that third-party observers of harmful actions attributed more free will to the perpetrator when the perpetrator was a political adversary harming a political comrade than when the perpetrator was a political comrade harming a political adversary, even when the harmful behavior was *identical* in both cases (Everett et al., 2020). Nothing between the actions under consideration differed except whether the victim and harmdoer were the third-party observers' in-group or out-group members, and people saw the out-group member who harmed the in-group member as *more* responsible than the in-group member who harmed the out-group member. Thus, no situational features, including counternormativity, varied between the actions except that people are more likely to care about harm to in-group members than harm to out-group members (e.g., Aboud, 2003; Clark et al., 2019; Clark & Winegard, 2020; Tajfel, 1982) and wish to excuse the harmful behavior of in-group members more than the harmful behavior of out-group members (e.g., Brandt et al., 2014; Claasen & Ensley, 2016; Jordan et al., 2014). In other studies, it was found that people attributed *more* free will to harmful actions that were judged as *less* counternormative than paired neutral actions (Clark et al, 2021). And in others, a reverse pattern was detected for one's own actions such that people attributed *less* free will to their own harmful behavior than to their own harmless behavior (Vonasch et al., 2017). Thus, in cases where one would wish to blame, people ascribe more responsibility, whereas in cases where one would wish to excuse, people ascribe less responsibility.

There remains some debate surrounding the meaning of apparent motivated attributions of responsibility, but overall, I find the conclusion that people's attributions of responsibility vary in accordance with their intuitive desires to blame (or excuse) most parsimoniously explains this body of work.

But the Punishment Should Also Fit the Crime

Rationalist Theories. But more *rational* features also influence attributions of responsibility. Motivated attributions of responsibility findings likely receive more attention in the literature than the effect sizes warrant because they seem somehow surprising, irrational, or normatively mistaken. For example, a meta-analysis of motivated free will attribution effects found a small to medium effect size, $r = .25$, and found evidence that such effects may not be particularly long-lasting (Clark et al., 2021). One can easily imagine cases in which a person might have extremely strong desires to blame or punish but find a causal agent completely free of responsibility (e.g., if a person killed one's sister in a car accident because they had a seizure while driving). According to the Blame Efficiency Hypothesis, these motivated attributions of responsibility are likely *minor adjustments* that occur on top of numerous otherwise more "rational" considerations. Many factors beyond intuitive desires to blame or punish influence whether people find others deserving of moral condemnation.

A Theory of Blame by Malle and colleagues (2014) contends that blame emerges when a person first identifies a norm-violating event or outcome and a causal agent for that event or outcome. Once such an agent is identified, a person considers whether the agent brought on the event intentionally, what their reasons were for acting, and whether they should and could have prevented the event. More intentionality, less justifiable reasons, and more obligation and capacity to prevent the event would all be associated with higher blame ascriptions. It is clear that people *do* take such circumstances into consideration when they decide how much to blame, and it is clear that people think people *should* take such circumstances into consideration when they decide how much to blame. The present chapter seeks to reconcile this model with motivated attributions of responsibility by considering *why*—from an evolutionary perspective—people would take circumstances such as intentionality into consideration while perhaps amplifying perceived intentionality and related responsibility-making attributions in cases of harmful behavior. My contention is that people morally condemn those whose future behavior can be shaped by moral condemnation, while erring on the side of assuming moral condemnation will work for harmful actions, because it would be a costlier error to underestimate responsiveness to moral condemnation than to overestimate it.

The Blame Efficiency Hypothesis

The Blame Efficiency Hypothesis might help resolve the apparent conflict between rationalist and intuitionist models of moral judgment, explaining why on the one hand, people make largely rational ascriptions of responsibility by considering intentionality and causal control, but on the other, people seem especially inclined to ascribe responsibility for harmful actions (relative to similar neutral and helpful ones).

Considerations for the Evolution of Blame. The human mind evolved to react and reason and guide human behavior in ways that promote fitness (Cosmides & Tooby, 1992). One recurrent adaptive problem for humans was and is how to reap the benefits of cooperation via social interaction while minimizing risk of exploitation and other harms. Consequently, humans evolved to detect and punish antisocial members of the social group (Axelrod & Hamilton, 1981; Fehr et al., 2002; Kurzban & Leary, 2001; Nowak & Sigmund, 1998; Trivers, 1971) because this helps sustain high levels of cooperation and minimizes risks of future personal victimization (Fehr & Fischbacher, 2004; Krasnow et al., 2016; Milinski et al., 2002).

Punishments (e.g., withholding freedoms and resources, delivering physical pain or discomfort, charging fines) could be delivered from a purely functionalist perspective—harmdoers must be punished so they learn their lesson and do not commit the infraction again (and third-party observers learn such infractions are prohibited). But humans do not merely punish fellow humans as a means of regulating harmful or risky behaviors. They also *blame* and *morally condemn* harmdoers. Many punishments involve not merely dispassionate deliverance of unpleasantness upon a harmdoer but also include emotionally and morally charged accusations about the harmdoer's behavior or character. Blame and moral condemnation imply that a harmdoer *deserves* punishment because they did something *morally wrong*. In fact, people experience such strong emotional impulses to punish others, they will do so even in cases where punishment will have no deterrent effect (e.g., Carlsmith et al., 2002; Crockett et al., 2014). Whereas one might scold a puppy for chewing a couch cushion in order to deter the puppy from chewing couch cushions in the future, one still might not *blame* the puppy in a way that implies that the puppy did something *morally wrong* or that the puppy is himself a *morally bad* puppy. In contrast, many human infractions elicit blame, moral outrage, and accusations of poor character (e.g., Ginther et al., 2021).

This kind of moral condemnation would be an effective deterrent (and thus beneficial for fitness) when directed toward those with concern for their moral reputations and the capacity to behave differently. The Blame Efficiency Hypothesis asserts that people will ascribe moral responsibility when a person (1) could conceivably avoid the bad behavior in similar situations and (2) cares about their own moral reputation, because absent these two conditions, moral condemnation would be a waste of one's energy.

Blaming Efficiently. The "rational" features that people deem relevant to blame are precisely those that indicate that blame and moral condemnation would be an effective strategy for regulating bad behavior. For example, people blame those who intend and desire to cause harm (e.g., Cushman, 2008; Malle et al., 2014; Malle & Knobe, 1997; Monroe & Malle, 2017). It makes less sense to blame others for harms they caused by accident because one cannot deter impulses that someone does not have in the first place. Thus, blame is a useful deterrent primarily for intended harms.

Similarly, blame would be less effective for behaviors people have no control over because they lack the capacity to alter their behavior in response to the blame. And indeed, people are less inclined to blame people for actions they cannot control. For example, blame is mitigated in cases of harmful behavior performed as a result of hypnosis or by a person with schizophrenia (Guglielmo et al., 2009). For the Blame Efficiency Hypothesis, the *perceived* level of control would be equally if not more important than the *actual* level of control. That is, people should blame behaviors that they (at least intuitively) *believe* people can control regardless of whether people actually can control those behaviors. This may partially explain why those who believe homosexuality is a choice find homosexuality more morally wrong (Haider-Markel & Joslyn, 2008), why those who find obesity and schizophrenia more controllable are more likely to blame people for such conditions (Chandrashekar, 2020), why higher perceptions of controllability (and lower perceptions of genetic causality) are associated with higher perceptions of moral wrongness and stronger desires to punish pedophilia, drug addiction, psychopathy, homosexuality, having a fetish, being racist, being transgender, obesity, depression, and schizophrenia (Mercier et al., 2019), why those who believe more in free will in general have stronger desires for vengeance (Shariff et al., 2014), and why those who perceive themselves as more able to control their own thoughts and mental states are more likely to moralize the mental states of others (Weiss et al., 2021).

Moral Condemnation as a Reputation-Damaging Strategy. Moral condemnation probably uniquely deters harmful behavior in humans because humans care deeply about maintaining positive moral reputations (e.g., Fehr, 2004; Sperber & Baumard, 2012; Tennie et al., 2010; Vonasch et al., 2018; Wu et al., 2016a, 2016b). People evolved to cooperate with valuable members of the social group and to punish and exclude costly members, and so people evolved to build and maintain positive reputations in order to reap social benefits and avoid social costs. Once people *cared* about maintaining positive reputations, *tarnishing* reputations or threatening to tarnish reputations would become an effective strategy for social regulation or shaping others' behavior in ways most beneficial to the self. And one way people can tarnish others' reputations is by ascribing moral responsibility to them for some negative outcome, for example, by asserting that the harmdoer caused harm *on purpose* because they are *mean* or *selfish*.

The Blame Efficiency Hypothesis predicts that people should be more likely to blame those who care more about their moral reputations and thus are likely to respond to blame by changing their behavior in future situations. More evidence is needed to support this component of the hypothesis, but there is some suggestive evidence for it. For example, it seems likely that babies and animals care little or not at all about their moral reputations and generally are not accused of immorality even when they cause harm (although, hundreds of years ago in Europe, animals were occasionally put on trial [Evans, 1906]). When animals or children misbehave, people frequently blame and hurl moral accusations at the owners or parents rather than the animals or children. Many modern legal systems reduce or eliminate entirely punishments for children and those with severe mental health disorders or cognitive disabilities (people who may have limited concern about their moral reputations), suggesting the possibility that people have reduced desire to blame or punish people who display minimal moral self-awareness. And the Black Sheep Effect describes a phenomenon whereby people more harshly judge in-group members than out-group members for identical transgressions (e.g., Marques et al., 1988). Presumably, people care more about their moral reputations among other in-group members, and so moral judgment is likely more effective at deterring bad behavior when it is directed at other in-group members. Some work also finds that people have stronger desires to punish those who intend to do good but cause harm than those who do not intend to do good and cause harm (Martin & Cushman, 2016). Good moral character might signal to others that one is concerned with one's moral reputation and so condemning a harmdoer with good moral character might be more effective than condemning a harmdoer with bad moral character.

I know of no research that directly tests the hypothesis that people are more likely to blame and condemn people with concern for their moral reputations. But a couple of predictions straightforwardly follow: people might be less inclined to blame and attribute moral responsibility to otherwise competent individuals who demonstrate little concern for their moral reputations, and people might be more inclined to blame and attribute moral responsibility to individuals who signal concern for their moral reputations (e.g., capacity for guilt; Svensson et al., 2013). For one intuitive example, imagine that a husband comes home from boys' night out noticeably intoxicated after he promised to cap it at two beers. The wife might wait until the next day when he wakes up sober to unleash the castigation. Although there could be numerous explanations for such a pattern, one possibility is that drunk people have reduced concern for their moral reputations (and thus are minimally affected by moral judgment), and so making moral accusations toward drunk people while they are still drunk is likely less useful than making moral accusations toward drunk people after they sober up.

People might have an intuitive moral system (Clark & Winegard, 2019a) that allows them to distinguish between those for whom blame and moral condemnation is effective, and those for whom it is not, and reserve moral condemnation for the former sort of people, because blaming and condemning the latter would be a waste. This would mean that moral responsibility is attributed both to those who appear to be capable of controlling their behavior in future situations and to those who appear to be controllable—likely to change their behavior in response to harsh moral judgment. In other words, people should most harshly condemn those who are *capable* of changing their future behavior and who would *want* to do so in order to avoid moral condemnation.

Error Management and The Don Corleone Principle. As with other evolved human tendencies, our tendencies to ascribe moral responsibility are subject to error management principles, such that we have a bias toward minimizing costlier errors. When faced with ambiguous information environments, human cognition evolved to favor less costly errors. For example, Haselton and Buss (2000) found that whereas men tend to overestimate a woman's sexual interest in him, women tend to underestimate a man's commitment to her. The argument is that for a man, it is costlier to miss out on a successful mating opportunity than to make an unwanted sexual advance toward a woman, whereas for a woman, it is costlier to risk pregnancy from a man who will abandon her and any potential future offspring immediately after sex than to miss out on a sexual opportunity with a man who might commit to her and then provide resources for her and her offspring. So in ambiguous mating contexts, men err on the side of assuming a woman is sexually interested in him, whereas women err on the side of assuming a man is not committed to her.

In the context of ascribing moral responsibility to others, it may be costlier *to not blame* and morally condemn a harmdoer whose future bad behavior would be deterred by moral condemnation than *to blame* and morally condemn a harmdoer whose future bad behavior would not be deterred by moral condemnation. When "responsibility" for bringing about a particular outcome is ambiguous, people might err on the side of assuming a harmdoer was morally responsible. Letting harmdoers off the hook could signal to others that one is an easily exploitable pushover, which would be highly costly for one's fitness. In contrast, being a bit too harsh in one's moral responsibility judgments might not be particularly costly (although read on for a crucial caveat described in greater detail below). Indeed, having a reputation as a harsh punisher could be evolutionarily advantageous as people might work harder to avoid harming such people. I call this The Don Corleone Principle:

> I'm a superstitious man, and if some unlucky accident should befall Michael, if he is to be shot in the head by a police officer, or be found hung dead in a jail cell … or if he should be struck by a bolt of lightning, then I'm going to blame some of the people in this room, and then I do not forgive.
> –Don Corleone, The Godfather

By indicating that he will seek vengeance even for accidental harms, The Godfather likely intimidates potential enemies and others from crossing him. Thus, identifying morally culpable agents, even when there may not be one, could be evolutionarily advantageous (Clark & Winegard, 2019b), whereas *not* identifying a morally culpable agent when there is one could be evolutionarily disastrous.

It is unclear that this cost asymmetry exists for underestimating (vs. overestimating) another's responsibility for bringing about neutral or helpful outcomes. Failing to properly ascribe responsibility to someone who does good might reduce others' tendencies to behave altruistically toward the self, but it would not put a target on one's back the same way being known as a sucker would. And no consequences come to mind for failing to ascribe responsibility to a person for bringing about neutral outcomes. Thus, in cases of harmful actions, people should err on the side of ascribing more responsibility than might be warranted rather than less. For helpful actions and especially for neutral actions, people should not have extra motivation to ascribe responsibility. And so we should observe that people ascribe more responsibility to harmful actions than to otherwise similar helpful or neutral ones.

Motivated attributions of responsibility show precisely this: people ascribe more intentionality, causal control, free will, etc. to people who cause harmful consequences than to similarly situated people who cause neutral or helpful consequences (e.g., Alicke, 1992, et al., 2008; Knobe, 2003; Reeder & Spores, 1983). And further, consistent with the possibility that failing to ascribe responsibility for morally good actions has relatively small but not non-existent costs, people attribute more free will to morally good actions than to morally neutral actions (Clark et al., 2018). This error management perspective may also explain why we observe similar moral responsibility maintenance biases when harms are directed toward the self or good others than bad others (Clark et al., 2014), in concrete rather than abstract cases (Nichols & Knobe, 2007; Struchiner et al., 2020), and in their own social worlds rather than in other worlds (Roskies & Nichols, 2008). The costlier it would be to fail to ascribe moral responsibility in ambiguous cases, the more inclined people should be to err on the side of moral responsibility.

Like most biases, these apparent asymmetries in responsibility-making attributions (e.g., free will, causal control, intentionality) should be larger in more ambiguous cases (e.g., Kopko et al., 2011; Munro et al., 2010), for example, when the harmful outcome was a side-effect of an action, when the harmful outcome was improbable (such as an accident caused by negligent or other irresponsible behavior), or when there were other extenuating circumstances that make the action difficult to interpret. Blatant biases, double standards, unfairness, and hypocrisy can injure a person's reputation and prestige (e.g., Jordan et al., 2017; Monroe & Malle, 2019), and so biases tend to reveal themselves in more ambiguous information environments (Clark et al., 2021). In the context of moral responsibility judgments, if a person were to harshly blame and punish someone who very clearly was not responsible for causing a harm, third-party observers might punish the punisher, making blatantly *unwarranted* blames costly (Clark et al., 2017; Malle et al., 2014). And so people should only "err on the side of moral responsibility" in ambiguous cases where third-party observers would be unlikely to deem the blame excessive.

However, moral judgments are *often* ambiguous (e.g., Clark & Winegard, 2020)—one cannot read minds or know with certainty whether a person intended to cause a harm or had ill will—and so such judgments should frequently be vulnerable to biased interpretations. This may explain why people judge completely ambiguous actions as immoral (Hester et al., 2020). And this may explain why many classic demonstrations of motivated attributions of responsibility rely on ambiguous cases, such as harmful side-effects resulting from more neutral behaviors (e.g., Knobe, 2003) or improbable outcomes from more neutral behaviors (e.g., Alicke, 1992).

Overall then, the Blame Efficiency Hypothesis may explain why ascriptions of moral responsibility and blameworthiness appear largely rational, but with a slight bias toward ascribing responsibility in cases of harmful behavior (in comparison with neutral or helpful behaviors). Blaming efficiently means reserving blame for cases in which blame will deter bad behavior in the blamed party and third-party observers, while minimizing the costly error of underblaming in ambiguous cases.

The Blame Efficiency Hypothesis and Free Will Belief

Finally, the Blame Efficiency Hypothesis may help explain the stubborn persistence of belief in free will. Many attributions of responsibility are evaluated on a case-by-case basis. Did this person *intend* to cause the harm? Could this person have avoided causing the harm? Would other people have not caused the harm? Unlike considerations of intentionality or causal control, free will feels different because many believe that the broad capacity for human moral responsibility relies on the existence of human free will. In other words, if people *in general* do not have free will, then *nobody* is *ever* morally responsible. Along with the other "Big Questions" such as the origin of the cosmos and the role of consciousness in human behavior, scholars have puzzled over whether people have free will for centuries or perhaps millennia (Baumeister et al., 2015; Baumeister et al., 2018). Scholars have debated what free will really is (e.g., Dennett, 2004; Frankfurt, 1969; Pereboom, 2006; van Inwagen,1983; Wolf, 1990), what laypeople *think* free will is (e.g., Feldman et al., 2014; Feldman & Chandrashekar, 2018; Feltz et al., 2009; Knobe et al., 2012; Monroe et al., 2014; Monroe & Malle, 2010; Nahmias et al., 2005; Nahmias et al., 2006; Nichols & Knobe, 2007; Vonasch et al., 2018), whether concepts of free will exist and vary across cultures (Berniūnas et al., 2021; Hannikainen et al., 2019; Sarkissian et al., 2010), as well as the causes of consequences of free will beliefs (Baumeister et al., 2009; Baumeister et al., 2015; Baumeister et al., 2018; Confer & Chopik, 2019; Feldman et al., 2016; Genschow et al., 2017; Genschow et al., 2020; Genschow & Vehlow, 2021; MacKenzie et al., 2014; Monroe et al., 2017; Nadelhoffer et al., 2020; Shariff et al., 2014; Vohs & Schooler, 2008). If we can draw anything from this (often contradictory) body of work, it is that people *care a lot* about the existence of free will and upholding the existence of free will, perhaps despite having no clear understanding of what it is (Clark et al., 2019).

Like motivated attributions of free will (e.g., Clark et al., 2017, 2018; Everett et al., 2020), the Blame Efficiency Hypothesis may explain motivated free will beliefs: people tend to report stronger *beliefs* in free will and resist science that challenges free will after exposure to others' harmful actions (e.g., Clark et al., 2014, 2021). The existence of free will may be the ultimate ambiguous moral judgment. We cannot fully comprehend all of the causes of human behavior, and so people err on the side of assuming people are capable of moral responsibility, especially when contemplating harmful actions.

Conclusion

The present chapter represents a first attempt at resolving seemingly contradictory perspectives on the folk psychology of blame: rationalist perspectives (which highlight how considerations of intentionality and causal control influence blame judgments) and intuitionist perspectives (which highlight how punitive desires influence judgments of intentionality and moral responsibility) by forwarding the Blame Efficiency Hypothesis. Through an evolutionary lens, we may view blame judgments as largely rational—based on whether blame serves as an effective deterrent for the harmdoer and similarly situated others—but with a small bias toward ascribing responsibility in ambiguous cases of harm to minimize the costly error of under-blaming.

References

Aboud, F. E. (2003). The formation of in-group favoritism and out-group prejudice in young children: Are they distinct attitudes? *Developmental psychology, 39*(1), 48–60.

Alicke, M. D. (1992). Culpable causation. *Journal of Personality and Social Psychology, 63*(3), 368–78.

Alicke, M. D. (2000). Culpable control and the psychology of blame. *Psychological Bulletin, 126*, 556–74.

Appelbaum, P. S. (2006). Law & psychiatry: Insanity, guilty minds, and psychiatric testimony. *Psychiatric Services, 57*(10), 1370–2.

Axelrod, R., & Hamilton, W. D. (1981). The evolution of cooperation. *Science, 211*, 1390–6.

Bauman, R. A. (2002). *Crime and Punishment in Ancient Rome*. New York: Routledge.

Baumeister, R. F., & Newman, L. S. (1994). Self-regulation of cognitive inference and decision processes. *Personality and Social Psychology Bulletin, 20*(1), 3–19.

Baumeister, R. F., Masicampo, E. J., & DeWall, C. N. (2009). Prosocial benefits of feeling free: Disbelief in free will increases aggression and reduces helpfulness. *Personality and Social Psychology Bulletin, 35*(2), 260–8.

Baumeister, R. F., Clark, C. J., & Luguri, J. (2015). Free will: Belief and reality. In A. Mele (Ed.), *Surrounding Free Will* (pp. 49–71). New York: Oxford University Press.

Baumeister, R. F., Lau, S., Maranges, H. M., & Clark, C. J. (2018). On the necessity of consciousness for sophisticated human action. *Frontiers in Psychology, 9*, 1925.

Berniūnas, R., Beinorius, A., Dranseika, V., Silius, V., & Rimkevičius, P. (2021). The weirdness of belief in free will. *Consciousness and Cognition, 87*, 103054.

Brandt, M. J., Reyna, C., Chambers, J. R., Crawford, J. T., & Wetherell, G. (2014). The ideological-conflict hypothesis: Intolerance among both liberals and conservatives. *Current Directions in Psychological Science, 23*(1), 27–34.

Carlsmith, K. M., Darley, J. M., & Robinson, P. H. (2002). Why do we punish? Deterrence and just deserts as motives for punishment. *Journal of Personality and Social Psychology, 83*, 284–99.

Claassen, R. L., & Ensley, M. J. (2016). Motivated reasoning and yard-sign-stealing partisans: Mine is a likable rogue, yours is a degenerate criminal. *Political Behavior, 38*(2), 317–35.

Clark, C. J., & Winegard, B. M. (2019a). Optimism in unconscious, intuitive morality. *Behavioral and Brain Sciences, 42*, e150.

Clark, C. J., & Winegard, B. M. (2019b). An evolutionary perspective on free will belief. *Science Trends*. https://sciencetrends.com/an-evolutionary-perspective-on-free-will.

Clark, C. J., & Winegard, B. M. (2020). Tribalism in war and peace: The nature and evolution of ideological epistemology and its significance for modern social science. *Psychological Inquiry, 31*(1), 1–22.

Clark, C. J., Luguri, J. B., Ditto, P. H., Knobe, J., Shariff, A. F., & Baumeister, R. F. (2014). Free to punish: a motivated account of free will belief. *Journal of Personality and Social Psychology, 106*, 501–13.

Clark, C. J., Chen, E. E., & Ditto, P. H. (2015). Moral coherence processes: Constructing culpability and consequences. *Current Opinion in Psychology, 6*, 123–8.

Clark, C. J., Bauman, C. W., Kamble, S. V., & Knowles, E. D. (2017). Intentional sin and accidental virtue? Cultural differences in moral systems influence perceived intentionality. *Social Psychological and Personality Science, 8*, 74–82.

Clark, C. J., Baumeister, R. F., & Ditto, P. H. (2017). Making punishment palatable: Belief in free will alleviates punitive distress. *Consciousness and Cognition, 51*, 193–211.

Clark, C. J., Shniderman, A., Luguri, J. B., Baumeister, R. F., & Ditto, P. H. (2018). Are morally good actions ever free? *Consciousness and Cognition, 63*, 161–82.

Clark, C. J., Winegard, B. M., & Baumeister, R. F. (2019). Forget the folk: Moral responsibility preservation motives and other conditions for compatibilism. *Frontiers in Psychology, 10*, 215.

Clark, C. J., Liu, B. S., Winegard, B. M., & Ditto, P. H. (2019). Tribalism is human nature. *Current Directions in Psychological Science, 28*(6), 587–92.

Clark, C. J., Winegard, B. M., & Shariff, A. F. (2021). Motivated free will beliefs: The theory, new (preregistered) studies, and three meta-analyses. *Journal of Experimental Psychology: General, 150*(7), e22.

Clark, C. J., Honeycutt, N., & Jussim, L. (in press). Replicability and the psychology of science. In S. Lilienfeld, A. Masuda, & W. O'Donohue (Eds.), *Questionable Research Practices in Psychology*. New York: Springer.

Chandrashekar, S. P. (2020). It's in your control: Free will beliefs and attribution of blame to obese people and people with mental illness. *Collabra: Psychology, 6*(1), 29.

Confer, J. A., & Chopik, W. J. (2019). Behavioral explanations reduce retributive punishment but not reward: The mediating role of conscious will. *Consciousness and Cognition, 75*, 102808.

Cosmides, L., & Tooby, J. (1992). Cognitive adaptations for social exchange. In J. Barkow, L. Cosmides, & J. Tooby (Eds.), *The Adapted Mind* (pp. 163–228). New York: Oxford University Press.

Crockett, M. J., Özdemir, Y., & Fehr, E. (2014). The value of vengeance and the demand for deterrence. *Journal of Experimental Psychology: General, 143*, 2279–86.

Cushman, F. (2008). Crime and punishment: Distinguishing the roles of causal and intentional analyses in moral judgment. *Cognition, 108*(2), 353–80.

Cushman, F., Knobe, J., & Sinnott-Armstrong, W. (2008). Moral appraisals affect doing/allowing judgments. *Cognition, 108*(1), 281–9.

Dennett, D. C. (2004). *Freedom Evolves*. New York: Penguin.

Ditto, P. H., & Lopez. (1992). Motivated Skepticism: Use of different decision criteria for preferred and nonpreferred conclusions. *Journal of Personality and Social Psychology, 63*, 568–84.

Ditto, P. H., Pizarro, D. A., & Tannenbaum, D. (2009). Motivated moral reasoning. *Psychology of Learning and Motivation, 50*, 307–38.

Ditto, P. H., Liu, B. S., Clark, C. J., Wojcik, S. P., Chen, E. E., Grady, R. H., ... & Zinger, J. F. (2019a). At least bias is bipartisan: A meta-analytic comparison of partisan bias in liberals and conservatives. *Perspectives on Psychological Science, 14*(2), 273–91.

Ditto, P. H., Clark, C. J., Liu, B. S., Wojcik, S. P., Chen, E. E., Grady, R. H., ... & Zinger, J. F. (2019b). Partisan bias and its discontents. *Perspectives on Psychological Science, 14*(2), 304–16.

Evans, E. P. (1906). *The Criminal Prosecution and Capital Punishment of Animals.* London: Heinemann.

Everett, J. A. C., Clark, C. J., Meindl, P., Luguri, J. B., Earp, B. D., Graham, J., ... & Shariff, A. F. (2020). Political differences in free will belief are associated with differences in moralization. *Journal of Personality and Social Psychology, 120*, 461–83.

Fehr, E. (2004). Don't lose your reputation. *Nature, 432*, 449–50.

Fehr, E., & Fischbacher, U. (2004). Social norms and human cooperation. *Trends in Cognitive Sciences, 8*, 185–90.

Fehr, E., Fischbacher, U., & Gächter, S. (2002). Strong reciprocity, human cooperation, and the enforcement of social norms. *Human Nature, 13*, 1–25.

Feldman, G., & Chandrashekar, S. P. (2018). Laypersons' beliefs and intuitions about free will and determinism: New insights linking the social psychology and experimental philosophy paradigms. *Social Psychological and Personality Science, 9*(5), 539–49.

Feldman, G., Baumeister, R. F., & Wong, K. F. E. (2014). Free will is about choosing: The link between choice and the belief in free will. *Journal of Experimental Social Psychology, 55*, 239–45.

Feldman, G., Chandrashekar, S. P., & Wong, K. F. E. (2016). The freedom to excel: Belief in free will predicts better academic performance. *Personality and Individual Differences, 90*, 377–83.

Feldman, G., Wong, K. F. E., & Baumeister, R. F. (2016). Bad is freer than good: Positive-negative asymmetry in attributions of free will. *Consciousness and Cognition, 42*, 26–40.

Feltz, A., Cokely, E. T., & Nadelhoffer, T. (2009). Natural compatibilism versus natural incompatibilism: Back to the drawing board. *Mind & Language, 24*(1), 1–23.

Fincham, F. D., & Jaspers, J. M. (1980). Attribution of responsibility: From man the scientist to man as lawyer. In L. Berkowitz (Ed.), *Advances in Experimental Social Psychology* (Vol. 13, pp. 82–139). New York: Academic Press.

Frankfurt, H. G. (1969). Alternate possibilities and moral responsibility. *The Journal of Philosophy, 66*(23), 829–39.

Genschow, O., & Vehlow, B. (2021). Free to blame? Belief in free will is related to victim blaming. *Consciousness and Cognition, 88*, 103074.

Genschow, O., Rigoni, D., & Brass, M. (2017). Belief in free will affects causal attributions when judging others' behavior. *Proceedings of the National Academy of Sciences, 114*(38), 10071–6.

Genschow, O., Hawickhorst, H., Rigoni, D., Aschermann, E., & Brass, M. (2020). Professional judges' disbelief in free will does not decrease punishment. *Social Psychological and Personality Science, 12*, 357–62.

Ginther, M. R., Hartsough, L. E., & Marois, R. (2021). Moral outrage drives the interaction of harm and culpable intent in third-party punishment decisions. *Emotion.*

Guglielmo, S., Monroe, A. E., & Malle, B. F. (2009). At the heart of morality lies folk psychology. *Inquiry, 52*(5), 449–66.

Haider-Markel, D. P., & Joslyn, M. R. (2008). Beliefs about the origins of homosexuality and support for gay rights: An empirical test of attribution theory. *Public Opinion Quarterly, 72*(2), 291–310.

Haidt, J. (2001). The emotional dog and its rational tail: A social intuitionist approach to moral judgment. *Psychological Review, 108*(4), 814–34.

Haidt, J. (2012). *The Righteous Mind*. New York: Penguin Books.

Hannikainen, I. R., Machery, E., Rose, D., Stich, S., Olivola, C. Y., Sousa, P., ... & Zhu, J. (2019). For whom does determinism undermine moral responsibility? Surveying the conditions for free will across cultures. *Frontiers in Psychology, 10*, 2428.

Haselton, M. G., & Buss, D. M. (2000). Error management theory: A new perspective on biases in cross-sex mind reading. *Journal of Personality and Social Psychology, 78*(1), 81–91.

Heider, F. (1958). The naive analysis of action. In F. Heider (Ed.), *The Psychology of Interpersonal Relations* (pp. 101–124). New York: Wiley.

Hester, N., Payne, B. K., & Gray, K. (2020). Promiscuous condemnation: People assume ambiguous actions are immoral. *Journal of Experimental Social Psychology, 86*, 103910.

Jones, E. E. & Davis, K. E. (1965). From acts to dispositions: The attribution process in person perception. In L. Berkowitz (Ed.), *Advances in Experimental Social Psychology* (Vol. 2, pp. 219–66). New York: Academic Press.

Jordan, J. J., McAuliffe, K., & Warneken, F. (2014). Development of in-group favoritism in children's third-party punishment of selfishness. *Proceedings of the National Academy of Sciences, 111*(35), 12710–15.

Jordan, J. J., Sommers, R., Bloom, P., & Rand, D. G. (2017). Why do we hate hypocrites? Evidence for a theory of false signaling. *Psychological Science, 28*(3), 356–68.

Kant, I. (1998). *Groundwork for the Metaphysics of Morals*. M. Gregor (Ed., Tr.). New York: Cambridge University Press.(Original work published in 1785).

Kant, I. (2005). *The Critique of Pure Reason*. P. Guyer & A. W. Wood (Tr.) New York: Cambridge University Press.(Original work published in 1781).

Kelley, H. (1973). The processes of causal attribution. *American Psychologist, 28*, 107–28.

Knobe, J. (2003). Intentional action and side effects in ordinary language. *Analysis, 63*(3), 190–4.

Knobe, J. (2006). The concept of intentional action: A case study in the uses of folk psychology. *Philosophical Studies, 130*(2), 203–31.

Knobe, J., & Fraser, B. (2008). Causal judgment and moral judg- ment: Two experiments. In *Moral psychology (Vol. 2): The cognitive Science of Morality: Intuition and diversity* (pp. 441–7). Cambridge, MA: MIT Press.

Knobe, J., Buckwalter, W., Nichols, S., Robbins, P., Sarkissian, H., & Sommers, T. (2012). Experimental philosophy. *Annual Review of Psychology, 63*, 81–99.

Kopko, K. C., Bryner, S. M., Budziak, J., Devine, C. J., & Nawara, S. P. (2011). In the eye of the beholder? Motivated reasoning in disputed elections. *Political Behavior, 33*(2), 271–90.

Krasnow, M. M., Delton, A. W., Cosmides, L., & Tooby, J. (2016). Looking under the hood of third-party punishment reveals design for personal benefit. *Psychological Science, 27*(3), 405–18.

Kunda, Z. (1990). The case for motivated reasoning. *Psychological Bulletin, 108*, 480–98.

Kurzban, R., & Leary, M. R. (2001). Evolutionary origins of stigmatization: The functions of social exclusion. *Psychological Bulletin, 127*, 187–208.

Leslie, A. M, Knobe, J., & Cohen, A. (2006). Acting intentionally and the side-effect effect: Theory of mind and moral judgment. *Psychological Science, 17*, 421–7.

Liu, B. S., & Ditto, P. H. (2013). What dilemma? Moral evaluation shapes factual belief. *Social Psychological and Personality Science, 4*(3), 316–23.

MacKenzie, M. J., Vohs, K. D., & Baumeister, R. F. (2014). You didn't have to do that: Belief in free will promotes gratitude. *Personality and Social Psychology Bulletin, 40*(11), 1423–34.

Malle, B. F., & Knobe, J. (1997). The folk concept of intentionality. *Journal of Experimental Social Psychology, 33*(2), 101–21.

Malle, B. F., Guglielmo, S., & Monroe, A. E. (2014). A theory of blame. *Psychological Inquiry, 25*(2), 147–86.

Malti, T., & Krettenauer, T. (2013). The relation of moral emotion attributions to prosocial and antisocial behavior: A meta-analysis. *Child Development, 84*(2), 397–412.

Marques, J. M., Yzerbyt, V. Y., & Leyens, J. P. (1988). The "black sheep effect": Extremity of judgments towards ingroup members as a function of group identification. *European Journal of Social Psychology, 18*(1), 1–16.

Martin, J. W., & Cushman, F. (2016). Why we forgive what can't be controlled. *Cognition, 147*, 133–43.

Mercier, B., Clark, C. J., & Shariff, A. F. (2019). *Correlates of Perceived Mental Illness* [Unpublished manuscript]. Department of Psychological Science, University of California, Irvine, Irvine, CA.

Mercier, H. & Sperber, D. (2011). Why do humans reason? Arguments for an argumentative theory. *Behavioral and Brain Sciences, 34*, 57–111.

Milinski, M., Semmann, D., & Krambeck, H. J. (2002). Reputation helps solve the "tragedy of the commons." *Nature, 415*, 424–6.

Monroe, A. E., & Malle, B. F. (2010). From uncaused will to conscious choice: The need to study, not speculate about people's folk concept of free will. *Review of Philosophy and Psychology, 1*(2), 211–24.

Monroe, A. E., & Malle, B. F. (2017). Two paths to blame: Intentionality directs moral information processing along two distinct tracks. *Journal of Experimental Psychology: General, 146*(1), 123–33.

Monroe, A. E., & Malle, B. F. (2019). People systematically update moral judgments of blame. *Journal of Personality and Social Psychology, 116*(2), 215–36.

Monroe, A. E., & Ysidron, D. W. (2020). Not so motivated after all? Three replication attempts and a theoretical challenge to a morally motivated belief in free will. *Journal of Experimental Psychology: General, 150*, e1–e12.

Monroe, A. E., Dillon, K. D., & Malle, B. F. (2014). Bringing free will down to Earth: People's psychological concept of free will and its role in moral judgment. *Consciousness and Cognition, 27*, 100–8.

Monroe, A. E., Brady, G. L., & Malle, B. F. (2017). This isn't the free will worth looking for: General free will beliefs do not influence moral judgments, agent-specific choice ascriptions do. *Social Psychological and Personality Science, 8*(2), 191–9.

Motley, J. L. (1883). *The Rise of the Dutch Republic*. Netherlands: Bickers & Son.

Munro, G. D., Weih, C., & Tsai, J. (2010). Motivated suspicion: Asymmetrical attributions of the behavior of political ingroup and outgroup members. *Basic and Applied Social Psychology, 32*(2), 173–84.

Nadelhoffer, T. (2006). Bad acts, blameworthy agents, and intentional actions: Some problems for juror impartiality. *Philosophical Explorations, 9*(2), 203–19.

Nadelhoffer, T., Shepard, J., Crone, D. L., Everett, J. A., Earp, B. D., & Levy, N. (2020). Does encouraging a belief in determinism increase cheating? Reconsidering the value of believing in free will. *Cognition, 203*, 104342.

Nahmias, E., Morris, S., Nadelhoffer, T., & Turner, J. (2005). Surveying freedom: Folk intuitions about free will and moral responsibility. *Philosophical Psychology, 18*(5), 561–84.

Nahmias, E., Morris, S. G., Nadelhoffer, T., & Turner, J. (2006). Is incompatibilism intuitive? *Philosophy and Phenomenological Research, 73*(1), 28–53.

Nichols, S., & Knobe, J. (2007). Moral responsibility and determinism: The cognitive science of folk intuitions. *Nous, 41*(4), 663–85.

Nietzsche, F. (1954). *Twilight of the Idols*. W. Kaufmann (Tr.). New York: Penguin Books. (Original work published 1889).

Nowak, M. A., & Sigmund, K. (1998). Evolution of indirect reciprocity by image scoring. *Nature, 393*, 573–7.

O'Connor, C. (2016). The evolution of guilt: A model-based approach. *Philosophy of Science, 83*(5), 897–908.

Pereboom, D. (2006). *Living without Free Will*. New York: Cambridge University Press.

Reeder, G. D., & Spores, J. M. (1983). The attribution of morality. *Journal of Personality and Social Psychology, 44*(4), 736–45.

Roskies, A. L., & Nichols, S. (2008). Bringing moral responsibility down to earth. *The Journal of Philosophy, 105*(7), 371–88.

Roth, M. P. (2014). *An Eye for an Eye: A Global History of Crime and Punishment*. London: Reaktion Books.

Sarkissian, H., Chatterjee, A., De Brigard, F., Knobe, J., Nichols, S., & Sirker, S. (2010). Is belief in free will a cultural universal? *Mind & Language, 25*(3), 346–58.

Sayre, F. B. (1932). Mens rea. *Harvard Law Review, 45*(6), 974–1026.

Schein, C., & Gray, K. (2018). The theory of dyadic morality: Reinventing moral judgment by redefining harm. *Personality and Social Psychology Review, 22*(1), 32–70.

Shariff, A. F., Greene, J. D., Karremans, J. C., Luguri, J. B., Clark, C. J., Schooler, J. W., … & Vohs, K. D. (2014). Free will and punishment: A mechanistic view of human nature reduces retribution. *Psychological Science, 25*(8), 1563–70.

Shaver, K. G. (1985). *The Attribution of Blame*. New York: Springer-Verlag.

Sperber, D., & Baumard, N. (2012). Moral reputation: An evolutionary and cognitive perspective. *Mind & Language, 27*, 495–518.

Struchiner, N., De Almeida, G. D. F., & Hannikainen, I. R. (2020). Legal decision-making and the abstract/concrete paradox. *Cognition, 205*, 104421.

Svensson, R., Weerman, F. M., Pauwels, L. J., Bruinsma, G. J., & Bernasco, W. (2013). Moral emotions and offending: Do feelings of anticipated shame and guilt mediate the effect of socialization on offending? *European Journal of Criminology, 10*(1), 22–39.

Tajfel, H. (1982). Social psychology of intergroup relations. *Annual Review of Psychology, 33*(1), 1–39.

Tennie, C., Frith, U., & Frith, C. D. (2010). Reputation management in the age of the world-wide web. *Trends in Cognitive Sciences, 14*, 482–8.

Trivers, R. L. (1971). The evolution of reciprocal altruism. *The Quarterly Review of Biology, 46*, 35–57.

Van Inwagen, P. (1983). *An Essay on Free Will*. Oxford: Oxford University Press.

Vohs, K. D., & Schooler, J. W. (2008). The value of believing in free will: Encouraging a belief in determinism increases cheating. *Psychological Science, 19*(1), 49–54.

Vonasch, A. J., Clark, C. J., Lau, S., Vohs, K. D., & Baumeister, R. F. (2017). Ordinary people associate addiction with loss of free will. *Addictive Behaviors Reports, 5*, 56–66.

Vonasch, A. J., Reynolds, T., Winegard, B. M., & Baumeister, R. F. (2018). Death before dishonor: Incurring costs to protect moral reputation. *Social Psychological and Personality Science, 9*, 604–13.

Vonasch, A. J., Baumeister, R. F., & Mele, A. R. (2018). Ordinary people think free will is a lack of constraint, not the presence of a soul. *Consciousness and Cognition, 60*, 133–51.

Walster, E. (1966). Assignment of responsibility for an accident. *Journal of Personality and Social Psychology*, *3*(1), 73–9.

Weiner, B. (1995). *Judgments of Responsibility: A Foundation for a Theory of Social Conduct.* New York: Guilford Press.

Weiss, A., Forstmann, M., & Burgmer, P. (2021). Moralizing mental states: The role of trait self-control and control perceptions. *Cognition.*

Winegard, B. M., & Clark, C. J. (2020). Without contraries is no progression. *Psychological Inquiry*, *31*(1), 94–101.

Wolf, S. (1990). *Freedom within Reason*. New York: Oxford University Press.

Wu, J., Balliet, D., & Van Lange, P. A. (2016a). Reputation management: Why and how gossip enhances generosity. *Evolution and Human Behavior, 37,* 193–201.

Wu, J., Balliet, D., & Van Lange, P. A. (2016b). Reputation, gossip, and human cooperation. *Social and Personality Psychology Compass, 10,* 350–64.

3

Mental State Control and Responsibility

Corey Cusimano and Geoffrey P. Goodwin

Introduction

On October 13, 1988, at the start of the second presidential debate, Democratic Nominee Michael Dukakis took a question from the moderator challenging his long-held and widely known anti-death penalty stance, "Governor, if Kitty Dukakis were raped and murdered, would you favor an irrevocable death penalty for the killer?" Dukakis, true to his principles, responded, "I think you know that I've opposed the death penalty all of my life." As he continued laying out the reasons behind his opposition, he remained practiced, professional, and composed—which was exactly the problem. Potential voters who were watching were outraged at his unemotional reaction to the thought of his wife's hypothetical rape and murder. Dukakis' popularity dropped overnight. Outrage at Dukakis did not reflect objections to his principles or even doubts about his perceived commitment to his wife. In the words of a columnist at the time, "[it] is well-known that the Governor feels about Kitty the way Antony felt about Cleopatra and Romeo about Juliet" (McGrory, 1988, November 10). Everyone knew that he loved his wife, that the question itself was incendiary, and that his answer was nonetheless a good one, supported by strong evidence and reflecting deeply held moral commitments. Rather, the outrage reflected his "inadmissibly impersonal" reaction that failed to "merchandise his emotions" (McGrory, 1988, November 10). In short, he was blamed for having the wrong emotional reaction. This extraordinary moment in US politics betrays something quite mundane: we sometimes blame others for having the wrong attitudes, beliefs, wants, and feelings.

The case of Michael Dukakis raises both a *psychological* and a *philosophical* question about the nature of blame. The psychological question asks: in everyday life, what are the intuitive preconditions for blame? In other words, what occurred in the minds of the American populace that led them to think Michael Dukakis should be blamed for his emotionless reaction? The philosophical question asks: what is the most defensible theory about whether, and on what basis, someone can be said to deserve blame? In other words, assuming that Michael Dukakis's emotional reaction was bad, were people right to blame him for it? These two questions are distinct—after all, in everyday life, people may blame others in ways that seem mistaken after careful philosophical reflection. But there is also an important way in which the two questions are related, which is that philosophers have often treated everyday practices of blame as providing evidence for different philosophical positions (Knobe & Doris, 2010). Following Strawson (1962), many philosophers have constructed normative accounts of blameworthiness that aim to make the best sense of ordinary practices of blaming. Accordingly, the intuitive basis on which people blamed Dukakis might be treated as a starting point for a normative view of blame that ultimately serves to validate people's reactions.

Our focus in this chapter is why people sometimes assign blame for mental states such as Dukakis's. For reasons that we outline below, the question of mental state blame occupies a privileged position in both empirical and normative debates about moral responsibility. The reason is that while different theories of moral responsibility converge on the question of how people assign blame for behaviors, they make divergent predictions regarding whether, and on what basis, people blame others for their mental states. Thus, examining blame for mental states offers a means of adjudicating between these rival theories. Looking ahead, many theories suggest that our everyday practices of blame presuppose that people have *control* over whatever it is they are being blamed for. Yet, many philosophers point to everyday examples of mental state blame, such as people's reaction to Dukakis, as posing a counterexample to these theories. They claim that emotions (and other mental states) are not controllable, and so the fact that people regularly blame others for them suggests that normative accounts of blame should not presuppose control either. Here we offer a novel resolution to this debate. Based on recent empirical work, we conclude that scholars have mischaracterized the everyday practices of blame by assuming an incorrect basis for why people assign blame for mental states. We argue that people do readily blame others for their mental states, but they do so precisely because they think mental states are under people's control.

Control as a Precondition for Moral Responsibility

When those around us cause harm, or act inappropriately, we tend to hold them *morally responsible* for doing so. Holding someone morally responsible, accountable, or in other words, blaming them, often involves expressing anger toward them, criticizing them, demanding that they explain themselves or make amends, or otherwise making them feel bad (Coates & Tognazzini, 2013; Malle, Guglielmo, & Monroe, 2014). These behaviors communicate to the blamed party that what they did was unacceptable, they establish our expectations moving forward, and they provide motivation to the transgressor to fulfill those expectations. However, it is only acceptable to blame someone, and so confront them about their behavior and make them feel bad for it, if they deserve it—that is, if they are blame*worthy*. Indeed, blaming someone who does not meet this standard is itself blameworthy. This observation forms the grounds for the psychological and philosophical questions above: in everyday practice, what do people think is required for an agent to deserve blame? And, normatively, what is the most defensible, principled view of what would make someone legitimately blameworthy?

The dominant view in both psychology and philosophy appears to be that someone is morally responsible for their conduct, and so only blameworthy for bad conduct, if they had control over it. The commonly cited intuition behind this proposal is that it seems wrong to criticize someone for something that they could not have done anything to avoid. That is, it is only fair to blame people for their behavior if they could have chosen to behave otherwise; and likewise, it is only fair to blame people for unfortunate events or harms if those individuals could have stopped or prevented them from occurring. Thus, assessing others' blameworthiness is principally a matter of assessing others' choices (c.f. Fischer & Ravizza, 1998; Nelkin, 2011; Wallace, 1994; Wolf, 1990). If someone could have acted in line with good moral reasons, but chose not to do so, then they are blameworthy. And accordingly, people are blameworthy for causing bad events in the world insofar as those events reflect morally bad choices that they made.

A great deal of evidence from the past fifty years attests to the role of control in everyday evaluations of blameworthiness (see Alicke, 2000; Malle et al., 2014; Weiner, 1995). Early empirical studies of blame measured perceived culpability for harm based on the various ways that a harmful outcome could be traced back to someone's decision-making (Fincham & Jaspers, 1980; Weiner, 1995). The results of these studies provided strong support for control-based views. People were shown to treat intentional harms as highly blameworthy, with blame decreasing as an agent's control over the harm decreased, and as it reflected their decision-making less and less. For instance, if someone did not intentionally bring about harm, but behaved with disregard for harm they knew was likely, they received lower (but still substantive) blame than someone who caused harm intentionally. And if someone caused some harm that was unforeseeable, then they tended to receive no blame at all (Fincham & Jaspers, 1979; Shultz, Schleifer, & Altman, 1981; Shultz, Wright, & Schleifer, 1986).

Later studies showed that people actively seek out information about control when evaluating someone's blameworthiness (Alicke, 2000; Malle, et al., 2014). For instance, Guglielmo and Malle (2017) found that when an observer learns that another agent caused some harm, they seek out information about whether the agent chose to do so intentionally. And, after learning that person did not intentionally cause harm, observers then tend to seek out information about the person's past (controllable) choices, and then evaluate blameworthiness based on whether that person could have prevented the harm. Furthermore, relative to the blame people assign when the intentionality of a norm violation is ambiguous, people increase blame when they learn that that the violation was intentional (and therefore more controllable) and decrease blame when they subsequently learn that it was unintentional (and therefore less controllable; Monroe & Malle, 2019).

Finally, psychologists have routinely found that people defend themselves from blame by preferentially citing factors relating to their personal control over their behavior or the outcome in question. When held accountable for some behavior, people will argue that their behavior was unintentional, that they could not have foreseen the consequences, or that they could not have behaved otherwise, in order to convince others they are not blameworthy (Markman & Tetlock, 2000; Weiner, Amirkhan, Folkes, & Verette, 1987). Indeed, even when people know that they had control over their behavior or the outcome in question, they withhold that information from others and (deceptively) argue that they lacked control in order to avoid blame (Weiner, Figueroa-Munoiz, & Kakihara, 1991). And recently, McNeer and Machery (2019) found that most people (around 80 percent) explicitly endorse control as a necessary precondition of blameworthiness when asked about it in the abstract. Thus, not only do people's intuitions about blame reflect considerations of control, but people are explicitly aware of the importance of control and use it as a basis for assigning others blame and negotiating their own liability.

As noted above, these findings about the everyday practice of blame inform normative theories. For instance, Wallace (1994), who offers one of the definitive accounts of control-based theories of moral responsibility, motivates his theory by considering "our ordinary judgments of excuse and exemption from responsibility" (p. 15). The resulting moral theory then tries to honor and explain everyday individuals' adherence to control as a precondition of blame. Of course, this is not to say that normative theories do (or should) reflect a simple polling of everyday intuitions. Nevertheless, many normative moral theories get off the ground by trying to identify and make the most sense out of the implicit commitments that characterize everyday practice. The empirical data presented above strongly suggest that control comprises such a commitment, and that normative theories that want to capture everyday practices of blame need to incorporate control in some manner.

Nevertheless, both psychologists and philosophers have challenged the dominance of control in everyday moral judgment. The social psychology literature has focused on a few narrow cases, such as blame for severe accidental harms.[1] However, the most potent challenge against control, to which we now turn, comes from moral philosophy.

The Mental State Challenge

The most potent challenge against control-based theories of blame reflects a common observation within moral philosophy that people appear to be blameworthy for their objectionable mental states. For instance, in one of the first and most forceful versions of this idea, Adams (1985) suggests that we commonly blame others for, "jealousy, hatred, and other sorts of malice; contempt for other people, and the lack of a hearty concern for their welfare; or in more general terms, morally objectionable states of mind, including corrupt beliefs as well as wrong desires" (p. 4). However, mental states of this sort seem uncontrollable—in Adam's words, *involuntary sins*. Since Adams, others have made similar observations, with each one of them contributing new examples wherein people seem to blame others for seemingly involuntary emotions, beliefs, motives, or evaluative judgments (see, e.g., Hieronymi, 2008; Pizarro, Tannenbaum, & Uhlmann, 2012; Sher, 2006; Smith, A., 2005, 2008; Smith, H., 2011; Sripada, 2017). Summarizing this challenge, which we call the "mental state challenge," Angela Smith (2008) proposes that, "in our day-to-day lives we simply take for granted that people are responsible and answerable for much more than what they voluntarily choose to do" (p. 382).

It is helpful to consider why these authors suggest mental states are worthy of blame despite their apparent uncontrollability. Notwithstanding subtle differences between them, these authors commonly appeal to an intuition that at least some mental states indicate something *morally significant* about a person. For instance,

Blame for Ignorance. Finally, many scholars point to cases of unknowingly causing (or failing to prevent) harm (i.e., causing harm as a function of ignorance) as posing a threat to control-based theories. According to control theories, someone is only blameworthy for unknowingly causing harm if the reason they did not know they were causing harm can be traced back to an earlier bad choice (Rosen, 2004; Smith, H., 1983). So, for instance, a parent who hears their young child start the bath but refuses to investigate, is liable for their child drowning even if they are, in that moment, ignorant of what their child is doing. Their ignorance of the threat to their child's life can be traced back to their earlier choice not to investigate—this choice creates a culpable willful ignorance and represents an unjustified decision to disregard the foreseeable risks.

But some cases of ignorance appear blameworthy even when they cannot be traced back to intentional choices in this way (Sher, 2006; Smith, A., 2005; Smith, H., 2011; Vargas, 2005; but see Fischer & Tognazzini, 2009, for a response to these challenges). For instance, people appear blameworthy when they fail to *remember*, such as when someone forgets to call their mother on her birthday or forgets to buy their spouse an anniversary gift (Smith, A., 2005). Relatedly, people appear to be blameworthy when they cause harm by *failing to notice* something that they should have noticed. Smith (2011) and Sher (2006) illustrate this with the imaginary case, *Ryland*, telling an unintentionally hurtful joke:

> Ryland is very self-absorbed. Though not malicious, she is oblivious to the impact that her behavior will have on others. Consequently, she is bewildered when her rambling anecdote about a childless couple, a person with a disability, and a financial failure is not well received by an audience that includes a childless couple, a person with a disability, and a financial failure.

Smith and Sher suggest that Ryland is blameworthy for upsetting her audience. However, Ryland did not choose to fail to notice that her joke would upset her audience. And, unlike the cases of willful ignorance above, Ryland's ignorance does not stem from some prior conscious choice to ignore information. This inability to trace back Ryland's ignorance to some prior choice raises the question of what does explain her ignorance, and on what basis she is responsible for it.

A likely diagnosis is that Ryland failed to notice that her joke would be upsetting because of the attitudes that she holds, namely, her low degree of care and concern for others. Indeed, one's cares, concerns, and values affect what one attends to and wonders about. Had Ryland been the sort of person who cares more about others' feelings, she would have wondered how her joke would affect this particular audience. This naturally would have led her to attend to who was in the audience, notice that (for instance) a person with a disability was there, spend a moment to think about how the joke would affect that person, and then realize that her joke would offend them. In light of this observation, Sher and Smith have a ready explanation for why Ryland seems blameworthy for causing harm through failing to notice: she is blameworthy for having the wrong kinds of cares, concerns, and values (which explains her failure to notice the harm she was causing). The same logic applies to everyday failures to remember: when someone forgets a birthday or anniversary, it is reasonable to infer that they do not care sufficiently about their friend or spouse—if they did care, they would have remembered.

To our knowledge, little work has directly investigated people's reactions to harms caused by failures to notice. Some preliminary work comes from Murray and colleagues (2019) who gave participants a story about a man who needs to pick up materials for a birthday party on his way home from work. For a variety of reasons, including his getting excited or stressed about some piece of news, he does not notice the store on his drive home, passes it, and so fails to pick up the ingredients. Importantly, participants tended to say that it would be right for his spouse to blame him for forgetting to pick up the ingredients.

Summary. We have reviewed several cases in which people appear to blame others for possessing objectionable mental states. One sort of case involves attitudes, desires, or affective reactions that are outright immoral—such as when someone experiences *schadenfreude* or possesses a desire for harm to occur. Another sort of case involves objectionable beliefs, that are either immoral, politically or religiously incendiary (to a given observer), or simply false. And a still further case involves behaviors that are not unambiguously immoral (e.g., forgetting a birthday), but that seem blameworthy because they reveal objectionable mental states. Though experimental data are sparse, the emerging evidence does vindicate philosophers' speculations—people often do blame others for these kinds of objectionable mental states, suggesting that this sort of blame is part and parcel of our ordinary social practices.

This naturally then raises the question of *why* people blame others for mental states. According to theorists who regard mental state blame as posing a challenge to control-based theories, people blame others in these situations despite thinking that the mental state in question is mostly outside the control of the person who holds it. If this is true, then blame is being assigned simply because a person possesses bad dispositions (or character). However, it is not a given that this is what ordinary people are doing, and until recently, there was little evidence speaking to this question. An alternative perspective, contra to that held by philosophers who hold up these examples as undermining control theories, is that ordinary people regard the objectionable mental states in these examples as quite controllable and assign blame in proportion to their judged controllability. If this is true, then these cases of everyday blame would not constitute a threat to control-based theories, and would in fact bolster such theories. As we review below, this is indeed what we have observed in recent research. People attribute control to others over their mental states (objectionable and otherwise), and assign blame in line with these judgments of control.

Empirically Investigating Everyday Mental State Evaluation

Empirical Data on Attributions of Control

When asked directly, people tend to say others have some degree of intentional control over their mental states. For instance, in one study we recently conducted (Cusimano & Goodwin, 2019), we asked college undergraduates to write down the first emotions, beliefs, desires, and attitudes that they could think of. College students nominated the sorts of attitudes one would expect them to encounter and evaluate in their everyday

Experimental Philosophy and Manipulation Arguments

In the past years, experimental philosophers have collected data on people's intuitions about manipulation cases and have used it to push forward both *hard-line* and *soft-line* responses.

Experimental Philosophy and the Hard-Line Response

Feltz (2013) investigated folk intuitions about Pereboom's four cases argument. After controlling for a potential confounding factor that had nothing to do with determinism (namely, the presence of the manipulator's intention), Feltz observed that participants tended to consider that agents in manipulation arguments were in fact morally responsible for their actions. Feltz thus argued that his results might justify a hard-line response to Pereboom's argument: if we do not have the intuition that agents in manipulation cases are not morally responsible for their actions, then the very first premise of the argument is threatened.

Experimental Philosophy and the Soft-Line Retort

Other experimental studies have provided the ground for soft-line responses to manipulation arguments. In a seminal paper, Sripada (2012) argued that, to the extent that participants consider agents in manipulation cases not to be morally responsible for their actions, it is because they think that manipulated agents differ from everyday agents in one crucial respect: they do not act in accordance with their "deep self" (i.e., their "real," deeply-held values and attitudes). Sripada conducted a first study in which participants receive either the *Manipulation* or *Control* case (see Table 4.1).

In both cases, participants were asked about the agent's moral responsibility, but also about the concordance between his actions and his Deep Self (e.g., "Bill's killing of Mrs. White does not reflect the kind of person who he truly is deep down inside"). The results showed that participants considered Bill in the *Manipulation* case to be less responsible for his actions than Bill in the *Control* case, but that this difference was mediated by participants' deep self ratings: participants considered that Bill in the *Manipulation* case was not necessarily acting in accordance with his Deep Self.

In a second study, Sripada introduced a *Modified* manipulation case, which was identical to the *Manipulation* case, except that the following paragraph was added at the end:

> Bill is like anyone else in many respects. As he was growing up, Bill was educated about morality, the difference between right and wrong, and various ways he might conduct his life. Additionally, Bill was not simply fed lies about Mrs. White—he knows the truth about who she is and he knows exactly why he dislikes her. Bill is not a robot who simply does as others instruct. Nor is he under the grip of an irresistible impulse. Rather, Bill is a person, with desires, values, hopes, and dreams just like anyone else. But Bill's desires include killing Mrs. White. And his core values permit killing Mrs. White. So that is exactly what he does.

Table 4.1 Vignettes used by Sripada (2012).

No Manipulation Condition	Manipulation Condition
One day, Bill sees a woman named Mrs. White as she is jogging in the park. Bill hates this woman, and deliberates about what to do. After weighing his options, Bill decides he should	
kill her. Bill's mind is not clouded by rage or other extreme emotions. Rather, Bill thinks clearly and carefully about his own desires and values, and only then makes a decision. After he kills Mrs. White, Bill reflects on his action. He wholeheartedly endorses what he has done.	
But there is more you need to know about Bill, and how he came to be the person that he is now:	
There is a man named Dr. Z who is a scientific genius and who is an expert at indoctrination. Dr. Z hates Mrs. White and formed the following plan. Dr. Z would take an infant	
from an orphanage and raise the child himself. He would teach and reward just the right behaviors in the child so the child would hate Mrs. White and want her dead. He would script all the major events in the child's life to nurture and cultivate in the child the goal of doing whatever it would take to kill Mrs. White. Dr. Z tried this plan previously on five other children, and each time the child grew up to kill Dr. Z's intended targets.	
Dr. Z was getting ready to implement his plan for Bill. He was about to take Bill from an orphanage when Bill was an infant. But at the last minute Bill was adopted by another family. But completely by chance, it turned out that Bill came to hate Mrs. White without any influence from Dr. Z at all. Once Bill had grown up, Bill had the desire to do whatever it takes to kill Mrs. White. Thus Bill turned out exactly how Dr. Z planned all along, but Dr. Z did not actually implement his plan at all.	Dr. Z implemented his plan for Bill. He took Bill from an orphanage when Bill was an infant. The plan worked—once Bill had grown up, Bill had the desire to do whatever it takes to kill Mrs. White. Dr. Z's plan was kept completely hidden from Bill. Bill never knew that Dr. Z implemented the plan.

Compared to the first *Manipulation* case, adding this information about Bill's Deep Self led participants to see Bill as more responsible for his action. In fact, a majority of participants now answered that Bill killed Mrs. White *of his own free will*.

Together, these results suggest the following soft-line responses to manipulation arguments: to the extent that participants see manipulated agents as unfree, it is not because they perceive them as determined, but as acting against their own deeply held values. Thus, unless someone is able to show that determinism precludes people from acting on the basis of their deeply held values, we are not justified in transferring our intuitions about manipulation cases to cases involving agents in deterministic worlds.

Of course, one might object that these results are philosophically relevant. After all, we should take as a starting point the intuitions of experts and not of untutored, naive laypeople. However, it is not clear that this response is as effective as it might seem at first sight: past research in the philosophy of free will has tried to keep as close as possible to our intuitive conception of moral responsibility. Indeed, proving that moral responsibility is or is not possible might not prove practically relevant and worthwhile if the conception of moral responsibility one is using has cut all relationships to this intuitive conception. After all, if people's intuitions about manipulation case are that manipulated agents are free and morally responsible, why should they even begin to worry about Pereboom's argument?

But even if we consider that only expert intuitions are relevant to philosophical discussions about free will, this does not undermine Sripada's argument. Indeed, Sripada's argument is not that people's intuitions about manipulation cases are not in line with those of experts, but that intuitions about manipulation cases (when they agree with those of experts) are not explained by determinism but by considerations compatibilism can accommodate. Of course, one could still object that experts' intuitions are driven by completely different mechanisms than those of laypeople. However, this seems a gratuitous assertion for which there is at the moment no empirical evidence—and thus, some dose of skepticism is warranted. Moreover, we will see in the final discussion that some of the results presented in this paper warrant the idea that laypeople and experts' intuitions about free will seem to follow similar patterns.

Here Comes a New Challenger: the Zygote Argument

So far, all cases of manipulation that experimental philosophers have put to the test share one common feature: agents are manipulated *after their birth*. This might seem like a trivial observation, but one might actually argue that this is what leads participants to see a dissonance between manipulated agents and their Deep Self: after all, they already had desires and values before being manipulated. Thus, participants might see manipulated agents as divided or torn between two sets of desires and values: their original ones and the one that have been added by manipulation. This conception of agents' minds as divided might then drive them to consider the new desires and values added by manipulation as non-authentic and to some extent akin to brainwashing (Sripada, 2012).

If this hypothesis is true, then this means that it would be possible to avoid the kind of objection Sripada and other experimental philosophers have raised to manipulation arguments by turning to manipulation arguments in which agents are manipulated *before* being born, and thus before having any kind of preexisting desires and values that might be considered as the agents' "true" desires and values. One such case of argument is Alfred Mele's Zygote argument.

The Zygote argument begins with a thought experiment:

> Consider the following story. Diana creates a zygote Z in Mary. She combines Z's atoms as she does because she wants a certain event E to occur thirty years later. From her knowledge of the state of the universe just prior to her creating Z and the laws of nature of her deterministic universe, she deduces that a zygote with precisely Z's constitution located in Mary will develop into an ideally self-controlled agent who, in thirty years, will judge, on the basis of rational deliberation, that it is best to A and will A on the basis of that judgment, thereby bringing about E. If this agent, Ernie, has any unsheddable values at the time, they play no role in motivating his A-ing. Thirty years later, Ernie is a mentally healthy, ideally self-controlled person who regularly exercises his powers of self-control and has no relevant compelled or coercively produced attitudes. Furthermore, his beliefs are conducive to informed deliberation about all matters that concern him, and

he is a reliable deliberator. So he satisfies a version of my proposed compatibilist sufficient conditions for having freely A-ed.

(Mele, 2008:279).

For the Zygote argument to begin, we have to assume that you have the intuition (or that you agree) that Ernie is not morally responsible for his A-ing in this case. Once this crucial premise is accepted, the Zygote argument runs like this:

1. Because of the way his zygote was produced in his deterministic universe, Ernie is not a free agent and is not morally responsible for anything.
2. Concerning free action and moral responsibility of the beings into whom the zygotes develop, there is no significant difference between the way Ernie's zygote comes to exist and the way any normal human zygote comes to exist in a deterministic universe.
3. So determinism precludes free action and moral responsibility. (Mele, 2008:280)

Thus, from the intuition that agents in Zygote cases (such as Ernie's) are not morally responsible for their actions, the Zygote argument concludes that moral responsibility is incompatible with determinism.

Goal of the Present Paper and Some Methodological Considerations

In this paper, my goal is to empirically investigate people's intuition about Zygote cases. My main driving hypothesis is that, even if manipulation intervened before the agent's birth, people *still have* (at least implicitly) the intuition that manipulated agents in Zygote cases are not able to act on the basis on their true desires and values, and that this explains why some people have the intuition that agents in Zygote cases are not morally responsible for their actions.

Before moving on to the empirical part of the paper and to my data-driven assessment of Mele's Zygote argument, there are a few methodological points I would like to highlight, even if I do not have enough space to fully develop them:

1. I will not focus on participants' judgments about free will, but on their judgments about moral responsibility. The reason is that I am primarily interested in FREE WILL, but FREE WILL in the sense that it is currently discussed by most philosophers, that is: the kind of control one must exert upon one's actions to be morally responsible for them. There might be a folk concept of free will (though it is not clear that there is one in every language; see Berniūnas et al., 2021), but it is not directly superposable to the one I am interested in. For example, in Nahmias and colleagues (2006)'s experiments, free will attributions tended to be *lower* than moral responsibility attributions, even when the very same participants answered both questions. I still collected participants' free will judgments for those interested, but I won't comment on them.

2. The Deep Self measures I will be using are slightly different from those used in the literature. They have been rephrased to avoid all references to *concordance* between action and deep self and to rather insist on the *provenance* of one's action from one's deep self. Indeed, my own spin on the Deep Self hypothesis (i.e., the Deep Self Provenance hypothesis) is that one is responsible for actions that stem from one's Deep Self, even if there is no concordance between the final outcome and one's Deep Self (see Cova, 2011).

3. I am not committed to the claim that the effect of manipulation on attributions of moral responsibility will be *fully* mediated by participants' scores on Deep Self measures. Because Sripada's Deep Self account (Sripada, 2010) has been tested using mediation analysis, some have argued that the Deep Self explanation of intuitions about manipulation argument fails because Deep Self scores only *partially* mediate the effect of Deep Self on moral responsibility (Björnsson, 2016). However, we should expect Deep Self scores to *fully* mediate the effect of manipulation only in case our measures of Deep Self beliefs and attributions of moral responsibility are accurate enough. Using simulations (Cova, forthcoming), I have observed that introducing some measurement error prevents Deep Self scores from fully mediating the effect of manipulation, even when attributions of responsibility are fully driven by considerations about the Deep Self. Given that Deep Self measures are phrased in metaphoric terms and that we should expect participants not to have full access to their internal representation of such cases, expecting full mediation seems an unreasonable demand.

4. Rather than focusing only on mediation analysis, I prefer to put the Deep Self Concordance model to the test by showing that it makes very specific and novel predictions and testing these predictions. In this paper, this prediction is the following: *the effect of manipulation on attributions of moral responsibility should be lower for good actions than for bad actions*. Indeed, let's suppose that the reason why some people consider agents in manipulation cases not to be morally responsible is because they perceive them as not acting from their own true, deeply held values. The effect of manipulation should be lower when it is *easier* to think that the action performed comes from one's true values. However, a vast literature has documented the following fact: people find it easier to think that people's deep selves are *morally good* than to consider that people can be "rotten to the core" (Newman et al., 2014; Strohminger et al., 2017). Thus, we should expect people to find it easier to believe that a manipulated agent acts upon one's true values when these values are morally good.

In the next section, I present results suggesting that this bold hypothesis actually works in the case of classical manipulation cases, thus suggesting that the Deep Self Provenance model is a good explanation of participants' intuitions about manipulation cases. Then, in Studies 1 and 2, I extend this hypothesis to Zygote cases.

Materials and Data

Materials and data for all studies are available at osf.io/qnp86/

Pilot Study—The Effect of Manipulation on Moral Responsibility Depends on the Action's Moral Valence

In this pilot study, the goal was simply to test one key prediction of my Deep Self Provenance model: that the effect of manipulation on judgments of moral responsibility (when comparing a manipulation case to a control case) should be greater for bad actions, compared to good actions.

Materials and Methods

The study took the form of an online survey. Participants were presented with one of four vignettes. Two vignettes were Sripada's *Modified* and *Control* vignettes. The two others were modified versions of the *Modified* and *Control* vignette, in which the agents' action was morally good (saving Mrs. White) rather than morally bad (killing Mrs. White).[2] Thus, two dimensions were independently manipulated: whether the agent was manipulated, and his action's moral valence.

After reading the vignette, participants were presented with a series of statements. For each of them, participants were asked to indicate to which extent they agreed (-3: Strongly disagree, 3 = Strongly agree):

> *(Resp.)* Bill is morally responsible for killing [saving] Mrs. White. (Participants were asked to justify their answer.)
> *(Blame/Praise)* Bill deserves blame for killing [praise for saving] Mrs. White.
> *(Desert)* Bill deserves to be punished for killing [rewarded for saving] Mrs. White.
> *(Free Will)* Bill killed [saved] Mrs. White of his own free will.
> *(Deep Self 1)* It is Bill's very own desires and values that led him to kill [save] Mrs. White.
> *(Deep Self 2)* It's what Bill really wanted deep down that caused him to kill [save] Mrs. White.
> *(Deep Self 3)* It is because of the kind of person he's truly deep down inside that Bill killed [saved] Mrs. White.
> *(Deep Self 4)* Bill's killing [saving] of Mrs. White had nothing to do with what he really wanted to do.
> *(Bypass 1)* Bill's own decisions played no role in his killing [saving] Mrs. White.
> *(Bypass 2)* What Bill wanted had no effect on his killing [saving] Mrs. White.
> *(Bypass 3)* What Bill believed had no effect on his ending up to kill [save] Mrs. White.
> *(Control)* Bill had no control over his killing [saving] Mrs. White.
> *(Throughpass)* When earlier events caused Bill's actions, they did so by affecting what he believed and wanted, which in turn caused him to act in a certain way.

After that, participants answered four comprehension checks and completed a scale (the Geneva Sentimentality Scale; Cova & Boudesseul, 2021) in which two attention checks were hidden.

Results

491 participants were recruited on Prolific Academic and paid £0.70 for their participation completed our survey. After exclusion based on four comprehension checks and two attention checks, we were left with 391 participants (235 men, 152 women, and 4 others; M_{age} = 25.73, SD_{age} = 7.82).

Responsibility Ratings. Responsibility ratings, blame/praise ratings, and desert ratings were aggregated to form a single aggregated responsibility score (ARS; α =.72). A 2-way ANOVA with Outcome Valence (Bad/Good) and Case (Modified vs. Control) as factors and ARS as dependent variable found a significant interaction effect: $F(1,387)$ = 33.86, p <.001, η_p^2 = 0.08, a significant main effect of Outcome Valence: $F(1,387)$ = 45.14, p <.001, η_p^2 = 0.09, and a significant main effect of Case: $F(1,387)$ = 46.99, p <.001, η_p^2 = 0.11. Results are presented in Table 4.2.

Table 4.2 Mean, Standard Deviation, and % of answers above the midpoint (= 0) for each condition in Pilot Study. Stars(*) present the results of Welch t-tests comparing the two cases (Modified, and Control) for each variable and each outcome valence. Interaction between Outcome Valence and Case was significant for: ARS, Resp, Blame/Praise, Desert, and Throughpass; but not significant for: Free Will, Deep Self, Bypass, and Control.

	Bad		Good	
	Modified	Control	Modified	Control
ARS	1.29*** (1.33) 82%	2.61 (0.66) 98%	1.31 (1.04) 86%	1.44 (0.99) 89%
Resp.	1.03*** (1.62) 75%	2.68 (0.73) 98%	1.12* (1.71) 72%	1.61 (1.52) 84%
Blame/Praise	1.19*** (1.61) 76%	2.53 (0.92) 95%	1.60 (1.32) 81%	1.89 (1.13) 89%
Desert	1.65*** (1.31) 87%	2.62 (0.76) 96%	1.21 (1.32) 69%	0.82 (1.53) 61%
Free Will	0.65*** (1.77) 65%	2.52 (1.14) 95%	0.88*** (1.58) 65%	2.38 (0.91) 96%
Deep Self	-0.09*** (0.98) 47%	0.64 (0.93) 74%	0.42*** (0.82) 65%	0.90 (0.59) 91%
Bypass	-1.05*** (1.09) 11%	-1.78 (1.02) 4%	-0.97* (1.14) 17%	-1.30 (1.16) 10%
Control	-0.96*** (1.69) 24%	-2.29 (0.96) 1%	-0.94*** (1.62) 22%	-1.94 (1.17) 5%
Throughpass	1.39*** (1.17) 82%	-0.20 (1.77) 35%	0.89*** (1.59) 63%	0.21 (1.20) 46%
N	79	112	98	102

Discussion

As predicted by the Deep Self Provenance hypothesis, the effect of manipulation was stronger for bad actions than for good actions. This is explained naturally by the fact that people are less likely to think that someone committing a bad action acted in accordance with their Deep Self.

Thus, if people's intuitions about Zygote cases are explained by people's intuitions about the Deep Self, we should expect to observe the same pattern. This is what I set out to test in Study 1.

Study 1—Investigating Intuitions about the Zygote Argument

Materials and Methods

The study took the form of an online survey. At the beginning of the experiment, participants were randomly assigned to one of three cases (Manipulation, Indeterministic or Control) and to one of two outcome valences (Bad or Good). Then, depending on these factors, each participant was presented with one of six cases.

Table 4.3 Three different cases used in Study 1 (Bad Outcome version).

Manipulation	Indeterministic	Control
Imagine a world just like ours, except that there exist beings similar to the Greek and Roman gods. These beings are not all-powerful but they have strange powers: they can see into the future to determine with certainty what consequences their actions will have. They can also manipulate matter and even create life. These beings' existence is completely unknown to men.	Imagine a world just like ours, except that there exist beings similar to the Greek and Roman gods. These beings are not all-powerful but they have strange powers: they can see into the future to determine with great accuracy what consequences their actions will have. They can also manipulate matter and even create life. These beings' existence is completely unknown to men.	Imagine a world just like ours, except that there exist beings similar to the Greek and Roman gods. These beings are not all-powerful but they have strange powers: they can see into the future to determine with great accuracy what consequences their actions will have. They can also manipulate matter and even create life. These beings' existence is completely unknown to men.
Imagine that Diane is such a goddess. She knows with full certainty that, if she creates a certain zygote (a human embryo at a very early stage) and implants it in the uterus of Mary, a common human, on March 3, 2021 there is a 100% chance that this zygote will grow up to become a young man named Bill. Diane also sees that there is a 100% chance that, on his thirtieth	Imagine that Diane is such a goddess. She knows with full certainty that, if she creates a certain zygote (a human embryo at a very early stage) and implants it in the uterus of Mary, a common human, on March 3, 2021 there is a 98% chance that this zygote will grow up to become a young man named Bill. Diane also sees that there is a 95% chance that, on his thirtieth birthday,	Imagine that Diane is such a goddess. She knows with full certainty that, if she creates a certain zygote (a human embryo at a very early stage) and implants it in the uterus of Mary, a common human, on March 3, 2021 there is a 98% chance that this zygote will grow up to become a young man named Ted. Diane also sees that there is a 95% chance

birthday, Bill will eventually kill his aunt to inherit from her early.	Bill will eventually kill his aunt to inherit from her early.	that, on his thirtieth birthday, Ted will rob a bank.
Knowing all that Diane creates said zygote and implants it in Mary's uterus. After that, she never interferes again in the zygote's development and Bill's life.	Knowing all that Diane creates said zygote and implants it in Mary's uterus. After that, she never interferes again in the zygote's development and Bill's life.	Knowing all that, Diane decides not to create said zygote and never interferes in Mary's life. A few days later, Mary has sex with a man named John and gets pregnant.
Nine months later, Mary gives birth to Bill. Bill grows up to be an ordinary human being. He's as rational as other human beings and exerts as much self-control upon his actions. On his thirtieth birthday, after a long deliberation, and on the basis of his deeply held values, he kills his aunt to inherit from her early.	Nine months later, Mary gives birth to Bill. Bill grows up to be an ordinary human being. He's as rational as other human beings and exerts as much self-control upon his actions. On his thirtieth birthday, after a long deliberation, and on the basis of his deeply-held values, he kills his aunt to inherit from her early.	Nine months later, Mary gives birth to Bill. Bill grows up to be an ordinary human being. He's as rational as other human beings and exerts as much self-control upon his actions. On his thirtieth birthday, after a long deliberation, and on the basis of his deeply-held values, he kills his aunt to inherit from her early.

The three different cases in their Bad Outcome version are presented in Table 4.3. The Manipulation case is supposed to be a typical Zygote case: the agent is created by a goddess who predicts his action with a 100 percent chance. The Indeterministic case is similar, except that the goddess cannot perfectly predict the future. Finally, the Control case is a case in which the goddess still predicts the agent's future with near certainty, but in which she does not play a role in the production of this agent (rather, he is the normal product of human sexual intercourse).

I introduced the Indeterministic case because the Zygote argument assumes that determinism plays a key role in the intuition that the agent is not morally responsible in Zygote cases. However, if it turned out that people also had the intuition that agents still lack moral responsibility in modified Zygote cases in which the goddess' actions only have indeterministic effects, this would pose a problem to both versions of the Zygote argument. On the *no difference* version of the Zygote argument, this would lead us to conclude that moral responsibility is not only impossible in a deterministic universe, but also in indeterministic ones. Thus, we would not conclude to incompatibilism, but to some form of skepticism about moral responsibility. On the *explanation-based* version of the Zygote argument, this would lead us to conclude that determinism is not the reason why agents are not morally responsible in Zygote cases, and this would prevent us from concluding that determinism is incompatible with responsibility.[3]

In the Good outcome version of these vignettes, Bill's bad action (indicated in bold in Table X) was replaced by a morally good one ("giving the money he just inherited from his aunt to create a homeless shelter"). In the Control case, "robbing a bank" was also replaced by "saving someone from drowning").

After reading the vignette, participants were presented with roughly the same statements as in the Pilot Study, except that the action description was replaced by "killing his aunt" (in the Bad Outcome version) or "creating a homeless shelter" (in the Good Outcome version). The only statements to be modified more extensively were the following:

> *(Resp)* It would be fair to hold Bill morally responsible for having killed his aunt [created a homeless shelter].[4]
> *(Blame/Praise)* Bill deserves blame [praise] for killing his aunt [creating a homeless shelter].
> *(Desert)* Bill deserves to be punished [deserves credit] for killing his aunt [creating a homeless shelter].

Research Questions and Hypotheses

In this study and the next one, the questions I wanted to address were the following:

1. Do people really have the intuition that agents in Zygote cases are not morally responsible for their actions?
2. Does manipulation affect participants' attributions of moral responsibility?
3. Does the effect of manipulation depend on determinism? Or is manipulation without determinism enough to trigger the same intuitions?
4. Are agents in manipulation cases identical to agents in control cases? Or do people perceive differences between the two that could explain their different assessment of their moral responsibility?
5. Can the results be explained by the Deep Self Provenance hypothesis? Which can be broken down in three sub-questions:
   a. are attributions of moral responsibility correlated with Deep Self scores?
   b. do Deep Self scores mediate the effect of manipulation on attribution of moral responsibility?
   c. does the effect of manipulation depend on the action's moral valence?

Results

705 participants were recruited on Prolific Academic and paid £0.75 for their participation completed our survey. After exclusion based on four comprehension checks and two attention checks, I was left with 532 participants (272 women, 246 men, and 14 others; $M_{age} = 31.38$, $SD_{age} = 11.74$).

Q1. *Do people have the intuition that agents in Zygote cases are not morally responsible for their actions?* Responsibility ratings, blame/praise ratings, and desert ratings were aggregated to form a single aggregated responsibility score (ARS; $\alpha = .83$). Responsibility scores in the Manipulation condition were high ($M = 1.79$, $SD = 1.35$) and significantly above the midpoint: $t(147) = 16.16$, $p < .001$. Overall, 88 percent of participants obtained ARS superior to 0. Thus, it seems fair to conclude that most participants did not share the intuition that agents in Zygote cases were not morally responsible for their actions.

Q2. *Does manipulation affect participants' attributions of moral responsibility?* I conducted a 2-way ANOVA with Outcome Valence (Bad/Good) and Case (Control/Manipulation/Indeterministic) as factors and ARS as dependent variable. We found a main effect of Outcome Valence: $F(1,526) = 37.01$, $p < .001$, $\eta_p^2 = 0.06$, a main effect of Case: $F(2,526) = 11.48$, $p < .001$, $\eta_p^2 = 0.04$, and a significant interaction effect: $F(2,526) = 5.29$, $p = .005$, $\eta_p^2 = 0.02$. Thus, manipulation had an effect on aggregated responsibility ratings, but this effect depended on outcome valence (i.e., whether the action was good or bad). Thus, I analyzed bad outcomes cases and good outcomes separately, by performing two separate Tukey tests. As summarized in Table 4.4, I found no effect of manipulation for good outcome cases. However, for bad outcome cases, I found that scores in the Control condition were significantly higher compared to the Manipulation and Indeterministic condition. Thus, for bad outcomes only, manipulation had an effect on participants' ARS.

Q3. *Does the effect of manipulation depend on determinism?* Focusing on bad outcome cases, I found a significant difference in ARS between the Indeterministic and the Control conditions, but no significant difference between the Manipulation and Indeterministic conditions. Thus, it seems that manipulation can have an effect on participants' attributions of responsibility even in absence of determinism.

Q4. *Are agents in manipulation cases identical to agents in control cases?* Focusing on bad outcome cases, I used two Tukey tests to compare Deep Self scores (α =.82) and Bypassing scores (α =.73) across conditions. Both tests found significant differences between the Manipulation and Control cases (see Table 4.4): Deep Self scores were lower in the Manipulation condition while Bypassing scores were higher in the Manipulation condition. This suggests that participants did not perceive agents in the Manipulation condition as identical to those in the Control condition.

Table 4.4 Mean, Standard Deviation and % of answers above the midpoint (= 0) for each condition in Study 1. Superscripts present the results of Tukey tests comparing the three cases (Manipulation, Indeterministic, and Control) for each variable and each outcome valence. When superscripts are present, two conditions that do not share a common letter in superscript significantly differ from each other. When no superscript is present, this means that there was no difference between conditions. Interaction between Outcome Valence and Condition was significant for: ARS, Blame/Praise, and Desert; but not significant for: Resp., Free Will, Deep Self, Bypass, Control, and Throughpass.

	Bad Outcome			Good Outcome		
	Manip.	Indet.	Control	Manip.	Indet.	Control.
ARS	1.90[a] (1.51) 86%	2.23[a] (1.03) 96%	2.73[b] (0.63) 98%	1.66 (1.14) 91%	1.87 (0.86) 97%	1.82 (1.01) 90%
Resp.	1.76[a] (1.79) 84%	2.20[a] (1.11) 94%	2.75[b] (0.88) 97%	0.91 (1.83) 63%	1.34 (1.66) 77%	1.47 (1.54) 73%

Blame/Praise	1.74ª (1.83) 81%	2.28ᵇ (1.03) 94%	2.76ᶜ (0.71) 96%	2.01 (1.13) 93%	2.10 (0.82) 95%	1.83 (1.05) 85%
Desert	2.21ª (1.34) 88%	2.21ª (1.07) 93%	2.67ᵇ (0.73) 97%	2.06 (1.21) 91%	2.19 (0.77) 97%	2.14 (1.10) 92%
Free will	1.60ª (1.89) 79%	2.00ª (1.26) 91%	2.72ᵇ (0.67) 97%	1.34ª (1.79) 75%	1.79ª (1.42) 82%	2.27ᵇ (1.09) 92%
Deep Self	1.29ª (1.30) 83%	1.53ª (1.13) 90%	1.94ᵇ (0.94) 94%	1.45ª (1.38) 85%	1.72ᵃᵇ (1.10) 92%	1.90ᵇ (0.89) 94%
Bypass	-1.25ª (1.38) 15%	-1.84ᵇ (1.13) 06%	-2.06ᵇ (1.03) 05%	-1.30 (1.39) 13%	-1.56 (1.16) 08%	-1.75 (1.08) 04%
Control	-1.21ª (1.89) 18%	-2.10ᵇ (1.30) 06%	-2.66ᶜ (0.70) 01%	-1.25ª (1.87) 19%	-1.63ᵃᵇ (1.47) 10%	-2.17ᵇ (1.21) 05%
Throughpass	0.44 (1.72) 50%	0.46 (1.65) 54%	0.20 (2.02) 50%	0.44 (1.97) 53%	0.48 (1.79) 49%	0.28 (1.67) 49%

Q5. Can the results be explained by the Deep Self Provenance hypothesis?
   a. <u>Interaction between condition and valence:</u> As predicted by the Deep Self Provenance hypothesis, the effect of manipulation was stronger for bad outcomes than for good outcomes.
   b. <u>Correlations:</u> There was a significant correlation ($r = .60$) between ARS and Deep Self scores (see Table 4.5).
   c. <u>Mediation analysis:</u> I used structural equation modeling (in R's {lavaan} package) to investigate whether Deep Self scores mediated the effect of manipulation on ARS. I focused on bad outcome cases, and on the two following comparisons: Manipulation vs. Control and Indeterministic vs. Control. Results are presented in Figure 4.1. In both cases, the effect of manipulation on ARS was significantly mediated by Deep Self ratings. However, in both cases, a direct effect remained.

Thus, my three sub-hypotheses were corroborated by my data. Does this mean that participants' judgments of responsibility are best explained by participants' perception of agents' deep self? Not necessarily, as there is also some contradictory evidence. For example, in positive outcome cases, there was no difference in responsibility judgments between the Manipulation and Control cases, but there was a significant difference in Deep Self scores.

Table 4.5 Inter-correlations between variables in Study 1.

	Free Will	Deep Self	Bypass	Control
ARS	.74***	.60***	-.53***	-.63***
Free Will	-	.67***	-.55***	-.68***
Deep Self	-	-	-.65***	.64***
Bypass	-	-	-	.68***

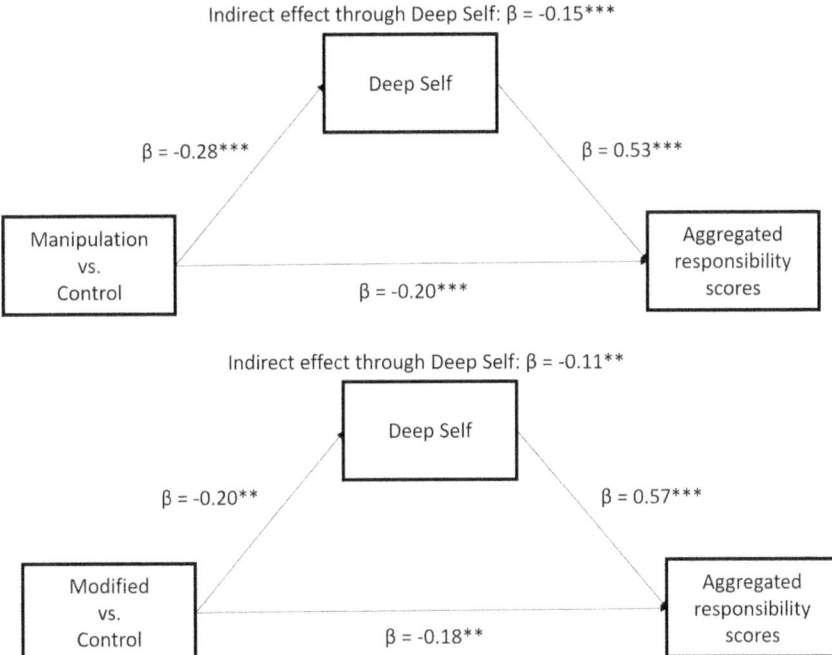

Figure 4.1 Deep Self scores as mediators of the effect of manipulation (Manipulation vs. Control and Modified vs. Control) in Study 1.

Discussion

In this study, I investigated participants' intuitions about Zygote cases. The results of this study suggest the following conclusions:

1. The results suggest both a soft- and a hard-line answer to the Zygote argument. On the hard-line side, most participants actually had the intuition that agents were morally responsible for their actions in the Zygote cases. On the soft-line side, even the answers of the minority who considered that agents in Zygote cases were not morally responsible can be explained away by the fact that agents in the Zygote cases are not perceived as identical to participants in the Control cases.
2. Our results suggest that at least part of the effect of manipulation in Zygote cases has nothing to do with determinism, as there was also a difference between the Manipulation and the Control case.

Overall, this suggests that laypeople's intuitions about Zygote cases do not support Mele's argument. Nevertheless, one might object that my formulation of the Manipulation case failed to elicit the appropriate intuitions because it failed to highlight the relevant considerations. For example, maybe it did not make clear the fact that Diane's ability to predict the future was premised on some form of determinism.

Another objection might be that, because I used particularly bad and good deeds (killing a person vs. giving all one's money to charity), their desire to blame (or praise) agents might have led participants to ignore other relevant features of these scenarios.

In the next study, I modified my presentation of the Zygote argument to address these issues.

Study 2—Replication and Extension of Previous Findings

Materials and Methods

In this study, the three types of vignettes used in Study 1 were modified to make it more salient that the goddess was able to predict the future because she has perfect knowledge of the current state of the world and of the laws of nature. The probabilities in the Indeterministic case were modified: the goddess now saw that the zygote had a 99 percent chance to grow up and become Bill and that Bill had a 67 percent chance of performing the target action. The Control case was also rewritten to exclude all reference to Ted and to simply be a case in which the goddess predicts (with a 67 percent chance) that Bill would perform the target action, without her having anything to do with Bill's birth. A fourth type of vignette was included, in which the goddess did not create Bill but was able to predict his future behavior with perfect certainty. This way, I was able to manipulate Manipulation (M) and Determinism (D) orthogonally by having four cases: Manipulation (M+/D+), Indeterministic (M+/D-), Deterministic (M-/D+), and Control (M-/D-). This would allow me to determine the respective weights of Manipulation and Determinism in people's intuitions about Zygote cases.

Compared to Study 1, I also modified the type of actions performed by Bill, so that they would be less upsetting and more closely matched across conditions. In the Bad Outcome version, Bill finds a wallet full of money and keeps it for himself. In the Good Outcome version, Bill returns the wallet to its rightful owner.

As an example, here is the Good version of the Deterministic case:

Deterministic (M-/D+), Good: Imagine a world just like ours, except that there exist beings similar to the Greek and Roman gods. These beings are not all-powerful but they have strange powers: they can use their perfect knowledge of what is currently happening in the world and combine it with their perfect knowledge of the laws of nature to deduce with absolute certainty what will happen in the future and what consequences their actions will have. They can also manipulate matter and even create and destroy life. These beings' existence is completely unknown to men.

Imagine that Diane is such a goddess. One day, March 3rd, 2021, she notices that Mary, a common human, has just got pregnant. Based on her knowledge of the current state of the world and the laws of nature, she knows with full certainty that, if she leaves the zygote (a human embryo at a very early stage) in Mary's uterus to grow without interfering, there is a 100 percent chance that this zygote will grow up to become a young man named Bill. Diane also sees every action that Bill will perform in his life. For example, she sees that there is a 100 percent chance that, on his 30th birthday, Bill will find a wallet containing $500 in the street and that he will decide not to keep the money for himself but to return it to its rightful owner.

Knowing all that Diane decides not to interfere and to leave the zygote grow in Mary's uterus. Moreover, she never interferes again in the zygote's development and Bill's life.

Nine months later, Mary gives birth to Bill. Bill grows up to be an ordinary human being. He's as rational as other human beings and exerts as much self-control upon his actions. On his 30th birthday, he finds a wallet containing $500 in the street. After a long deliberation, and on the basis of his deeply-held values, he decides not to keep the money for himself but to return it to its rightful owner.

After reading the vignette, participants were asked to rate the same statements as in Study 1. The *Throughpass* statement was removed as it did not seem to track exactly what it was supposed to be tracking.[5] The only statement to be modified beyond action description was:

(*Resp*) Bill is the one who is morally responsible for having kept [returned] the money.

Results

1350 participants were recruited on Prolific Academic and paid £0.63 for their participation completed our survey. After exclusion based on three comprehension checks,[6] I was left with 1111 participants (611 women, 483 men, and 17 others; M_{age} = 32.93, SD_{age} = 11.70).

Q1. *Do people have the intuition that agents in Zygote cases are not morally responsible for their actions?* Responsibility ratings, blame/praise ratings, and desert ratings were aggregated to form a single aggregated responsibility score (ARS; α =.71). Responsibility scores in the M+/D+ condition were high (M = 1.25, SD = 1.36) and significantly above the midpoint: $t(301)$ = 15.95, p <.001. Overall, 78 percent of participants in the M+/D+ condition obtained an ARS superior to 0. Thus, it seems fair to conclude that most participants did not share the intuition that agents in Zygote cases were not morally responsible for their actions.

Q2. *Does manipulation affect participants' attributions of moral responsibility?* I conducted a 2-way ANOVA with Outcome Valence (Bad/Good) and Case (M+/D+, M+/D-, M-/D+ and M-/D-) as factors and ARS as dependent variable. There was no significant interaction effect: $F(3,1103)$ = 1.24, p =.29, η_p^2 = 0.003. After dropping the interaction term, we found a significant effect of Valence: $F(1,1106)$ = 219.71, p <.001, η_p^2 = 0.15, but no significant effect of Case: $F(3,1106)$ = 1.98, p =.12, η_p^2 = 0.005. Thus, there was no difference between the Manipulation (M+/D+) and Control (M-/D-) cases, even when analyzing both outcome valences separately.

Table 4.6 Mean and Standard Deviation for each condition in Study 2. Superscripts present the results of Tukey tests comparing the four cases for each variable and each outcome valence. When superscripts are present, two conditions that do not share a common letter in superscript significantly differ from each other. When no superscript is present, this means that there was no difference between conditions. There was no significant interaction effect.

	Valence	Case			
		Manipulation (M+/D+)	Indet. (M+/D-)	Deterministic (M-/D+)	Control (M-/D-)
ARS	Bad	0.85 (1.43)	0.99 (1.18)	0.92 (1.29)	1.11 (1.20)
	Good	1.82 (1.06)	1.80 (0.88)	2.09 (0.87)	1.99 (0.87)
Resp.	Bad	1.48 (1.92)	1.87 (1.28)	1.83 (1.45)	1.93 (1.46)
	Good	2.08^a (1.14)	2.08^a (1.04)	2.49^b (0.77)	2.46^b (0.74)
Blame/Praise	Bad	1.04 (1.80)	1.02 (1.69)	1.05 (1.76)	1.32 (1.59)
	Good	1.55 (1.39)	1.50 (1.25)	1.84 (1.24)	1.65 (1.27)
Desert	Bad	0.02 (1.77)	0.09 (1.61)	-0.13 (1.58)	0.07 (1.62)
	Good	1.83 (1.32)	1.83 (1.15)	1.93 (1.05)	1.86 (1.27)
Free Will	Bad	1.98 (1.44)	2.10 (1.14)	2.12 (1.24)	2.24 (1.11)
	Good	1.74^a (1.43)	2.03^{ab} (1.10)	2.29^{bc} (1.06)	2.41^c (0.89)
Deep Self	Bad	1.46 (1.17)	1.56 (1.02)	1.42 (1.09)	1.59 (1.04)
	Good	1.51^a (1.15)	1.60^{ab} (0.96)	1.86^b (0.87)	1.87^b (0.82)
Bypass	Bad	-1.51 (1.26)	-1.56 (1.13)	-1.49 (1.20)	-1.60 (1.18)
	Good	-1.41^a (1.18)	-1.14^b (1.33)	-1.46^{ab} (1.24)	-1.53^{ab} (1.20)
Control	Bad	-1.86 (1.46)	-2.05 (1.08)	-1.95 (1.21)	-2.17 (1.21)
	Good	-1.75 (1.47)	-1.91 (1.11)	-2.22 (0.97)	-2.29 (0.99)
N	Bad	139	129	119	115
	Good	118	115	116	260

Table 4.7 Inter-correlations between variables in Study 2.

	Free Will	Deep Self	Bypass	Control
ARS	.44***	.46***	-0.28***	-0.36***
Free Will	-	.55***	-.41***	-.64***
Deep Self	-	-	-.57***	-.60***
Bypass	-	-	-	.57***

In absence of a significant main effect of Case and/or of a significant interaction effect between Cases and Outcome Valence, it was impossible to investigate my other research questions. This is why I decided to run additional data.

Additional Data

Aggregate responsibility scores were abnormally low in the Control (M-/D-) condition, particularly when the outcome was bad ($M = 1.11$). This might simply have been because participants did not consider keeping the wallet as a serious offense worth blaming and punishing. But it might also have been because this condition was not an adequate control condition—maybe the mere presence of superior entities able to (roughly) predict and prevent human action was already perceived as a threat to humans' moral responsibility. After all, given that our goddess could have prevented Bill from keeping the wallet, why not think *she* is partly responsible for it?

To adjudicate between these two possibilities, I decided to collect more data by introducing two *pure control* cases (that I called *normal* cases), in which there is absolutely no reference to any god or goddess (see Table 4.8).

I recruited 300 additional participants on the same online platform, using the same demographic constraint, and launching the additional study at the same hour I launched the original study. Based on three comprehension checks, forty-five participants were excluded, leaving us with 255 participants (133 women, 116 men, and 6 others; $M_{age} = 33.00$, $SD_{age} = 12.26$).

Participants received one of our two normal cases at random, then answered the same questions as in Study 2 (only comprehension checks were changed). Then, I compared participants' answer to these normal cases with participants' answer to the Manipulation (M+/D+) cases in Study 2.

For ARS, an ANOVA with Outcome Valence (Bad/Good) and Case (Manipulation vs. Normal) as factors revealed a marginally significant interaction effect: $F(1,508) = 3.13$, $p = .078$, $\eta_p^2 = 0.006$, a significant main effect of Outcome Valence: $F(1,508) = 64.84$, $p < .001$, $\eta_p^2 = 0.109$, and a significant main effect of Case: $F(1,508) = 5.06$, $p = .025$, $\eta_p^2 = 0.010$.

So, using these *Normal* cases as comparison cases for our Zygote cases, I was able to find some effect of manipulation on participant's judgments about moral responsibility. This allowed me to investigate my research questions further, by focusing on Bad Outcome cases, as there was no significant difference in ARS between the two cases for Good Outcome cases.

Table 4.8 The two *Normal* cases used in Study 2 to collect additional data.

Normal (Bad)	Normal (Good)
Imagine a world just like ours.	Imagine a world just like ours.
One day, March 3, 2021, Mary, a common human, gets pregnant. The zygote (a human embryo at a very early stage) in Mary's uterus grows up to become a young man named Bill.	One day, March 3, 2021, Mary, a common human, gets pregnant. The zygote (a human embryo at a very early stage) in Mary's uterus grows up to become a young man named Bill.
On his thirtieth birthday, Bill finds a wallet containing $500 in the street. After a long deliberation, and on the basis of his deeply held values, he decides to keep the money for himself rather than return it to its rightful owner.	On his thirtieth birthday, Bill finds a wallet containing $500 in the street. After a long deliberation, and on the basis of his deeply held values, he decides not to keep the money for himself but to return it to its rightful owner.

Table 4.9 Mean and Standard Deviation for each condition in follow-up to Study 2. Stars(*) present the results of Welch t-tests comparing the two cases (Manipulation and Normal) for each variable and each outcome valence.

	Bad		Good	
	Manipulation	Normal	Manipulation	Normal
ARS	0.85* (1.43)	1.25 (1.09)	1.82 (1.06)	1.87 (0.89)
Resp.	1.48* (1.92)	1.98 (1.59)	2.08 (1.14)	2.32 (0.90)
Blame/Praise	1.04** (1.79)	1.55 (1.36)	1.55 (1.39)	1.60 (1.25)
Desert	0.02 (1.77)	0.22 (1.56)	1.83 (1.32)	1.68 (1.25)
Free Will	1.98*** (1.44)	2.51 (0.95)	1.74*** (1.43)	2.42 (0.71)
Deep Self	1.46* (1.17)	1.75 (0.93)	1.51 (1.15)	1.58 (0.85)
Bypass	-1.51*** (1.26)	-2.00 (0.93)	-1.41 (1.18)	-1.57 (1.17)
Control	-1.86*** (1.46)	-2.51 (0.73)	-1.75** (1.47)	-2.28 (1.08)
N	139	122	118	133

Q3. *Does the effect of manipulation depend on determinism?* As we saw earlier, for Bad Outcome cases, there was no significant difference in ARS between the M+/D+ and M+/D- cases. Thus, it is not clear that Determinism plays a role in undermining agents' moral responsibility in Zygote cases.

Q4. *Are agents in manipulation cases identical to agents in control cases?* Focusing on bad outcome cases, I used two Welch t-tests to compare Deep Self scores ($\alpha = .82$) and Bypassing scores ($\alpha = .73$) across conditions. Both tests found significant differences between the Manipulation and Normal cases (see Table 4.9): Deep Self scores were lower in the Manipulation condition while Bypassing scores were higher in the Manipulation condition. This suggests that participants did not perceive agents in the Manipulation condition as identical to those in the Normal condition.

Q5. *Can the results be explained by the Deep Self Provenance hypothesis?*
   a. <u>Interaction between condition and valence:</u> There was a marginally significant interaction effect. Moreover, the effect of manipulation was significant for bad outcomes but not for good outcomes. This is in line with my predictions.
   b. <u>Correlations:</u> For bad outcomes, there was a significant correlation ($r = .43$) between ARS and Deep Self scores.
   c. <u>Mediation analysis:</u> I used structural equation modeling (in R's {lavaan} package) to investigate whether Deep Self scores mediated the effect of manipulation on ARS. I focused on bad outcome cases, and on the comparison between the Manipulation and Normal cases. Results are presented in Figure 4.2. The effect of manipulation on ARS was significantly mediated by Deep Self ratings. No significant direct effect remained.

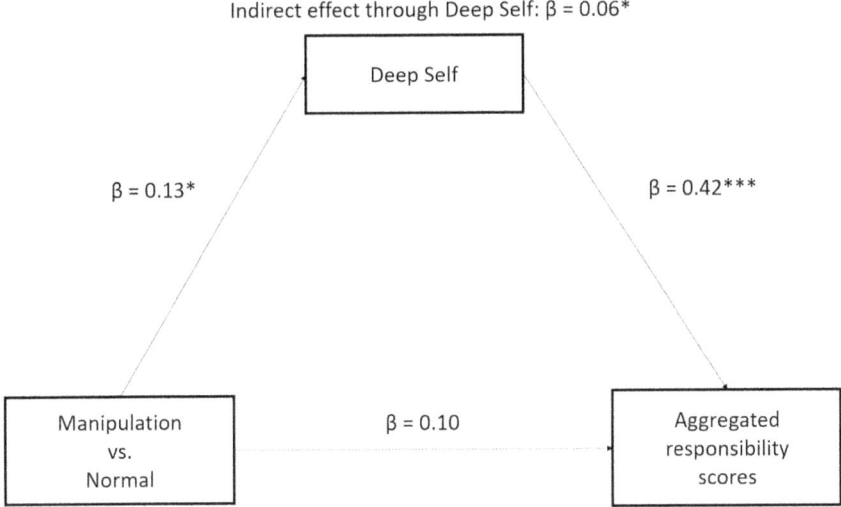

Figure 4.2 Deep Self scores as mediators of the effect of manipulation (Manipulation vs. Normal) in follow-up to Study 2.

Conclusion: "the Goddess you need can't be me"

In this paper, my goal was to investigate people's intuitions about the Zygote argument, and to see whether they supported the argument. Overall, my data did not really support the Zygote argument, as it allowed for both a *hard-line* and *soft-line* response to the Zygote argument.

Regarding the *hard-line* response, it is striking to observe that most participants did attribute moral responsibility to agents in Zygote cases. When the outcome was good, there was no significant difference in moral responsibility attributions between Zygote and control cases. Thus, it seems that the very starting point of the Zygote argument—that we have the intuition that agents in Zygote cases are not morally responsible for their actions—is simply a non-starter.

Of course, defenders of the Zygote argument could simply argue that folk intuitions about the Zygote cases are irrelevant, and that intuitions from trained, impartial philosophers with a good knowledge of the debate and the ability to understand the subtleties of such cases are what counts. This is precisely Mele's contention:

> Suppose an intuition check were to be run on premise (1). Would incompatibilists uniformly deem 1 true whereas compatibilists uniformly deem (1) false? Some philosophers and psychologists run controlled intuition checks on untutored subjects. I myself am doubtful about the significance of the judgments such subjects make about complicated theoretical matters. A more suitable audience for the question about premise (1) of the zygote argument might be people who have

thought long and hard about freedom and moral responsibility and are agnostic about compatibilism. I call them *reflective agnostics*.

(Mele, 2008, pp. 280–1)

But we also have grounds for a *soft-line* response to the argument: indeed, participants did not consider agents in Zygote cases to be identical in all relevant respects to agents in control cases. If we focus on Bad Outcome cases (the ones for which we found an effect of manipulation), we can see that participants in Studies 1 and 2 were less likely to see agents in Zygote cases as being acting from their deep self, and more likely to see their mental states as "bypassed." Moreover, these differences seemed to play a role in participants' judgments: the effect of manipulation was mediated by Deep Self considerations, but also by participants' Bypass ratings (as I observed in additional, *post-hoc* analyses). Finally, we saw that the effect of manipulation was stronger for Bad Outcomes, compared to Good outcomes—exactly as I predicted based on the Deep Self Provenance model. Thus, even if participants' attributions of moral responsibility were affected by manipulation, this effect can be explained away by considerations available to compatibilists.

Once again, defenders of the Zygote argument could object that the relevant intuitions, for example those of Mele's *reflective* agnostics, are not likely to be driven by the same considerations as those of non-specialists. But is it really the case? When discussing the intuitions of *reflective agnostics* (among whom he counts himself), Mele makes the following prediction:

Thus far, I have not said what the event is that Ernie was built to produce (in the original story), event E. Different specifications of it may affect the strength of intuitions about the story. Suppose that E is the death of Ernie's aunt and that Ernie poisoned her in order to inherit her money so that he could get himself out of serious financial trouble. Some reflective agnostics will feel pulled toward the judgment that Ernie is not blameworthy for the killing because Diana assembled his zygote as she did to ensure that he would do precisely that and because her creative activity did ensure that he would do that. Furthermore, because they judge that if Ernie had been morally responsible for the killing or had killed his aunt freely, he would have been blameworthy for the killing, they feel pulled toward the judgment that the action was not free and not one for which Ernie is morally responsible. These same agnostics might have a different attitude if E were a homeless shelter's receiving a $200 donation and A were Ernie's donating that money. Other reflective agnostics may be more powerfully moved by Ernie's bad will in the killing scenario than by the details of his creation and be pulled toward the judgment that he is blameworthy and morally responsible for the killing and freely kills his aunt.

(Mele, 2008, p. 283).

So, Mele predicts that reflective agnostics' intuitions about Zygote cases will depend on the kind of action performed by the agent. And, in this paragraph, he clearly suggests that reflective agnostics are more likely to think that some reflective agnostics will be more likely to consider the agent in Zygote cases to be morally responsible when the outcome is good (e.g. donating to a homeless shelter) than when the outcome is bad (e.g. killing one's aunt). But, this is exactly what I observed in Study 1. Thus, it does not seem that these hypothetical reflective agnostics' intuitions are much more different than laypeople's intuitions. So why think they have different psychological underpinnings?

Moreover, Mele does not offer any plausible mechanism that would explain why these reflective agnostics would be more willing to attribute moral responsibility when the agent is giving money compared to when they kill their aunt. To my knowledge, the only available explanation we have at the moment is the Deep Self Provenance hypothesis, which predicted these very same results. As such, it seems legitimate to conclude (at least temporarily) that the intuitions of Mele's reflective agnostics are also driven by (implicit) considerations about whether agents in Zygote cases act on the basis of their Deep Self, which allows to reject Mele's claim that we have the intuition that agents in Zygote cases lack moral responsibility even when they fulfill all (non-historical) compatibilist requirements. Rather, it is probably because we perceive them (consciously or not) as being prevented to act on their own deeply held desires and values.

Finally, the data presented in this paper give us a third reason to be skeptical of the Zygote argument: indeed, the evidence suggests that the intuition that agents in Zygote cases are not morally responsible for their actions has nothing particular to do with determinism. In Study 1, the Indeterministic case was not significantly different from the Manipulation case, but was significantly different from the Control case. In Study 2, there was no significant difference between the Manipulation and Indeterministic case. Thus, it seems that, whatever drives participants' intuitions about Zygote cases, it has nothing to do with determinism. Thus, determinism cannot be counted as the best explanation why agents in Zygote cases are not morally responsible, and the explanatory version of the Zygote argument is no more successful than the direct one.

Of course, all these counterarguments to the Zygote argument might once again be dismissed on the ground that folk intuitions do not matter, and only experts' intuitions are conducive to truth. However, I would resist this defense on two grounds. The first ground is meta-philosophical: doing so seems to assume that there is some kind of metaphysical (or rather, moral) truth about moral responsibility only expert philosophers would have access to (or to which expert philosophers would have better access). I must say that I have always failed to see what would warrant such a view of the philosophical enterprise: our notion of moral responsibility is not a technical one, but rather comes from attitudes and practices that preexist the philosophical enterprise. The second ground is dialectic: as an expert in the field myself, I have never shared the intuition at the basis of the Zygote argument, and I am not the only expert in this case. Knowing that common sense is on my side, why should I even worry with the Zygote argument to begin with?

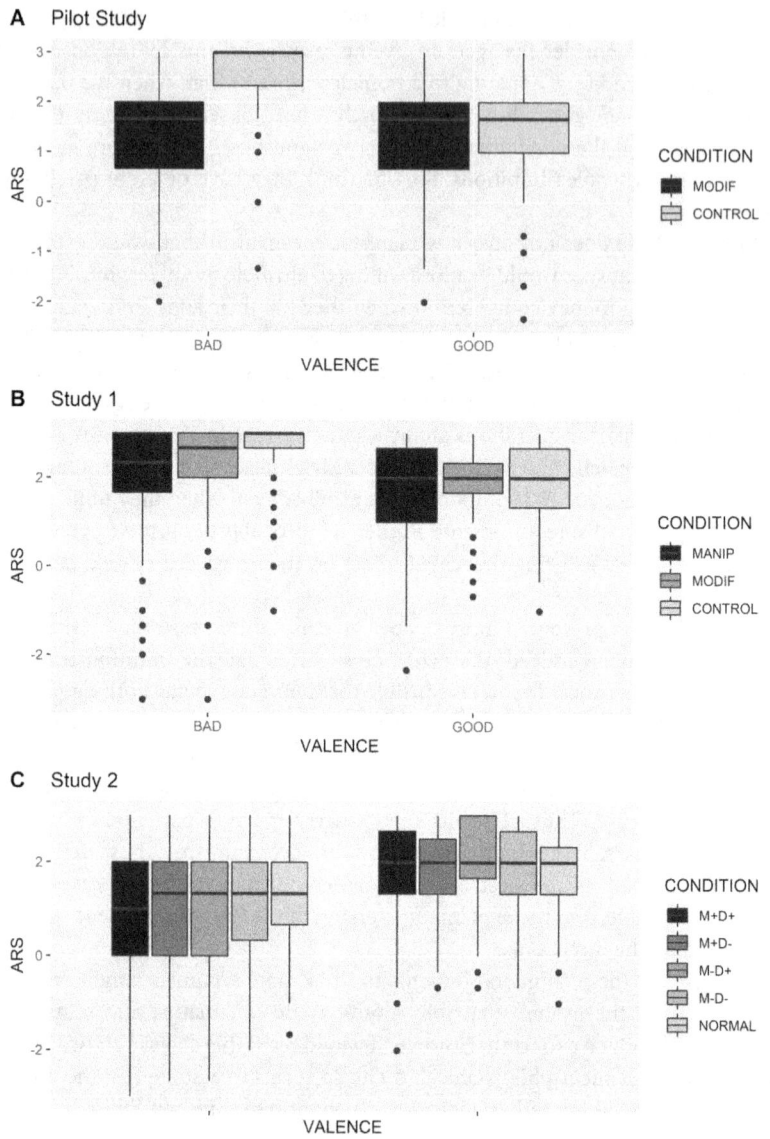

Figure 4.3 Boxplots of Aggregate Responsibility Scores (ARS) in function of CONDITION and OUTCOME VALENCE for all three studies.

Notes

1. Mickelson (2017) distinguishes a third type of manipulation argument, based on *generalization*. For the sake of simplicity, and because I won't need them for my discussion of experimental results, I won't develop such arguments here.

2   Originally, I also planned to add two versions of Sripada's *Manipulation* case. However, due to human error, the Good version of the *Control* case was inserted in place of the Good version of the *Manipulation* case. I thus excluded the *Manipulation* cases from analysis.
3   For the idea that the Zygote argument fails if determinism plays no role in the intuition that agents lack moral responsibility, see Kearns (2012).
4   This cumbersome formulation was chosen because analysis of participants' open-ended justifications in Pilot Study revealed that, in the Good Outcome cases, a lot of participants interpreted the question about whether Bill was responsible for saving Mrs. White as being about whether it was Bill's duty and obligation to save Mrs. White. This ambiguity in the expression "being morally responsible for" is a serious problem and has already plagued other studies (such as Turri, 2017a, 2017b).
5   Introduced by Björnsson and Pereboom, D. (2014), this item was supposed to measure the belief that "the agent's deliberation is not bypassed." However, the results of the Pilot Study show that Throughpass scores are way higher in the manipulation than in the Control case, suggesting that the statement rather measures to which extent the agent is manipulated by external forces. For further discussion, see Cova (forthcoming).
6   There were actually four comprehension checks, but the last one was failed by a lot of participants. Comments sent spontaneously by participants on Prolific Academic indicated that they found the sentence ill-phrased and that they were unsure what to answer. The sentence (that they had to rate as TRUE or FALSE) was "Diane predicted that there would be a 100 percent chance that the zygote would grow up to give birth to Bill". According to a lot of participants, it was not correct to say that the zygote "gave birth" to Bill.

References

Berniūnas, R., Beinorius, A., Dranseika, V., Silius, V., & Rimkevičius, P. (2021). The weirdness of belief in free will. *Consciousness and Cognition*, 87, 103054.

Björnsson, G. (2016). Outsourcing the deep self: Deep self discordance does not explain away intuitions in manipulation arguments. *Philosophical Psychology*, 29(5), 637–53.

Björnsson, G., & Pereboom, D. (2014). Free will skepticism and bypassing. In W. Sinnott-Armstrong (Ed.), *Moral Psychology* (Vol. 4, pp. 27–35). Cambridge, MA: MIT Press

Cova, F. (2011). *L'Architecture de la cognition morale*. PhD thesis. EHESS.

Cova, F. (forthcoming). A defense of natural compatibilism. In J. Campbell, K. M. Mickelson, & V. A. White (Eds.), *Blackwell Companion to Free Will*. Oxford: Blackwell.

Cova, F., & Boudesseul, J. (2021). "That feels deep!": Feelings of being moved play a role in perceptions of depth and profundity (feat. the Geneva Sentimentality Scale). Unpublished manuscript, University of Geneva.

Feltz, A. (2013). Pereboom and premises: Asking the right questions in the experimental philosophy of free will. *Consciousness and Cognition*, 22(1), 53–63.

Kane, R. (1985). *Free Will and Values*. Albany, NY: State University of New York Press

Kearns, S. (2012). Aborting the zygote argument. *Philosophical Studies*, 160(3), 379–89.

Levy, N. (2011). *Hard Luck: How Luck Undermines Free Will and Moral Responsibility*. New York: Oxford University Press.

Mele, A. R. (2005). A critique of Pereboom's' four-case argument for incompatibilism. *Analysis*, *65*(1), 75–80.

Mele, A. (2006). *Free Will and Luck*. New York: Oxford University Press.

Mele, A. R. (2008). Manipulation, compatibilism, and moral responsibility. *The Journal of Ethics*, *12*(3–4), 263–86.

Mele, A. R. (2019). *Manipulated Agents: A Window to Moral Responsibility*. New York: Oxford University Press.

Mickelson, K. (2015). The zygote argument is invalid: Now what? *Philosophical Studies*, *172*(11), 2911–29.

Mickelson, K. (2017). The manipulation argument. In M. Griffith, K. Timpe, & N. Levy (Eds.), *The Routledge Companion to Free Will*, pp. 166–78. New York: Routledge.

Nahmias, E., Morris, S. G., Nadelhoffer, T., & Turner, J. (2006). Is incompatibilism intuitive? *Philosophy and Phenomenological Research*, *73*(1), 28–53.

Newman, G. E., Bloom, P., & Knobe, J. (2014). Value judgments and the true self. *Personality and Social Psychology Bulletin*, *40*(2), 203–16.

Pereboom, D. (1995). Determinism al dente. *Noûs*, *29*(1), 21–45.

Sripada, C. S. (2010). The deep self model and asymmetries in folk judgments about intentional action. *Philosophical Studies*, *151*(2), 159–76.

Sripada, C. S. (2012). What makes a manipulated agent unfree? *Philosophy and Phenomenological Research*, *85*(3), 563–93.

Strohminger, N., Knobe, J., & Newman, G. (2017). The true self: A psychological concept distinct from the self. *Perspectives on Psychological Science*, *12*(4), 551–60.

Turri, J. (2017a). Compatibilism can be natural. *Consciousness and Cognition*, *51*, 68–81.

Turri, J. (2017b). Compatibilism and incompatibilism in social cognition. *Cognitive Science*, *41*, 403–24.

5

Moral Responsibility without (Some Kinds of) Freedom

Walter Sinnott-Armstrong

Wars over free will have raged for millennia. Neither side seems able to imagine how their opponents could possibly disagree with them, so neither is willing to surrender. To end this ongoing feud, we need to help them understand each other and find some treaty that appeases both sides by giving each part of what it wants. This paper will scout out that road to peace.

The Challenge

Both antagonists respond in different ways to the same simple argument:

1—Every act is either determined or random.[1]
2—Any agent whose act is determined is not free.[2]
3—Any agent whose act is random is not free.[3]
4—*Therefore*, no agent is ever free.
5—Any agent who is not free is not responsible.[4]
6—*Therefore*, no agent is ever responsible.
7—We should never imprison any agent who is not responsible.[5]
8—*Therefore*, we should never imprison any agent.

Almost nobody wants to reach Conclusion 8, because it implies that we should never imprison any convicted murderers and rapists for their heinous acts. However, this argument is logically valid, so we cannot consistently deny its conclusion without rejecting at least one of its premises. Nonetheless, the premises all seem individually plausible, at least initially to many people. That is the problem.

To solve this problem, different philosophers reject different premises. *Libertarians* about freedom typically claim that some human actions are not determined (Kane, 2007). But if these undetermined actions were simply random, such as effects of quantum mechanical perturbations, then their occurrence and probability would not be controlled by the agent in any way that could plausibly ground moral responsibility.

For such reasons, libertarians typically go further and claim that some human actions are also not random. Instead, they see these actions as based on reasons rather than causes, so the act, decision, or agent is a rational uncaused cause. Thus, Libertarians typically claim that these acts are neither determined nor random, so they deny Premise 1.[6] This is how they try to escape Conclusions 4, 6, and 8.

In contrast, *Compatibilists* about freedom typically deny Premise 2 (Fischer, 2007). They claim that agents can be free even if their acts and wills are determined. One could instead deny Premise 3 and claim that freedom is compatible with randomness (though perhaps not determinism, if one accepts Premise 2), but that position is rare. In any case, compatibilists usually interpret freedom in terms of some kind of control that can exist in a determined universe (see below). Premise 2 is then false on their interpretation, so they can consistently reject Conclusions 4, 6, and 8.

The third common position is *Hard Determinism* (or hard incompatibilism; Pereboom, 2007). Hard determinists *about freedom* accept Premises 1, 2, and 3, so they have to accept Conclusion 4. Hard determinists *about responsibility* go on to accept Premise 5 and Conclusion 6, so they claim that no agent is ever responsible for anything. Nonetheless, they usually admit that at least some convicted murderers and rapists should be imprisoned as the only realistic means to prevent crime (by means of deterrence, incapacitation, rehabilitation, or reinforcing moral norms). Some hard determinists do oppose all *punishment* in any sense that requires retribution for desert and thus differs from mere penalties, civil commitment, quarantine, and caging animals for safety. However, Premise 7 is about imprisonment rather than punishment in this retributive sense, so even these hard determinists deny Premise 7. Their denial of Premise 7 is what enables them to avoid Conclusion 8.

This challenging argument and these responses are old hat—and none is fully satisfying. That is the point. This traditional debate seems unresolvable. To escape this dead end (and find a new hat or a new road), we need to make two moves. First, we need to question Premise 5, which all three traditional approaches assume (cf. van Inwagen, 2017, p. 215). Second, we need to ask what freedom means in Premises 2–5.

Responsibility without Freedom

Premise 5 claims that no agent can be responsible (for an act) without being free (to do and not to do that act). *Semi-compatibilists* deny this premise and claim that it is possible for an agent to be responsible without having either freedom of action or freedom of will (Fischer, 2007, p. 56). This basic claim of semi-compatibilism is about the relation of freedom and responsibility, so it is neutral on whether freedom is compatible with determinism (and, hence, on Premise 2) and also neutral on whether any agent is free (and, hence, on Sub-conclusion 4). However, instead of remaining neutral on 1–4, others who deny Premise 5 also accept Premises 1–3 and Sub-conclusion 4, so they conclude that no agent is free. I will call this combination of claims *partial compatibilism* in order to distinguish it from semi-compatibilism.

Many opponents dismiss semi- and partial compatibilism as nonstarters. They see Premise 5 as so obvious that it does not need any justification or they just implicitly assume Premise 5 in motivated reasoning of the form, "We have to have freedom in order to save responsibility" (e.g., van Inwagen, 1983, pp. 206-13). When opponents bother to give any argument for Premise 5, it is often simply an appeal to legal or other traditions (e.g., List, pp. 18-19), although actual laws almost never refer explicitly to free will. Some opponents give a quick example, even though it is clearly too hasty to generalize from one example—or even several examples—to Premise 5, which is a universal claim about *all* actions. Someone who is pushed off a roof and falls onto a pedestrian does not jump or fall freely and is not responsible for hitting the pedestrian, but that does not show that she lacks responsibility *because* she lacks freedom. There might be *other* reasons why she is not responsible (such as that she was pushed off the roof). Moreover, other agents in other cases still might be responsible without being free. For such reasons, examples like this are not enough to establish Premise 5, and it is hard to find any stronger argument for Premise 5.

Premise 5 still might seem obvious, but its veneer of truth begins to fade when we notice differences between the natures of freedom and responsibility. As Gazzaniga (2012) argued, whether an agent, act, or will is free seems to be an issue of *metaphysics* or *science*, at least on many common interpretations (see below for other interpretations). In contrast, responsibility seems to be a *normative* or *moral* issue about whether it is legitimate for others to act in certain ways toward the agent.[7] Because freedom and responsibility differ in such essential ways, it would be surprising if responsibility conceptually entailed freedom, as Premise 5 claims. Of course, even if responsibility depends on other factors, such as norms, it is still *possible* that freedom is a necessary condition for any (even minimal) responsibility.[8] Nonetheless, anyone who asserted such a universal connection between what is metaphysical or scientific and what is normative or moral would owe us a strong argument. As mentioned, no strong argument has been given in centuries of debate.[9]

Surveys

Additional reasons to doubt Premise 5 come from surveys of popular opinion. Of course, popular opinion does not prove or disprove philosophical truths. Premise 5 might be true, even if many or even most people deny it. Nonetheless, Premise 5 is supposed to be so obvious that it needs no argument. If enough people ascribe responsibility without freedom, then Premise 5 is at least not as obvious as its defenders assume, and then it seems to need support from at least some argument. Of course, people do make mistakes about even simple conceptual truths, such as when they deny that modus tollens is valid. However, those conceptual truths can be supported by arguments, such as truth tables for modus tollens. Those conceptual truths need support, and they have it. The point here is that Premise 5 also needs to be supported by some kind of argument. It is not clear what kind of argument could satisfy that need, but the need is pressing if enough people ascribe responsibility without freedom.

Several recent surveys suggest that many people are indeed willing to ascribe responsibility without freedom (e.g., Figdor & Phelan 2015; Vierkant, Deutschländer, Sinnott-Armstrong, & Haynes 2019). In the largest and most diverse study on this issue, Hannikainen et al. (2019) surveyed 5268 participants in twenty countries and sixteen languages. About half (2381) of their participants read this "actual sequence" (AS) scenario from Nichols and Knobe (2007):

> Imagine a universe in which everything that happens is completely brought about by whatever happened before it. This is true from the very beginning of the universe, so what happened in the beginning of the universe brings about what happened next, and so on right up until the present. For example, one day John decided to have vegetable soup at lunch. Like everything else, this decision was completely brought about by what happened before it. So, if everything in this universe was exactly the same up until John made his decision, then it had to happen that John would decide to have vegetable soup at lunch.
>
> In this universe, a man named Bill has become attracted to his secretary, and he decides that the only way to be with her is to kill his wife and three children. Before he leaves on a business trip, he sets up a bomb that destroys his house and kills his family while he is away.

The phrases "completely brought about" and "had to happen" signal a strong version of determinism to which some compatibilists might object, but that makes it even more significant if participants assert freedom and responsibility in this scenario.

Participants were asked two questions related to freedom and two questions related to responsibility[10]:

(Q1) Did the agent (Bill) act freely when he killed his wife? (1: yes, 0: no)
(Q2) How much control did he have over killing his victim? (1: no control—7: complete control)
(Q3) To what extent was he was blameworthy? (1: not at all—7: extremely)
(Q4) How much punishment did he deserve? (1: no punishment—7: severe punishment).

The key finding reported in Hannikainen et al. (2019) is that participants tended to judge that the agent in AS is neither free nor in control (mean answer to Q1 = 0.47 out of 0–1, and mean answer to Q2 = 3.31 out of 1–7; both significantly *below* the midpoint). Nonetheless, they also tended to judge that the agent was still responsible (mean answer to Q3 = 4.67, and mean answer to Q4 = 5.04; both significantly *above* the midpoint).[11]

These reported results still do not show how many participants ascribed responsibility without freedom, so I asked Ivar Hannikainen to fill these gaps, and he did.[12] The relevant results are in Table 5.1.

Participants on the first row said that Bill was free, so they were in no position to say that Bill was responsible but not free. The only participants who were able to ascribe responsibility without freedom in this case are on the second row, so that is the crucial group. Out of the 876 participants who passed their comprehension checks and denied that Bill acted freely (No to Q1), 571 (65 percent) answered above 1 on Q3. Since an answer of 1 to Q3 indicated that Bill was not at all blameworthy, participants

Table 5.1 Responses to Q1 and Q3 about Bill in AS in Hannikainen et al. (2019).

Responses	1 to Q3	2 to Q3	3 to Q3	4 to Q3	5 to Q3	6 to Q3	7 to Q3
Yes to Q1	49	14	31	64	43	102	461
No to Q1	305	60	67	113	69	68	194

who answered above 1 said that Bill was at least *somewhat* blameworthy, even though these 571 had just said that Bill did not act freely. Defenders of premise 5 might deny that a little bit of blame goes a long way in this argument.[13] Nonetheless, participants who answered at or above the midpoint (4) to Q3 said that Bill was *substantially* blameworthy, and this response was given by 444 (51 percent) out of the 876 who passed their comprehension checks and said that Bill did not act freely. Indeed, 194 (22 percent) of those 876 said that Bill was *extremely* blameworthy (7 to Q3). Thus, many (though not all) of these participants ascribed responsibility (or at least blameworthiness) without freedom.

These judgments conflict with Premise 5 in the opening argument, which claims that any agent who is not free (to do or not do an act) cannot be responsible (for that act). These judgments also align with semi- and partial compatibilism, which deny Premise 5 and claim that agents can be responsible for their acts even if they are not free. The participants in these surveys did not report whether or not they accepted determinism in our actual world, so they did not endorse partial compatibilism, which asserts determinism, infers lack of freedom, and still asserts responsibility. Nonetheless, these participants did make judgments about a deterministic universe that imply that responsibility (or at least blameworthiness) is compatible both with determinism and with lack of freedom.

Admittedly, the fact that so many survey participants make judgments in this pattern does not prove that their judgments are true or even coherent or defensible. They might be confused or mistaken. Moreover, not all participants' judgments fit these patterns. Some of them endorsed neither freedom nor responsibility, while others endorsed both freedom and responsibility. Nonetheless, enough of them endorsed responsibility without freedom to pose a serious challenge to Premise 5. After all, Premise 5 is not supposed to be an obscure fact that the public could not be expected to know. It is supposed to be a relatively simple conceptual truth that should be obvious to anyone with an adequate grasp of common concepts. Although people do get confused about some simple conceptual truths, such as modus tollens, enough disagreement still shows that these claims need some support from some argument (see above). Unless defenders of Premise 5 give adequate reasons to show that these participants who ascribed responsibility without freedom misunderstood what they said, their survey answers create significant doubts about Premise 5.

Some defenders of Premise 5 might respond that these survey participants *must* be confused, because these opponents stipulatively define the relevant kind of freedom as whatever is needed for responsibility in addition to other necessary conditions for responsibility, whatever those other conditions are (e.g., Wolf, 1990, pp. 3–4; Mele,

2006, p. 17). This stipulation openly begs the question against those who deny that freedom is needed for responsibility. Philosophers can define their terms however they want, but the surveys show that this definition of freedom in terms of responsibility is not what many ordinary folk mean by freedom.[14] If philosophers define their terms in ways that differ in crucial respects from how many people use those terms, then those philosophers will be unable to talk directly about what those other people care about. Moreover, even if many philosophers and common folk define freedom as necessary for responsibility, this kind of freedom might not be the *only* relevant kind, as we will see after the next section.

Freedom without Ability to Do Otherwise

Although our main focus so far has been on Premise 5, we also need to ask about Premise 2, which claims that any agent whose action (or will) is determined is not free. Partial compatibilists, who deny freedom, often use Premise 2 (along with Premises 1 and 3) to argue against freedom (by reaching Sub-Conclusion 4).

One popular argument for Premise 2 (e.g., van Inwagen 2017, p. 82) runs something like this:

(2.1) If any act is determined, then its agent cannot do otherwise.
(2.2) If an agent cannot do otherwise, then that agent is not free to do that act.
Therefore, (2) if any act is determined, then its agent is not free to do that act.

This argument is again logically valid, but it justifies its conclusion only if its premises are true. Like Premise 5, Premise (2.2) is supposed to be a conceptual truth that should be obvious to anyone with an adequate grasp of its component concepts. On this view, survey participants who understand the concepts should not be willing to ascribe freedom of action to any agent who cannot do otherwise.

Perhaps surprisingly, many people are willing to do this, as shown by another survey in Hannikainen et al. (2019). They presented the other half (2887) of their participants with this counterfactual intervener (CI) scenario (adapted from Frankfurt, 1969):

> The year is 3072. A group of mad scientists has invented a sophisticated device that can monitor what is going on in a person's mind. The device works at a distance by sending and receiving signals from a special chip that can be easily implanted into a person's brain. With the device, the scientists can change a person's decisions to engage in specific actions by simply sending signals to the special chip implanted in the person's head and thereby manipulating the activation of the person's neurons.
>
> One day, the scientists had a person infiltrate a clinic to find people so that the chip could be secretly implanted in them. Martin is one of the subjects who receive the implant.
>
> The next day, while monitoring Martin's thoughts, the scientists see that Martin is deliberating on a matter of great concern: whether to kill his friend Adam, who is having an affair with Martin's wife. The scientists agree that they

will let Martin make his own decision, but that, if he decides not to kill Adam, they will make him change his mind by sending signals that reinforce his desire and reasons to kill Adam. In other words, regardless of Martin's own final decision, Martin will kill Adam, because the scientists are set on interfering if necessary. Martin decides to kill Adam and ends up killing Adam. The scientists didn't have to interfere.

Martin presumably can *decide* not to kill Adam, but he cannot *act* otherwise, because the intervener will "make him change his mind" if he decides to do otherwise.

The crucial next question is whether the agent (Martin) acted freely. Hannikainen et al. (2019) asked their participants (Q1)–(Q4) above. Their central findings here were that participants tended to judge that Martin in this counterfactual intervener scenario acted freely and had control (mean answer to Q1 = 0.83 on a scale of 0–1, and mean answer to Q2 = 5.00 on a scale of 1-7; both significantly above the midpoint). They also tended to judge that the agent was blameworthy and deserved punishment (mean answer to Q3 = 5.90, and mean answer to Q4 = 5.98; both significantly above the midpoint). Thus, many (83 percent) of these participants said that Martin acted freely even though he lacked the ability to do otherwise.[15] These results pose a serious challenge to Premise 2.2 and thereby also Premise 2, just as the previous results challenged Premise 5.

As before, one might try to show how these participants were confused or mistaken. One also might wonder what they mean by acting freely if it is compatible with being unable to act otherwise. I will turn to that topic in the next section. But these studies already suggest that Premises 2 and 5 in the opening argument are at least not so obvious that everybody who understands them accepts them, so they need to be supported by some argument.

Some Kinds of Freedom[16]

Freedom comes in many flavors, but they share a certain abstract structure. Freedom is always freedom *to* do something (instead of something else),[17] and it is always freedom *from* some kind of barrier (as opposed to other kinds of barrier). Schematically, freedom is freedom *to* ___ and freedom *from* ___. Both blanks need to be filled with contrasts (Feinberg, 1973; MacCallum, 1967; Sinnott-Armstrong, 2013) in order to specify the kind of freedom at issue.

To illustrate degrees of freedom *to*, a prisoner is not free to leave his jail cell instead of staying in his cell, but he is still free to walk around inside his jail cell instead of sitting in one corner. If the prisoner is released on bail, then he might become free to move around a city even if he is not free to leave the city because of restrictions on his bail. And if he is acquitted, then he might become free to leave the city but still not free to leave the country, if he has no passport. This series shows that freedom comes in degrees that vary with the range of actions that an agent is (or is not) free to do in a given circumstance (or, in the case of free will, the range of decisions or choices that the agent is free to make). As a result, we should not ask simply whether a person is free to do (or to will to do) something without specifying the relevant range of alternatives, foils, or contrasts.

Freedom *from* also comes in degrees, because a range of barriers can restrict actions and choices. To call mints on a hotel counter free is to say that you can take them without paying, so cost is not a barrier to your taking a mint (even if standards of politeness are a barrier to taking the whole bowl of mints). Similarly, to call a seat in a theater free is to say that it is not reserved, so the rules of the theater and of etiquette are not barriers to sitting there (though those rules are still barriers to destroying the seat). A country has free speech to the extent that its citizens can say what they want about politics and other issues without risking punishment by the government, so its laws are not barriers to these kinds of speech (even if laws are still barriers to perjury or false advertising). In general, then, a claim that something is free is not positive but negative insofar as it claims that certain barriers, obstacles, or restrictions are *not* present. Different barriers are relevant in different cases, but freedom is always the absence of some kind of barrier.[18]

Of course, freedom *to* is closely related to freedom *from*. Each barrier that removes freedom *from* also removes freedom (*from* that barrier) *to* do a certain range of acts. Each barrier prevents some acts but not others. A lack of freedom from financial barriers can remove a person's freedom (*from* financial barriers) *to* send their children to expensive private schools without restricting their freedom (*from* financial barriers) *to* send their children to (free!) public schools or their freedom (*from* financial barriers) *to* protest against economic inequality. Thus, freedom *from* each barrier makes the agent free *from* that barrier *to* do certain acts, even if the person is not free *from* other barriers *to* do those or other acts.

Some barriers can also remove freedom of action without removing freedom of will. As John Locke pointed out long ago (1689), a person who is locked in a room but who does not know that the only door is locked can stay in the room of her own free will, so the locked door is not a barrier to free will in such cases. The locked door is not a barrier to her *choosing* to stay, even if it is a barrier to her *act* of leaving. She might choose to leave, walk over to the door, and try but fail to open the door. That shows her that she is not free to leave (because the locked door is a barrier to that action), but she still was free to try and to will to leave (because the locked door is not a barrier to that choice as long as she does not know she is locked in). Later, after she learns that the door is locked and that she cannot leave, then she cannot will or choose to do what she knows she cannot do, at least in this case. She has to be free from this barrier—knowledge that she cannot leave—in order to be free to will to leave. Of course, she is still free to will to scream for help or to will to read a book patiently until she is released, so she retains some freedom of action and will even after known barriers remove her freedom both to leave and to will to leave.[19]

These points about the form or structure of freedom are not intended to settle any substantive disputes, but they do help us understand many disputes. When people argue about freedom of action or will, we can avoid misunderstanding and confusion by asking, "Which kind of barrier is relevant?", "What are you denying?", "Free as opposed to what?", and "Free to do what as opposed to what else?" In particular, the debates between incompatibilists and compatibilists about premises 2 and 5 in the opening argument can be clarified by asking which barrier each side has in mind.

Who Cares about Which Kind?

Incompatibilists are most concerned with barriers like determination. They see determinism as incompatible with freedom of action, because no agent whose actions are completely determined is able to do otherwise (Kane, 2007). They are right in this sense: if every act is completely determined, then no agent is *free from determination*. That much is obvious by definition.[20]

Other incompatibilists allow that some acts are free from determination but still claim that no act is free from causation. An act can be caused without being determined if its cause increases its probability without completely determining that its agent will do that particular act (Hitchcock, 2018). Such probabilistic causation still strikes many as incompatible with moral responsibility at least when the agent has no control over the probabilities or over which possibility is actualized, because then what the agent does is a matter of luck (Levy, 2011). When their acts are caused probabilistically, agents are again supposed to be unable to do otherwise, because they lack control over whether they do otherwise, even if it is possible that they might do otherwise. Thus, if every event is caused, but some causes are only probabilistic, then some agents might be free from determination, but no agent is *free from causation*. That much should again be clear by definition.

Freedom from determination and causation are usually seen as relevant to responsibility because responsibility is assumed to require an ability to do otherwise. If determination and causation both remove an agent's ability to do otherwise, and if every act is determined or caused, then no agent is *free from inability* to do otherwise. Yet again, that much should be clear by definition. Moreover, an agent might be free from both determination and causation but not free from inability to do otherwise if an act is not caused by anything and the agent has no control over whether the act or an alternative is done. Thus, these three kinds of freedom—freedom from *determination*, freedom from *causation*, and freedom from *inability* to do otherwise—are distinct, and all three are necessary for responsibility, according to at least some incompatibilists.

In contrast, when compatibilists claim that an act is free even while it is determined and caused, they are not talking about freedom from determination or causation. They must know this, because it is obvious by definition that universal determinism and causation are not compatible with any freedom from determination or causation. They also wonder why they should want to be free from causation, whether deterministic or probabilistic, since freedom from causation would mean that their decisions and actions would not result from their desires or values and would not respond to their reasons for and against those decisions and actions.

Instead, when compatibilists call an act free, they seem to be saying that it is *free from constraint*. The relevant kind of constraint is anything that prevents the agent from doing what the agent really wants to do or which aligns best with the agent's basic desires, values, or reasons (though, as we will see, disputes arise about which of these are real or basic). For example, suppose that an agent fed peanut soup to a victim with a known peanut allergy. If she fed him peanut soup only because an enemy threatened to kill her if she did not feed the victim peanut soup, then her act was not free from constraint because she did not really want to feed him peanut soup. She really wanted not to be threatened. Thus, *coercion* is a constraint. Another constraint is serious *mental illness*, at least in some cases. If the agent who fed peanut soup to the victim was deluded and believed that the victim was a devil, then her act is not free from constraint because she did not really want to feed him peanut soup. She wanted to feed peanut soup to a devil, but he was not a devil. Other conditions—such as pushing or tripping, mistakes or accidents, and defense of self or others—can also be understood as constraints insofar as they also prevent the agent from doing what the agent really wants to do. These are the kinds of barriers that most of us want to avoid and have reason to avoid, so compatibilists see them as relevant to the kind of freedom worth wanting (in the memorable phrase of Dennett, 1984).

These constraints are also normally seen as excuses in the sense of conditions that reduce or remove moral responsibility. The law sometimes contrasts excuses with justifications (like coercion), but here I am using the notion of excuses broadly enough to include justifications, because an agent who is justified in doing an act is less blameworthy and less responsible for at least some harmful consequences of that act. In this broad sense, coercion and mental illness along with reasonable mistakes and other constraints are usually seen as excuses, because they are assumed to remove or reduce an agent's moral responsibility. Nonetheless, this assumption is substantive and does not follow merely from the definition of a constraint, which does not explicitly mention responsibility. Consequently, the notion of *freedom from excuse* is conceptually distinct from the notion of freedom from constraint, even if the two are closely connected, and even though most compatibilists are concerned with both of these kinds of freedom.

Crucially, compatibilists admit that *some* kinds of causes (such as cell bars or phobias) do remove freedom from constraint and excuse, but they do not generalize hastily to the conclusion that *all* kinds of causation or determination are barriers that remove freedom from constraint and excuse. In their view, some other kinds of causes do not constrain agents or provide any excuse that reduces responsibility, so they do not remove freedom from constraint or excuse (Sinnott-Armstrong, 2016). To see why, imagine that the agent fed peanut soup to the victim in order to steal his money. Then she did really want to feed him peanut soup, even though she wanted this not for its own sake but only as a means to steal his money. Assume also that she did not want to care about him or to have any different desires. Then her desire to do what she did was not a constraint, and her act was free from constraint, at least according to most people.

Most people would also see her desire as no excuse at all, even if it caused her action. If she argued that she was not responsible because "My desire made me do it," we would think that she must be joking. And if you were her victim, you would be angry with her and would blame her, your anger and blame would be justified, and you would see her as morally responsible. Why? Because this kind of cause—her desire and lack of concern for her victim—is not an excuse for what she did. Thus, she is free from excuse in addition to being free from constraint.

Nonetheless, if her desire caused her action, then she was not free from causation. And if her desire determined her action, then she was also not free from determination. Many examples like these, thus, provide strong reasons to believe that some causes, even if they determine what the agent does, do not count as constraints or excuses.[21] Normal desires are then not barriers that remove freedom from constraint or excuse, which are the kinds of freedom that matter to compatibilists.

Of course, intransigent incompatibilists still might bite the bullet and deny that the unconstrained poisoner for money is responsible or free from constraint or excuse. However, if examples like these do not convince opponents, then it is hard to imagine what could convince anyone. Such examples show at least that most people tend not to count all desires as constraints, which places a heavy burden on incompatibilists to show both why most people are wrong about such cases and also that incompatibilists are talking about the same kind of freedom as common folk. Besides, in their everyday lives, even incompatibilists do not excuse aggressors who harm them simply because the aggressors want to harm them and do not care about them. They get angry at such acts and feel justified in their anger like everyone else does, and they do not feel justified in being so angry at people who are tripped and fall onto them. Incompatibilists' own actions and feelings thus suggest that they themselves recognize that not all causes are excuses or constraints.

Admittedly, it is easier to show that *some* causes are not constraints or excuses than to specify *which* causes are constraints or excuses and why. The full story is long and complex, because some abnormal desires do remove freedom from constraint and excuse. For example, heroin addicts who struggle against their desires to take heroin, still do what they want when they take heroin, but those acts are usually not seen as free from constraint or excuse (regardless of whether they are determined). Why not? Compatibilists disagree about this.

One answer (Frankfurt, 1971) is that unwilling addicts' struggles show that they have a second-order desire not to desire heroin, so they do not identify with their desire to take heroin, and their drug use does not show what they are really like as a person. They are only sick temporarily, so their actions do not express their real, true, or deep self (Sripada, 2016). An act is free on this view only when it is related in the right way to the agent's deep self, values, or second-order desires.

A different answer is that unwilling addicts take heroin even when they know that they have overriding reasons not to do so, such as that police are watching and they are likely to overdose or ruin their health. This pattern of emotion and behavior shows that these addicts are unable to stop using heroin, just as the fact that I would not succeed in lifting a car that is on top of my child, when I know I have overriding reason to lift it, shows that I am unable to lift it. This inability to respond to reasons is a barrier that prevents these addicts from avoiding their harmful behaviors, even if they really want to, so it thereby removes their freedom from constraint and excuse, according to these compatibilists (Fischer, 2007; Gert & Duggan, 1979).

Sometimes both conditions are met. Some acts of taking drugs by some addicts both fail to mesh with their deep self, values, or second-order desires and also result from mechanisms that are not responsive to reasons. Such addicts are not free or responsible according to any of these versions of compatibilism. Other drug users are free or responsible according to all of these versions of compatibilism, because they both endorse their drug use and can respond to reasons. Hence, compatibilists who disagree about other cases and issues can still agree at least that these agents are free from constraints and excuse, even if they are caused and determined. That is enough to show that compatibilists in both camps are not talking about freedom from determination or causation.

Notice also that expression of one's deep self and responsiveness to reasons both come in degrees. Desires can be more or less central to one's self or the kind of person one is, and one's second-order desires can mesh more or less well with one's first-order desires. Similarly, individual agents can respond to some reasons sometimes without responding to all reasons always. Hence, compatibilist kinds of freedom—freedom from constraint and from excuse—also come in degrees. In contrast, incompatibilist freedom from determination is dichotomous—either fully on or fully off—because actions and choices are either fully determined or not fully determined. Moreover, an act is either caused or not caused, even if causes can be probabilistic instead of deterministic (though some aspects of the action can be caused when other aspects are not). Thus, compatibilist and incompatibilist concepts of freedom are quite different in their logics and implications.

How to Have Both

Indeed, these concepts are so different that we can have them both. One compromise position (Sinnott-Armstrong, 2013) is that the incompatibilist kinds of freedom (from determination or causation) and the compatibilist kinds of freedom (from constraint or excuse) are all legitimate and useful concepts. Each serves its own purpose. Freedom from determination or causation is important to some issues, such as whether humans are significantly different from other animals or from inanimate computers with artificial intelligence (and maybe whether humans are more like God) and also whether our self-image of ourselves as able to do otherwise is compatible with science. On the other side, freedom from constraint or excuse is important to issues of moral responsibility and to which kinds of treatments or interventions can succeed in changing behaviors (such as by providing reasons).

When people debate furiously about freedom to act or to will, some people (including incompatibilists) seem to be talking about freedom from determination or causation, whereas others (including compatibilists) seem to be talking about freedom from constraint or excuse. Both are *correct* insofar as they are using their own concepts, but both are *incorrect* when they deny what their apparent opponents say, because they mistakenly think that their opponents are using the same concept as they are. Their arguments misunderstand and miss each other.

Recall, for example, these crucial premises in the opening argument:

2—Any agent whose act is determined is not free.
5—Any agent who is not free is not responsible.

If both of these premises are about freedom from determination, then Premise 2 is true by definition, because determinism requires everything to be determined; but then Premise 5 is not true, because determination by endorsed and reasons-responsive desires does not remove responsibility, as my example of the unconstrained poisoner for money showed. The reverse holds if these premises are about freedom from constraint or excuse, for responsibility does require freedom from constraint and excuse, so Premise 5 is true; but Premise 2 is not true, because determinism is compatible with an absence of constraint and excuse, such as when the agent's action is determined by the agent's own endorsed and reasons-responsive desires, again as in my example of the unconstrained poisoner for money. One of the premises fails for each kind of freedom, so the opening argument depends on an equivocation between these two meanings or kinds of freedom.

This distinction also unravels some mysteries about Premise 5 (Gazzaniga, 2012). As I argued above, it is not clear why we should believe Premise 5 if it claims a strong relation between the normative notion of moral responsibility and a metaphysical or scientific notion of freedom, such as freedom from determination or causation. In contrast, freedom from constraint and excuse are normative, so it is no longer any mystery how these normative kinds of freedom can be required by moral responsibility, as Premise 5 says. Relations between normative concepts are less surprising than relations between norms and science or metaphysics.

On this view, then, compatibilists and incompatibilists do not need to give up their favored concepts, but they do need to specify which of these concepts they are talking about. They also need to stop arguing. They can achieve peace by more charitably and accurately understanding what the other side means by freedom.

This distinction between kinds of freedom *from* allows us to go halfway toward semi- and partial compatibilism. We can agree with semi- and partial compatibilists that people can be fully responsible even if they are not free from determination or causation. However, we can also *dis*agree with semi- and partial compatibilists insofar as people cannot be fully responsible if they are not free from constraint and excuse, since that other kind of freedom is necessary for responsibility. Semi- and partial compatibilists deny Premise 5, but we can deny it for only some kinds of freedom but not for others.

The resulting view then might be called contrastive partial compatibilism, but surely there must be a shorter and better name. I will call it *the appeasement view* because its aim is to appease both sides by giving each part of what it wants. Whatever you call it, I hope that the view and its motivations are clear and plausible.

Surveys Revisited

The appeasement view can also explain the data discussed above. Hannikainen et al. (2019) asked participants about freedom *to* kill Bill's family or Adam, but they did not specify any contrasts to fill out the blanks in freedom *from* ___. As a result, it is not clear which kind of freedom participants meant or had in mind when they answered the short and simple survey questions. This vagueness leaves open the possibility that different participants meant different things by freedom or had different concepts of freedom in mind when they gave different responses in surveys.

Which contrast participants have in mind can be affected by which question they are asked. Some surveys ask *abstract* questions like "If every event in the world is determined, does anyone ever act freely?" (e.g., Nahmias, Coates, & Kvaran, 2007, Roskies & Nichols, 2008). Other surveys ask *concrete* questions, such as in Hannikainen et al. (2019): "If every event in the world is determined, does Bill act freely when he kills his wife?" Several studies have found large differences between the proportions of responses to these kinds of questions. These differences might be explained by various factors, including emotions, abstractness, and intrusion of prior beliefs (Nichols & Knobe, 2007; Rose, Buckwalter, & Nichols, 2017; Sinnott-Armstrong, 2008). I do not deny that these factors might explain part of these results, but I want to suggest a complementary contrastive explanation.

The *abstract* questions mention determinism but do not mention any particular agent who might be constrained or excused, any particular act to excuse any agent for, or any particular situation that might provide any constraint or excuse. Such abstract questions, thus, seem likely to make participants think of freedom from determination or causation instead of freedom from constraint or excuse. In contrast, *concrete* questions mention a particular agent who commits a particular act in a particular situation, such as Bill who kills his wife and children in order to be with his secretary. Such concrete questions thereby make it natural for participants to tend to think about whether that particular agent, act, and situation are free from constraint or excuse.

Participants who think about freedom from determination or causation will be more likely to *deny* freedom, at least in a deterministic universe, and participants who think about freedom from constraint or excuse will be more likely to *endorse* freedom, at least if they do not assume that all causes are constraints. Admittedly, other influences are present, and neither answer is given by everyone in any survey. Still, variation is compatible with my hypothesis, which is that these different kinds of question increase the probability (but do not guarantee) that participants are thinking about different barriers and different kinds of freedom, and these differences affect the percentages of participants who deny or endorse freedom in their answers to each question. More specifically, participants who answer either question by saying that agents are *not* free are more often thinking of freedom from determination (or maybe causation), whereas those who answer either question by saying that agents *are* free are more often thinking of freedom from constraint (or maybe excuse). Thus, when their answers to different questions appear to conflict—such as when they answer "No" to the abstract question " ... does anyone ever act freely?" but "Yes" to the concrete question "Did Bill act freely when he killed his wife?"—their answers are sometimes not really inconsistent, because they are talking about different topics triggered by the different questions.

This hypothesis might seem incompatible with the results in Hannikainen et al. (2019).[22] The AS scenario is concrete, but 876 (53 percent) of their 1640 participants who passed comprehension checks answered that Bill did not kill freely, so these seem to have been thinking about freedom from determinism instead of freedom from constraint or excuse. However, my hypothesis is *not* that most participants deny freedom when asked an abstract question or that most ascribe freedom when asked a concrete question. Instead, my claim is comparative: more participants will deny freedom when asked an abstract question than when asked a concrete question. This claim gains support by comparing Hannikainen et al. (2019) to other surveys (e.g., Nahmias, Coates, & Kvaran, 2007, Roskies & Nichols, 2008) that asked an abstract question about freedom in a deterministic world. Those other surveys regularly find that fewer participants—less that 51 percent—ascribe freedom when asked an abstract question about a similarly deterministic world. My contrastive hypothesis explains this difference between answers to abstract versus concrete questions.

My hypothesis is also *not* that the difference between abstract and concrete questions is the only relevant factor. Other factors undoubtedly also influence answers (Rose et al., 2017). Still, those other factors also might do so by way of making participants think about different kinds of freedom, so other factors might even support my general claim that different answers reflect different barriers or contrasts. Moreover, because many factors affect participants' answers, we should not expect uniformity. The point is not to explain each individual answer. It is only to understand why groups of participants give different answers at different rates.

My contrastive hypothesis can also explain why such a large percentage (83 percent) of those who received the CI scenario in Hannikainen et al. (2019) judged that Martin acted freely, even though Martin could not have acted otherwise, because the scientists would have changed his mind if he had decided not to kill Adam. This response would not make any sense if they were thinking in terms of freedom from inability to do otherwise.[23] In contrast, their answers would make perfect sense if they were thinking about freedom from constraint or excuse, because the counterfactual intervener never had to intervene, so nothing that actually happened constrained Martin's choice and action, and he had no excuse. The appeasement view again provides a natural explanation of otherwise surprising data.

Admittedly, these interpretations of the data require speculation. However, I am not trying to prove here that the appeasement view is correct or complete. My claim is only that the appeasement view can explain why different participants give the answers that they do, because they are thinking in terms of their own favored concepts of freedom. This view also avoids accusing the folk of widespread error or of misusing language.[24] These virtues provide some support for my claim that this appeasement view is at least plausible and promising.

To provide more support, we need more detailed and direct tests of the central claims in the appeasement view. In particular, the appeasement view rests on at least these central claims about when people are thinking about different contrasts:

i. When incompatibilists talk about freedom, and when common folk make judgments in line with incompatibilism, they are talking and thinking about freedom from determination or causation (or something like that).
ii. When compatibilists talk about freedom, and when common folk make judgments in line with compatibilism, they are *not* talking and thinking about freedom from determination or causation (or anything like that).

iii. When compatibilists talk about freedom, and when common folk make judgments in line with compatibilism, they are talking and thinking about freedom from constraint or excuse (or something like that).
iv. When compatibilists and common folk talk about constraints and excuses, they are *not* talking or thinking about causation by normal desires.
v. When compatibilists and common folk talk about constraints and excuses, they are talking or thinking about causes like physical force (pushing and tripping), mental illness (delusion and compulsion), mistakes or accidents, coercion, and defense of self or others.

We need to test these claims empirically in order to determine whether these assumptions behind the appeasement view are close to correct.

Evidence for the Hypotheses

To test hypotheses (i)–(v), our team conducted an online survey with 342 participants who passed comprehension checks.[25] We began by asking them all four questions about the AS and CI scenarios described above, and they replied as indicated in Table 5.2:

In these samples, a large majority ascribed freedom of action and of will as well as moral responsibility in the AS scenario where Bill's act is determined. An even larger majority did so in the CI scenario where Martin lacks the ability to do otherwise. This shows that determinism and inability to do otherwise do not exclude freedom or moral responsibility in their view.[26]

What about responsibility without freedom? Testing that relation was the point of asking directly about responsibility instead of blameworthiness or punishment. Only 53 (15.5 percent) of our participants ascribed moral responsibility while denying freedom of action and of will in the AS scenario, and only 18 (5 percent) did so in the CI scenario. These percentages might be so small (and smaller than those in Hannikainen et al., 2019) because participants can ascribe responsibility without freedom only when they deny freedom. Only 29 percent of our participants denied that Bill acted freely, and around a half of those did ascribe moral responsibility despite denying free action in a deterministic world. This subset of our participants implied the denial of Premise 5 in the opening argument.

Table 5.2 Number (percentage) of affirmative answers to questions on each row.

QUESTIONS:	AS scenario	CI scenario
Did he act freely when he killed?	243 (71%)	302 (88%)
Did he act of his own free will when he killed?	250 (73%)	301 (88%)
Was the agent morally responsible for killing?	289 (84.5%)	312 (91%)
Was the agent able to avoid killing?	161 (47%)	78 (23%)

Our innovation was to add counterfactual questions designed to test which concept of freedom—freedom from determinism or causation versus freedom from constraint or excuse—participants were thinking and talking about when they gave the above answers. Participants who said that Bill (or Martin) did act freely were asked whether Bill (or Martin) would not have acted freely if his act had been caused in certain ways. We asked about two causes (severe mental illness and coercive threats) that we expected most people *would* see as constraints and excuses and three other causes (desire, circumstances, and normal brain activity) that we expected most people *would not* see as constraints or excuses. The answers are indicated in Table 5.3:

One striking feature of these results is that many more participants agreed with the bottom two statements about causes that were constraints than with the top three statements about causes that were not constraints. A factor analysis of these results found that these two groups strongly clustered statistically, so these participants did distinguish constraints from other causes without any explicit mention or cue.

The question that is crucial to our hypotheses asks which kind of freedom these participants were thinking about. This group all initially said that Bill and Martin acted freely, so they must not have been thinking about freedom from *determinism* in the case of Bill or freedom from *inability* to do otherwise in the case of Martin. Moreover, if they were thinking in terms of freedom from *causation*, then they should have agreed with all five statements, since all five statements say that something caused the agent to kill. Very few of these participants agreed with all five (three (1 percent) for AS; six (2 percent) for CI) or even four out of five (seven (3 percent) for AS; 6 (2 percent) for CI) of the statements, so they seem not to have been thinking about freedom from causation either. These results support Hypothesis (ii), which claims that people who make judgments in line with compatibilism are *not* thinking about freedom from determination, causation, or inability to do otherwise.

Next, Hypothesis (iii) claims that those who ascribe freedom in such cases are instead thinking about freedom from something like constraint or excuse. If so, since only the bottom two but not the top three causes are constraints or excuses, they should say that

Table 5.3 Number (percentage) of the participants in the second survey who initially said that the agent acted freely who later agreed with the statement on that row.

STATEMENTS:	AS scenario	CI scenario
If the agent's desire to kill the victim(s) caused the agent to kill, then the agent did not act freely.	16 (7%)	13 (4%)
If the circumstances (secretary's beauty or Adam's affair) caused the agent to kill, then the agent did not act freely.	18 (7%)	20 (7%)
If normal neural activity in the agent's brain caused the agent to kill, then the agent did not act freely.	38 (16%)	35 (12%)
If the agent had a severe mental illness that caused him to kill, then the agent did not act freely.	141 (58%)	185 (61%)
If an enemy's threat to kill the agent if he did not kill the victim caused the agent to kill, then the agent did not act freely.	115 (47%)	164 (54%)

only the bottom two but not the top three causes make the agent not free. Our results provide some evidence for this hypothesis, because many more of these participants agreed that the bottom two causes (severe mental illness and coercive threats) removed freedom of action than agreed that the top three causes (desire, circumstances, and normal brain activity) remove freedom of action.

Admittedly, only 47–61 percent agreed that causation by severe mental illness and coercive threats remove freedom of action. However, those who did not agree with the bottom two statements could still have been thinking in terms of freedom from constraint, but they did not think of severe mental illness or coercive threats as constraints or as adequate to excuse the agent (at least not in the extreme case of murder). If this interpretation is correct, then these results cast some doubt on Hypothesis (v) or at least on its specific list of constraints and excuses. Other items on that list could still be paradigmatic constraints, but we did not test them.

One crucial case is causation by desire, which is supposed to be clearly not a constraint, according to my arguments above. Only a small number (<7 percent) of these participants agreed that causation by desire would remove freedom of action. That finding supports Hypothesis (iv), which claims people who make judgments in line with compatibilism are *not* thinking about freedom from causation by normal desires.

Finally, Hypothesis (i) is about people who make judgments in line with *in*compatibilism, so let's consider the other ninety-nine participants who initially said that Bill did *not* freely kill his family in his deterministic universe. When asked why, all but one agreed that "Bill did not act freely when he killed his family because Bill's act of killing his family was completely brought about by what happened before it." This reply ("completely") suggests that they were thinking in terms of freedom from determinism, so these results support Hypothesis (i) insofar as it claims that this group is thinking about freedom from determination.

To our surprise, however, only eight (8 percent) of these ninety-nine participants agreed with all five statements in Table 5.2, and only ten (10 percent) agreed with four or more of these statements. They should have agreed with all of those statements if they were thinking in terms of freedom from causation. Thus, no more than 10 percent who were thinking in terms of freedom from determinism were thinking in terms of freedom from causation. One potential explanation is that they allowed probabilistic causes and thought that only deterministic causes removed freedom (see Hitchcock, 2018). Another possible explanation is that they took determinism in the scenario to imply that the agent's mental states did not cause the action (see Nahmias, 2011 on bypassing; compare eliminativism, epiphenomenalism, and fatalism) and that misinterpretation of determinism is what made them think that determinism removes freedom. They could still have thought that, when acts really are caused by mental states (probabilistically?), those mental causes do not remove freedom of action. That could have led them to disagree with the statement that postulated desires as mental causes of the act in its antecedent: *if* the agent's <u>desire</u> to kill the victim(s) *really* caused the agent to kill, then the agent did not act freely. Regardless of what they were thinking, these results suggest that we need to distinguish freedom from determinism and freedom from causation, since many people seem to think about freedom from determinism without thinking about freedom from causation. Our results thereby cast doubt on Hypothesis (i) insofar as it claims that this group is thinking about freedom from causation.

Similarly, of the forty who said that Martin did not act freely in the CI scenario, thirty-three agreed that "Martin did not act freely when he killed Adam because he was not able to avoid killing Adam," which suggests that they were thinking about freedom from *inability* to do otherwise. However, only five of them (15 percent) agreed with four or more of the statements about which causes remove freedom, so they were probably not thinking about freedom from *causation*. Thus, we cannot understand their views if we assume that causation of an act makes the agent unable to do otherwise. They do not seem to think that that freedom from *inability* to do otherwise requires freedom from *causation*.

Conclusion

Overall, our surveys support the main claims behind the appeasement view. People whose judgments about freedom align with incompatibilism seem to be thinking about freedom from determinism but not freedom from constraint, whereas people whose judgments about freedom align with compatibilism seem to be thinking about freedom from constraint but not freedom from determinism. Because an agent can be free from constraint without being free from determinism, both sides of the ancient feud can be correct about the kind of freedom that they are thinking and talking about. Where they go wrong is in denying what the other side says. Both sides are mistaken in assuming that their opponents are thinking and talking about the same kind of freedom as them. If they give up that misinterpretation of their opponents, they can understand each other and live together in peace.

Of course, neither side will immediately accept this proposed treaty, and they shouldn't. My arguments and studies are admittedly far from complete or conclusive. Much more reflection and experimentation are needed before these ancient foes should be expected to give up fighting and then to get along with each other. That limitation should not, however, be surprising or too disappointing. We should not expect to end a millennia-old war in one paper. It should be enough to point us in a potentially right direction down a long road to peace.[27]

Notes

1   Acts here include choices, decisions, and willings, so free will is a special kind of free action.
2   Here I call agents (rather than acts) free or not, but an agent might be free to do some acts and not others. More precisely, Premises 2 and 3 claim that an agent is not free to do or not to do the act that is determined or random, and Conclusion 4 claims that no agent is ever free to do any act. These claims could be reformulated in terms of whether acts are free or not.

3   An act is random in the relevant sense if either it has no cause or its cause is only probabilistic and the agent has no control over what the probabilities are or over which possibility actually occurs.
4   More precisely, an agent who is not free to do or not to do a certain act is not responsible for doing that act or for its consequences. The kind of responsibility here is accountability or liability rather than attributability or answerability (Shoemaker, 2011) or role-responsibility in the sense in which parents have responsibilities or duties to their children (Hart, 1968).
5   More precisely, we should never imprison any agent *for doing an act* when that agent is not responsible for doing *that act* (or for its consequences). The agent still might be responsible for other acts and other consequences. We also might quarantine people in prison when they have a contagious disease, but that is not imprisoning them *for doing an act*. See below on prison versus punishment.
6   List (2019) argues for "compatibilist libertarianism" that is *libertarian* insofar as he denies Premise 1 *at the agential level*, because agents have "a genuine ability to choose between different actions" (9) on the basis of reasons. Nonetheless, List's view is *compatibilist* insofar as he accepts Premise 1 *at the physical level* and denies a mixed version of Premise 2, which claims that any agent whose act is determined *at the physical level* is not free *at the agential level*. I cannot discuss this subtle theory here, but it is compatible with my contrastive view insofar as what List calls freedom at the physical level is close to what I will call freedom from *determinism* and what List calls freedom at the agential level is close to what I will call freedom from *constraint* (see below).
7   Freedom and responsibility also differ in other ways. The issue of free will seems *intra*personal in the sense that it is about what goes on inside the agent, rather than about what other people in the agent's society do, except insofar as others cause or influence what happens inside the agent. In contrast, responsibility seems *inter*personal insofar as it depends on social settings, even when those social settings do not cause or influence what the agent chooses and does.
8   The claim that freedom (to do or not to do an action) is necessary for responsibility (for doing that action) is challenged by examples where agents intentionally make themselves unable to do what they ought to do (Sinnott-Armstrong, 1984) as well as examples where agents do not even try to do what they ought to do (as in CI below).
9   Of course, there might be some argument that we are not aware of. The bold claim in the text is intended as a challenge to opponents to find and present some argument for Premise 5.
10 Although these questions do not ask explicitly about responsibility, most people seem to think that responsibility is necessary for blameworthiness and for deserving punishment or at least severe punishment. Other studies (Figdor & Phelan, 2015; Vierkant et al., 2019; and our new study below) reached similar conclusions when asking directly about responsibility.
11 We cannot tell whether participants in this survey ascribed responsibility, blame, or desert on a backward-looking basis (solely because of Bill's past behavior) or a forward-looking basis (because holding Bill responsible by punishing him will have good consequences). Whatever their basis, the important point here is that they did say that Bill was blameworthy.
12 Thanks to Ben Eva for pressing me on this point and to Ivar Hannikainen for providing the data to respond to it. The numbers in this table total 1640, because of

the 2381 participants who received AS, only 1645 passed comprehension checks, and five of these did not answer all of the questions.
13 Even a little blameworthiness without freedom is incompatible with the claim that freedom is a minimal necessary condition of any blameworthiness and responsibility. When a father is kidnapped, and that is why he misses a family dinner, most say that the father is not responsible *at all* rather than that he is only a *little* responsible. That is why it matters how many answered above 1 on Q3.
14 Some common folk still might mean something like this by freedom, and this stipulated notion of freedom is close to what I will call freedom from excuse (see below).
15 Since Martin was able to decide otherwise but not able to do otherwise, this scenario might seem to separate freedom of will (or decision) from freedom of action. Compare Locke's example discussed below. Some participants in the survey might have mistakenly inferred that Martin acted freely because he decided freely. However, Q1 explicitly asked, "Did Martin *act* freely when he killed his wife?" It did not ask about his decision, choice, or will, and there is no evidence that these survey participants were thinking about free will when they ascribed free action. Thanks to Christian List for pressing me on this point (cf. List, 2019, 168–9n29).
16 Parts of this section and the next are modified from Sinnott-Armstrong (forthcoming).
17 An agent can be free *to* do something that the agent does not actually do. Some theorists talk about freedom *in* doing something or freely *doing* something when an agent actually does what the agent was free *to* do. These other notions also need to be relativized to contrast classes when they are understood in terms of freedom *to* do something.
18 For more detail and applications, see Sinnott-Armstrong 2012. David Lewis (2020) analyses ability in terms of the absence of obstacles understood as robust preventers. However, his notion of an obstacle as a robust preventer does not include the range of barriers that are needed to understand all of the kinds of freedom, in my view.
19 See note 15 as well as the CI scenario.
20 The event of the agent acting might be free from determination at the agential level but not at the physical level, according to List (2019). See note 6. I take freedom from determination to be close to what List calls freedom at the physical level.
21 Compare Lewis's point that not all preferences are obstacles in his sense (Lewis, 2020, p. 244; cf. Beebee et al., 2020, pp. 254–6).
22 Thanks to Paul Rehren for pressing me on this point.
23 Martin was able to *choose* otherwise, but the question asked whether he *acted* freely. See note 15.
24 Hence, the appeasement view is not a form of revisionism in the sense of Vargas (2007). Instead of redefining or finding ambiguity in "freedom," the appeasement view sees the meaning of freedom as inspecific. The claim that something is free means that it is free from relevant barriers to do something out of a set of relevant alternatives, but this claim is inspecific about which barriers and alternatives are relevant. The folk need not be mistaken or confused when they use this inspecific meaning, because it usually creates no problem in everyday contexts. However, philosophers need to make claims more precise by specifying the relevant contrasts in order to avoid puzzles that have plagued philosophical debates for centuries. Thus, the appeasement view is precisificationist instead of revisionist.

25 We conducted two surveys that reached similar results, but the first had flaws that made some results hard to interpret, so I omit it here. For details, see our accompanying scientific report (Simmons et al. in progress). I am very grateful to Claire Simmons and Paul Rehren for designing, running, and analyzing these studies and to MAD (Moral Attitudes and Decisions) lab at Duke University for helpful comments on our design and analysis.

26 Interestingly, our participants did not distinguish freedom of action from freedom of will, even though some philosophers claim that Martin has freedom of will but not freedom of action.

27 For helpful comments, I thank Robert Audi, Isabel Canfield, Ben Eva, Michael Ferejohn, Mike Gazzaniga, Ivar Hannikainen, John-Dylan Haynes, Jennifer Jhun, Christian List, Uri Maoz, Thomas Nadelhoffer, Shaun Nichols, Paul Rehren, David Rose, Jana Schaich Borg, Claire Simmons, and many audiences, including ones at Florida State, Duke, and the Neurophilosophy of Free Will research group. This publication was made possible through the support of a joint grant from the John Templeton Foundation and the Fetzer Institute. The opinions expressed in this publication are those of the author(s) and do not necessarily reflect the views of the John Templeton Foundation or the Fetzer Institute.

References

Beebee, H., Svedberg, M., & Whittle, A. (2020). *Nihil Obstat*: Lewis's compatibilist account of abilities. *The Monist*, *103*, 245-61.

Dennett, D. (1984). *Elbow Room: Varieties of Free Will Worth Wanting*. Cambridge, MA: MIT Press.

Feinberg, J. (1973). The idea of a free man. In J. F. Doyle (Ed.), *Educational Judgments* (pp. 104-24). London: Routledge and Kegan Paul.

Figdor, C., & Phelan, M. (2015). Is free will necessary for moral responsibility?: A case for rethinking their relationship and the design of experimental studies in moral psychology. *Mind & Language*, *30*(5), 603-27.

Fischer, J. M. (2007). Compatibilism. In J. M. Fischer, R. Kane, D. Pereboom, & M. Vargas (Eds.), *Four Views on Free Will*. Oxford: Blackwell.

Fischer, J. M. (2008). Blog post on The Garden of Forking Paths. https://gfp.typepad.com/the_garden_of_forking_pat/

Frankfurt, H. (1969). Alternate possibilities and moral responsibility. *The Journal of Philosophy*, *66*(23), 829-39.

Frankfurt, H. (1971). Freedom of the will and the concept of a person. *The Journal of Philosophy*, *68*(1), 5-20.

Gazzaniga, M. (2012). *Who's in Charge? Free Will and the Science of the Brain*. New York: Ecco Publishers.

Gert, B., & Duggan, T. J. (1979). Free will as the ability to will. *Noûs*, *13*(2), 197-217.

Hannikainen, I. R., Machery, E., Rose, D, Stich, S. et al. (2019). For whom does determinism undermine moral responsibility? Surveying the conditions for free will across cultures. *Frontiers in Psychology*, *10*, article 2428: doi.org/10.3389/fpsyg.2019.02428

Hart, H. L. A. (1968). *Punishment and Responsibility*. Oxford: Clarendon Press.

Hitchcock, C., "Probabilistic Causation," *The Stanford Encyclopedia of Philosophy* (Spring 2018 Edition), Edward N. Zalta (Ed.), https://plato.stanford.edu/archives/spr2018/entries/causation-probabilistic/

Kane, R. (2007). Libertarianism. In J. M. Fischer, R. Kane, D. Pereboom, & M. Vargas (Eds.), *Four Views on Free Will*. Oxford: Blackwell.

Levy, N. (2011). *Hard Luck. How Luck Undermines Free Will and Moral Responsibility*. Oxford: Oxford University Press.

Lewis, D. (2020). Outline of "*Nihil Obstat*: An analysis of ability." *The Monist*, 103, 241–4.

List, C. (2019). *Why Free Will Is Real*. Cambridge, MA: Harvard University Press.

Locke, J. (1689). *An Essay Concerning Human Understanding*, K. Winkler (Ed.). Indianapolis; Hackett Publishing, 1996.

MacCallum, G. C. (1967). Negative and positive freedom. *Philosophical Review*, 76(3), 312–34.

Mele, A. (2006). *Free Will and Luck*. New York: Oxford University Press.

Mill, J.S. (1843). *A System of Logic, Ratiocinative and Inductive, Being a Connected View of the Principles of Evidence, and the Methods of Scientific Investigation*, 8th Edition. London: John W. Parker.

Murray, D., & Lombrozo, T. (2017). Effects of manipulation on attributions of causation, free will, and moral responsibility. *Cognitive Science*, 41(2), 447–81.

Nahmias, E. (2011). Intuitions about free will, determinism, and bypassing. In R. Kane (Ed.), *The Oxford Handbook of Free Will, 2nd Edition* (pp. 555–76). New York: Oxford University Press.

Nichols, S., & Knobe, J. (2007). Moral responsibility and determinism: The cognitive science of folk intuition. *Noûs*, 41, 663–85.

Nahmias, E., Coates, J., & Kvaran, T. (2007). Free will, moral responsibility, and mechanism: Experiments on folk intuitions. *Midwest Studies in Philosophy*, 31, 214–42.

Pereboom, D. (2007). Hard incompatibilism. In J. M. Fischer, R. Kane, D. Pereboom, & M. Vargas (Eds.), *Four Views on Free Will*. Oxford: Blackwell.

Rose, D., Buckwalter, W., & Nichols. (2017). Neuroscientific prediction and the intrusion of intuitive metaphysics. *Cognitive Science*, 41, 482–502.

Roskies, A., & Nichols, S. (2008). Bringing moral responsibility down to Earth. *The Journal of Philosophy*, 105, 371–88.

Scanlon, T. M. (2008). Blog post on The Garden of Forking Paths.

Shoemaker, D. (2011). Attributability, answerability, and accountability: Toward a wider theory of moral responsibility. *Ethics*, 121(3), 602–32.

Simmons, C., Rehren, P., Haynes, J-D, Sinnott-Armstrong, W. (in progress). Freedom from what? Separating folk concepts of freedom.

Sinnott-Armstrong, W. (1984). "Ought" conversationally implies "can." *The Philosophical Review*, 93(2), 249–61.

Sinnott-Armstrong, W. (2008). Abstract + concrete = paradox. In J. Knobe & S. Nichols (Eds.), *Experimental Philosophy* (pp. 209–30). New York: Oxford University Press.

Sinnott-Armstrong, Walter. (2013). Free contrastivism. In M. Blaauw (Ed.), *Contrastivism in Philosophy* (pp. 134–53). New York: Routledge.

Sinnott-Armstrong, W. (2016). My brain made me do it—So what? In D. Edmonds (Ed.), *Philosophers Take on the World* (pp. 147–9). Oxford: Oxford University Press.

Sinnott-Armstrong, W. (forthcoming). What is freedom? In U. Maoz & W. Sinnott-Armstrong (Eds.), *Free Will: Philosophers & Neuroscientists in Conversation*. New York: Oxford University Press.

Sripada, C. (2016), Self-expression: A deep self theory of moral responsibility. *Philosophical Studies*, *173*, 1203–32.
van Inwagen, P. (1983). *An Essay on Free Will*. Oxford: Oxford University Press.
van Inwagen, P. (2017). *Thinking about Free Will*. Cambridge: Cambridge University Press.
Vargas, M. (2007). Revisionism. In J. M. Fischer, R. Kane, D. Pereboom, & M. Vargas (Eds.), *Four Views on Free Will*. Oxford: Blackwell.
Vierkant, T., Deutschländer, R., Sinnott-Armstrong, W., & Haynes, J-D. (2019). Responsibility without freedom? Folk judgments about deliberate actions. *Frontiers in Psychology*, 1–6. Doi: 10.3389/fpsyg.2019.01133
Wolf, S. (1990). *Freedom within Reason*. New York: Oxford University Press.

6

Folk Jurisprudence and Judgments about Free Will and Responsibility

Thomas Nadelhoffer and Andrew Monroe

Introduction

While philosophers disagree both about what free will requires and about whether or not we have it, there is wide-scale agreement that free will is important when it comes to moral responsibility.[1] Indeed, many philosophers simply define free will as whatever cognitive and volitional capacities are needed in order for an agent to be responsible for their behavior (Double, 1991; Ekstrom, 2000; Fischer, 1994; Haji, 1998; Levy, 2011; McKenna, 2013; Mele, 2006; Nelkin, 2011; Pereboom, 2001; Sartorio, 2016; Smilansky, 2000; Strawson, 1986; Vargas, 2013; Wolf, 1990).[2] On this common view, when agents lack free will they are not apt or fitting targets of reactive attitudes like resentment or retribution since they lack the kind of control that grounds these attitudes. On the other hand, when agents exercise their free will, they open themselves up to moral judgment. Moral responsibility therefore requires that agents have a certain amount of control over their behavior at the time they act—that is, their behavior must be up to them in the right kind of way. This up-to-usness just is what many philosophers have in mind when they discuss free will.

This standard view concerning the tight relationship between free will and responsibility isn't just a metaphysical abstraction dreamt up in the philosopher's armchair. Research in experimental philosophy and social psychology suggests that most people not only believe strongly in free will but they also believe that free will is important when it comes to determining whether someone is responsible for their behavior (Clark, Baumeister, & Ditto, 2017; Clark, Lugari, Ditto, Knobe, Shariff, & Baumeister, 2014; Clark, Winegard, & Baumeister, 2019; Feltz & Cova, 2014; Greene & Cohen, 2004; Knobe, 2014; Monroe, Dillon, & Malle, 2014; Nadelhoffer, Yin, & Graves, 2020; Nahmias, Morris, Nadelhoffer, & Turner, 2005; 2006; Nahmias & Murray, 2011; Nichols, 2006; Rose, Buckwalter, & Nichols, 2017; Shariff et al., 2014; Sripada, 2012; Viney, Parker-Martin, & Dotten, 1988; Viney, Waldman, & Barchilon, 1982). It is therefore unsurprising that the view that free will and responsibility are intimately connected finds expression in the criminal law—which is often understood as a codified repository of commonsense thinking about agency and responsibility.

As Rychlak & Rychlak (1997) observe, "the legal system's assumption of free will in human affairs is ubiquitous" (196).[3] For instance, the US Supreme Court has claimed that the belief in free will and moral responsibility is "universal and persistent"[4] and that "the law has been guided by a robust common sense which assumes the freedom of the will as a working hypothesis in the solution of its problems."[5] On this view, in order for the criminal law to serve both as a pricing system for discouraging certain forms of antisocial behavior and as a vehicle for giving offenders their just deserts, judges and jurors must be able to distinguish defendants who are responsible for their behavior from those who are not—since only the former are (a) sufficiently sensitive to the threats that serve as the law's only mechanism for incentivizing people to obey, and (b) sufficiently blameworthy to deserve the sorts of state-sanctioned harms that are associated with legal punishment. In short, according to the Supreme Court, punishment for most criminal offenses requires moral responsibility, which in turn requires free will.[6]

One area of the criminal law that highlights the tight relationship between free will and responsibility is the practice of excusing certain behaviors under extraordinary circumstances. By finding some defendants not guilty or blameless even though they were causally responsible for performing the prohibited act, the law is supposed to capture a fundamental feature of our ordinary moral judgments. According to our everyday practices, it only makes sense to blame people when they were both causally and morally responsible for their behavior. Imagine that someone purposely hits you with their car out of malice or spite. Now, imagine instead that they hit you with their car owing to a heart attack. We would not and should not hold them equally morally responsible even though they were both implicated in causing the accident. The various legal excuses are supposed to capture this feature of folk morality.

For instance, we excuse people in the case of infancy or insanity because, at the time of their action, they did not have the requisite cognitive and volitional capacities that are often taken to undergird free will and responsibility. A five-year-old child who shoots his sibling and a paranoid schizophrenic who shoots his neighbor as the result of a command hallucination aren't apt targets of moral disapprobation precisely because their moral agency is either underdeveloped (in the case of the child) or heavily impaired (in the case of the schizophrenic). Excuses like duress, necessity, automatism, and diminished responsibility similarly implicate the lack of free will. When people's circumstances are such that they aren't in the position to act upon their own choices, desires, and intentions—whether it's because they are being coerced (duress), because they had no alternative way of avoiding a serious harm (necessity), because they are temporarily not in control of their behavior (automatism), or because they were sufficiently impaired such that they couldn't properly premediate, deliberate, or form the requisite intent (diminished responsibility)—it doesn't make sense to hold them responsible for their behavior. This is true whether one adopts a consequentialist or a retributivist theory of punishment since people in these circumstances are not properly in control of their behavior and hence, they cannot be deterred and they don't deserve to suffer.

In short, the law cares about these types of extenuating circumstances because they impair or even completely undermine free will and hence moral agency. In this respect, the core capacities that constitute free will serve as a minimal threshold that defendants must cross before they can be found guilty for the crime they committed. Once it has been established that the defendant was causally responsible for the outcome in question and that his act was performed freely and voluntarily (the *actus reus* element of the criminal law), the jury is then asked to pass judgment on whether he acted with the requisite additional mental states required for the crime in question. In the United States, most courts follow the Model Penal Code in focusing on four basic *mens rea* mental states, which are associated with varying degrees of blameworthiness.

Consider, for instance, a man named Jim who fired a gun in his neighborhood. As a result, his neighbor's child was struck by the bullet and killed. Is Jim morally and legally responsible for the child's death and if so, how much punishment should he receive? That will depend in part on Jim's mental states at the time. Even if he didn't actually foresee the risk that he was creating by firing his gun, he could still be responsible since his negligence isn't exculpating. It is commonsense that firing guns in residential areas is dangerous—which is precisely why doing so is illegal. So, like any reasonable person, Jim should have foreseen something like this and acted accordingly. This kind of negligence grounds the minimal amount of blameworthiness. Imagine instead that Jim had foreseen that something like this could happen (recklessness) or knew that it was a practical certainty that something like this could happen (knowingly), then we would find him increasingly blameworthy in each respective case. Finally, imagine that Jim fired the gun precisely because he had a grievance with his neighbor and hence hoped his neighbor's child would be killed by the gunshot. In this case, we would find Jim maximally morally and legally responsible.

Notice that in all four cases, Jim exercises his free will in firing the gun—that is, he is an adult who engages in voluntary behavior, he is not coerced or compelled, he is free of delusions, he is not psychologically impaired, etc. This explains why he is an apt target for moral blame and legal punishment—namely, his decisions and actions were up to him in a way that opens him up for moral censure. Having first established that Jim acted freely, the *mens rea* elements can then be used to fine-tune our responsibility judgments concerning how blameworthy Jim is for what he did (and did not do). In this sense, free will is the minimal threshold a person must first clear to be found morally or legally guilty at all. But both how much guilt a person has and how much punishment he deserves is determined by looking at the cognitive, conative, and volitional states that served as the distal and proximate causes of the person's freely willed actions.

The way the law views the relationship between the *actus reus* and *mens rea* elements is supposed to at least partly capture how people ordinarily assign blame, excuse behavior, etc. Our goal was to see how well the decision procedures for assigning moral and legal responsibility that we have been discussing map on to folk intuitions. While a lot of research has been done on people's intuitions about free will and responsibility, much of this work has involved fantastical thought experiments involving deterministic universes where everything that happens has to happen (Nichols & Knobe, 2007), where supercomputers or neuroscientists have the power of perfect prediction (Nahmias et al., 2005), where nefarious agents use mind control devices to compel people to act (Sripada, 2012), where the universe can be "rolled back" over and over again yielding the same outcome every time (Nahmias et al., 2006), where a Book of Life contains a complete description of all of the events that will happen in the future, (Feltz & Milan, 2013), where people have the conditional—but not the unconditional—ability to do otherwise (Nadelhoffer, Yin, & Graves, 2020), etc. It is perhaps no surprise that some of the latest findings on intuitions about free will suggest that people have a hard time properly understanding the implications of these kinds of scenarios (Murray & Nahmias, 2014; Nadelhoffer, Rose, Buckwalter, & Nichols, 2020; Nahmias & Murray, 2011). As a result, some researchers have suggested that we should try to "bring free will down to Earth" (Monroe, Dillon, & Malle, 2014; see also Monroe & Malle, 2010; Nahmias et al., 2004; Stillman, Baumeister, & Mele, 2011)—that is, we should try to get at people's intuitions about free will and moral responsibility in more ecologically valid ways that don't focus on far-fetched scenarios that do not reflect the sorts of situations within which we ordinarily think about free will.

As we have seen, one real life situation where people are asked to think about free will and moral responsibility is the criminal law. Given the practical significance of this issue, it is surprising that relatively little empirical work has been done on this front (see, e.g., Appelbaum, Scurich, & Raad, 2015; Haynes, Rojas, & Viney, 2003; Nadelhoffer, Gromet, Goodwin, Nahmias, Sripada, & Sinnott-Armstrong, 2013; Nadelhoffer, Wright, Goya-Tocchetto, & McGuire, 2020; Scurich & Applebaum, 2015; Sharif et al., 2014; Tygart, 1994). So, we ran two preregistered studies in an effort to fill in some of the missing empirical pieces. Our results suggest that the criminal law does a fairly good job of capturing how people normally think about the relationship between free will and responsibility. When people think about responsibility in a legal context—which we are calling folk jurisprudence—they treat free will as a minimal threshold for determining *whether* an agent is responsible at all. But in determining *how much* responsibility an agent has for what he's done, people rely on the sorts of mental states associated with the *mens rea* elements of the criminal law.

The Present Research

Excuses, Free Will, and Responsibility

Participants

In presenting and discussing the experimental design and results from Study 1 and Study 2, we follow best scientific practices by reporting "how we determined our sample size, all data exclusions (if any), all manipulations, and all measures in the study" (Simmons, Nelson, & Simonsohn, 2012, p. 4).[7] All preregistrations, data sets, and supplemental material (including measures and stimuli) can be found at the following OSF page: https://osf.io/m72gu/.

To determine our sample size for Study 1, we used G*Power to run a power analysis. We ran two power analyses for our study (both ANOVA, fixed effects, main & interactions; power =.8): one assuming a very small effect size (f =.1 [equivalent to a Cohen's d = 0.2]) and a second assuming a small, but fairly normal effect size (f =.15 [equivalent to a Cohen's d = 0.3]). We got a recommended sample of 787 and 351, respectively. So, in an effort to strike a balance between statistical power and our budget, we recruited a sample of 625 (125 per condition). We recruited participants from Amazon's Mechanical Turk (MTurk).[8] Twenty-six participants were excluded for either failing to complete the study or failing one of the attention checks. This left us with 599 participants (46 percent female, 75 percent Caucasian).

Methods and Materials

For Study 1, we used a between-subjects design. Each participant was assigned to one of five conditions. They were then first told to imagine of the following scenarios:

Condition 1: Automatism
Bob Jones recently badly injured an innocent person. You see, Jones has a lifelong and well-document problem with sleep walking. It is not uncommon for Jones to engage in complex behaviors while asleep that would seem only to be possible if he were awake. And yet, science makes it clear that sleep walking is real and that people who might otherwise seem awake can actually be asleep. In the present case, one night Jones got into his car while sleepwalking and then ran over a neighbor down the road. The victim suffered serious injuries, including several broken bones. The State is prosecuting Jones for felony assault. The attorneys for Jones are arguing that because he was in an "automatistic" state, he should be cleared of all charges. On their view, sleep walking is a clear excuse from legal responsibility.

Condition 2: Duress
Bob Jones recently badly injured an innocent person. At the time of his offense, Jones was under duress. His wife and child had been abducted at gunpoint by John Smith, and Jones was told by Smith that if he didn't carry out this attack or if he went to the police his wife and child would be killed. Jones was devastated, but he didn't know what to do, so he carried out the attack as instructed causing serious injuries including several broken bones to the victim. The State is prosecuting Smith for assault. They are also trying to prosecute Jones as an accomplice. The attorneys for Jones are arguing that because he was under duress, he should be cleared of all charges. In their view, duress—that is, having one's family held at gunpoint—ought to be an excuse from legal responsibility.

Condition 3: Diminished Responsibility
Bob Jones recently badly injured an innocent person. However, there is compelling evidence that Jones's behavior was the result of a so-called "irresistible impulse." Jones suffered brain damage when he was a young child, and ever since he's struggled with impulse control—especially when it comes to controlling his temper. Owing to the damage to his frontal lobe, Jones often "flies off the handle." In the present case, the victim started an argument with Jones, and when the argument turned

violent, Jones fell into a rage and pushed the victim down some stairs in a parking garage. The victim was seriously injured, including several broken bones. The State is prosecuting Jones for felony assault. The defense attorneys for Jones claim that owing to his diminished capacity, Jones can't properly be said to have intended the attack as the law requires. In their view, because Jones has brain damage which impairs his ability to control his temper, this ought to mitigate or lessen (but not excuse) his responsibility.

Condition 4: Distal Mitigation but No Proximal Excuses
Bob Jones had a horrible childhood. His parents were negligent and abusive, they were in and out of jail, and they didn't express any interest in the welfare of Jones when he was growing up. Indeed, he was both physically and sexually abused by several family members. Perhaps unsurprisingly, Jones started getting in trouble at a young age. More recently, Jones badly injured an innocent person. This is the first time Jones has attacked or injured anyone else. In the present case, the victim started an argument with Jones, and when the argument turned violent, Jones fell into a rage and pushed the victim down some stairs in a parking garage. The victim was seriously injured including several broken bones. The State is prosecuting him for felony assault.

Condition 5: No Distal and No Proximal Excuses
Bob Jones had a normal childhood. His parents were loving, they had good jobs, and they make sure that Jones went to the best schools when he was growing up. Perhaps unsurprising, Jones was always well-behaved growing up. Yet, despite having a privileged life, Jones recently badly injured an innocent person. This is the first time Jones has attacked or injured anyone else. In the present case, the victim started an argument with Jones, and when the argument turned violent, Jones fell into a rage and pushed the victim down some stairs in a parking garage. The victim was seriously injured, including several broken bones. The State is prosecuting Jones for felony assault.

Having read one of the five vignettes, participants were then given the following directions:

Please read the following statements and questions and answer accordingly. There are no right or wrong answers, we just want your honest opinions:

1—7, strongly disagree to strongly agree
1. Mr. Jones had free will.
2. Mr. Jones had control over his actions.
3. Mr. Jones had the capacity for making choices.
4. Mr. Jones wanted to do what he did.
5. Mr. Jones was coerced or compelled.
6. Mr. Jones is fully morally responsible for his actions.
7. Mr. Jones has a legitimate excuse.
8. Mr. Jones' actions say something about who he really is.

1 through 7, none at all to a great deal

1. How much blame does Mr. Jones deserve for his actions?
2. How bad was Mr. Jones's behavior?
3. How wrong was Mr. Jones's behavior?
4. How much punishment does Mr. Jones deserve for his actions?

We then asked participants to respond to the following item:

> Select the following answer that best describes Mr. Jones's actions: (a) Mr. Jones acted negligently, (b) Mr. Jones acted recklessly, (c) Mr. Jones acted knowingly, or (d) Mr. Jones acted purposely.

Finally, we presented participants with The Free Will Inventory (Nadelhoffer, Shepard, Nahmias, Sripada, & Ross, 2014) and The Vengeance Scale (Stuckless, 1992) before asking them to voluntarily provide demographic information.[9]

Results

We first tested whether our manipulation affected people's attributions of free will. A one-way ANOVA revealed a significant effect, $F(4,293)$ 54.9, $p <.001$. People judged Jones to have the least free will in the automatism condition ($M = 3.88$, $SD = 1.73$), followed by the duress ($M = 4.69$, $SD = 1.78$) and diminished responsibility ($M = 4.97$, $SD = 1.50$) conditions, and complete free will in the distal mitigation ($M = 6.03$, $SD = 1.20$) and no excuse conditions ($M = 6.20$, $SD = 1.06$). Tukey post hoc test showed that free will attributions were significantly lower in the automatism condition compared to the duress and diminished responsibility conditions ($p <.001$), and the free will attributions were significantly lower in the duress and diminished responsibility conditions compared to the distal mitigation and no excuse conditions ($p <.001$).

Similar effects emerged for judgments of Jones' agency (average of control and choice attributions, Chronbach's α =.85), $F(4,293)$ 79.1, $p <.001$. Tukey post hoc test showed that participants judged Jones as lacking agency in the automatism condition ($M = 3.42$, $SD = 1.56$), having slightly more agency in the duress ($M = 4.78$, $SD = 1.50$) and diminished responsibility conditions ($M = 4.54$, $SD = 1.4$), and having full agency in the distal mitigation ($M = 5.83$, $SD = 1.09$) and no excuse conditions ($M = 5.98$, $SD = 0.93$) ($ps <.001$).

Judgments of moral responsibility (average of moral responsibility, blame, and punishment, Cronbach's α =.86),[10] however diverged somewhat from the patterns for free will and agency. We found an overall significant effect of condition, $F(4,295)$ 58.0, $p <.001$, but Tukey post hoc test revealed a slightly different clustering of conditions. People judged Jones as least morally responsible in the automatism ($M = 3.98$, $SD = 1.44$) and the duress conditions ($M = 3.84$, $SD = 1.39$), followed by the diminished responsibility condition ($M = 4.83$, $SD = 1.26$), and participants judged Jones as most morally responsible in the distal mitigation ($M = 5.57$, $SD = 0.97$) and no excuse conditions ($M = 5.67$, $SD = 1.08$) ($ps <.001$).

Discussion

Together these patterns suggest that people are only willing to deny that a person has free will when two conditions are met: the agent (a) lacks a *conscious desire* to for their behavior and (b) the person is unable to exert direct control over their behavior (i.e., automatism). The only condition where participants disagreed with the statement "Jones had free will" (i.e., mean free will ratings were below the midpoint of the scale) was the automatism condition where he lacked both the *desire* to harm and the ability to *consciously control* his actions. Thus, our data suggest that people treat free will as a threshold for determining *whether* an agent is responsible at all, and only profound debilitating circumstances are sufficient to cause people to deny free will to a person.

By contrast, when it comes to determining *how much* responsibility an agent has for what he's done, people rely on more fine-grained details like the sorts of mental states associated with the *mens rea* elements of the criminal law. Specifically, our data show that people are willing to substantially reduce an agent's moral responsibility for causing harm when the person lacks a desire to cause harm (i.e., automatism & duress conditions). When judging moral responsibility, the ability to control one's behavior or to produce a specific outcome is secondary to what the person wants to achieve—as evidenced by both the automatism and duress conditions producing comparable moral responsibility judgments. Broadly, our findings comport with legal treatment of mens rea and outcome information. Comparing the average sentencing guidelines for murder (twenty years to life), attempted murder (five to fifteen years), and involuntary manslaughter (two to four years) demonstrates that both the law and everyday moral judgments give precedence to an offender's mental states over the outcomes they cause for judging moral culpability.

Mens Rea, Free Will, and Responsibility

Participants

As with Study 1, we conducted two power analyses in G*Power (both ANOVA, fixed effects, omnibus, one-way analyses; power =.8): one assuming a very small effect size (f =.1 [equivalent to a Cohen's d = 0.2]) and a second assuming a small, but fairly normal effect size (f =.15 [equivalent to a Cohen's d = 0.3]). We got a recommended sample of 1096 and 492, respectively. So, in an effort to strike a balance between staying within our budget and making sure our study is adequately powered, we recruited a sample of 600[11] (150 per condition). We recruited participants from MTurk.

Methods and Materials

For Study 2, we used a between-subjects design. Each participant was assigned to one of four conditions. They were then first told to imagine of the following scenarios:

Condition 1: Negligence
Bob Jones recently seriously injured someone in a car accident. It was late at night and he was feeling impatient. The car in front of him was driving below the speed

limit. He honked the horn, but it didn't make a difference. Without giving it any thought or paying any attention, he tried to pass the car. It turned out another car was coming in the opposite lane. Jones hit the car head on, badly injuring the other driver. The State is prosecuting Jones for vehicular assault.

Condition 2: Recklessness
Bob Jones recently seriously injured someone in a car accident. It was late at night and he was feeling impatient. The car in front of him was driving below the speed limit. He honked the horn, but it didn't make a difference. He knew that visibility was low and that someone might be coming the other direction, but he tried to pass the car anyway. Sure enough, it turned out that another car was coming in the opposite lane. Jones hit the car head on, badly injuring the other driver while remaining unscathed. The State is prosecuting Jones for vehicular assault.

Condition 3: Knowingly
Bob Jones recently seriously injured someone in a car accident. It was late at night and he was feeling impatient. The car in front of him was driving below the speed limit. He honked the horn, but it didn't make a difference. He knew that visibility was low and that it was almost certainly the case that someone would be coming the other direction, but he didn't care. He tried to pass the car anyway. Sure enough, it turned out that another car was coming in the opposite lane. Jones hit the car head on, badly injuring the other driver while remaining unscathed. The State is prosecuting Jones for vehicular assault.

Condition 4: Purposely
Bob Jones recently seriously injured someone in a car accident. It was late at night and he was feeling impatient. The car in front of him was driving below the speed limit. He honked the horn, but it didn't make a difference. He knew that visibility was low and that it was almost certainly the case that someone would be coming the other direction, but he didn't care. Indeed, he was having the worst day of his life and he was looking to take it out on anyone he could, even if it put his own life in danger. So, he tried to pass the car anyway hoping a car would be coming his way. Sure enough, it turned out that another car was coming in the opposite lane. Jones hit the car head on, badly injuring the other driver while remaining unscathed. The State is prosecuting Jones for vehicular assault.

We then presented participants with the same dependent measures used in Study 1 (namely, the thirteen items about items free will, responsibility, and related constructs, The Free Will Inventory, and the Vengeance Scale) before asking them to voluntarily provide demographic information.

Results

We first tested whether our manipulation affected people's attributions of free will. A one-way ANOVA revealed a significant main effect, albeit substantially smaller than our effect in Study 1, $F(3,307)$ 4.45, $p = .004$. Overall, free will judgments of Jones were high across the negligence ($M = 5.64$, $SD = 1.40$), recklessness ($M = 5.84$, $SD = 1.37$), knowing ($M = 6.09$, $SD = 1.30$), and intentional ($M = 6.15$, $SD = 1.11$) conditions; however, Tukey post hoc tests revealed that judgments of free will in the negligence condition were significantly lower than in the intentional ($p = .007$) and the knowing ($p = .02$) conditions. Thus, while people affirm that Jones had free will across conditions—as evidenced by a mean free will score above 5 on a 1–7 scale—they still allowed for a slight gradation of free will when Jones was acting negligently.

In examining moral judgments of Jones, we separately analyzed *person-focused* moral judgments versus *event-focused* moral judgments (Malle, Guglielmo & Monroe, 2014). Person-centered moral judgments are moral evaluations that are typically directed at moral offenders (i.e., blame, punishment, and moral responsibility, α = .78), whereas event-focused moral judgments are typically evaluations of the moral status of a behavior, event, or outcome (i.e., badness or wrongness α = .90).[12]

A pair of one-way ANOVAs revealed a significant effect of the manipulation on person-focused moral judgments, $F(3,307)$ 6.92, $p < .001$ as well as event-focused moral judgments, $F(3,307)$ 7.82, $p < .001$. However, post hoc tests of the conditions showed substantially different patterns for the two types of judgments. Specifically, the severity of person-focused moral judgments increased linearly with moral judgments of negligence ($M = 5.38$, $SD = 1.18$) being the least extreme followed by judgments of recklessness ($M = 5.51$, $SD = 1.27$), knowingly causing harm ($M = 5.80$, $SD = 1.11$), and intentionally causing harm ($M = 5.92$, $SD = 1.05$) receiving the most extremely moral disapproval. Tukey post hoc tests showed that judgments of negligence, although not significantly different from recklessness ($p = .79$), were significantly lower than knowingly and intentionally harming ($ps < .01$), and judgments of reckless harm were significantly lower than judgments of intentional harm ($p = .015$).

Contrastingly, event-focused moral judgments clustered into two groups: judgments of negligent ($M = 5.21$, $SD = 1.48$) and reckless harm ($M = 5.30$, $SD = 1.58$) and judgments of knowing ($M = 5.78$, $SD = 1.35$) and intentional harm ($M = 5.88$, $SD = 1.32$). Tukey post hoc tests showed that judgments of negligence and recklessness were statistically identical to one another ($p = .95$), and significantly less extreme than judgments of knowing and intentional harm ($ps < .01$). This suggests different thresholds and uses for mental state information when making moral judgments about the blameworthiness of moral offenders compared to moral judgments that are primarily geared toward labeling and evaluating the moral status of events. Specifically, our data demonstrate that when making person-directed moral judgments (e.g., blame, punishment, moral responsibility) people make fine-grained distinctions between an agent's mental states—whether he negligently, knowingly, or intentionally caused harm—and use those distinctions to inform their moral judgments. By contrast, when making event-focused moral judgments, these standards loosen, and people treat negligent and reckless harm as similarly bad events, but still differentiate these from knowingly or intentionally harming others.

A final goal of this study is understanding the drivers of people's moral judgments, specifically, whether people's general belief in free will affects their willingness to ascribe moral condemnation, or if people's moral judgments are driven by ascriptions of choice and desire, which themselves are the building blocks of the folk concept of free will (Monroe & Malle, 2010). We tested these two possibilities using a multiple regression model with belief in free will entered in the first step of the model and ascriptions of choice and desire entered into the second step in the model. To compare the two predictions, we examined the total variance explained at each step of the model as well as the significance of the individual predictors.

The first step of the model revealed that people's general belief in free will did predict their moral judgments of Jones, $\beta =.22$, $t(555) = 4.76$, $p <.001$, and accounted for nearly 4 percent (3.93 percent) of the total variance in people's moral judgments. Adding choice and desire into the model in step 2 revealed that, controlling for free will beliefs, both choice, $\beta =.47$, $t(553) = 14.22$, $p <.001$ and desire, $\beta =.09$, $t(553) = 3.16$, $p =.002$ emerged as stronger predictors of moral judgments compared to belief in free will, while the strength of free will predicting moral judgments became substantially weaker, $\beta =.08$, $t(553) = 2.13$, $p =.03$ once choice and desire were entered into the model. Moreover, whereas free will belief explained 4 percent of the variance in people's moral judgments, choice and desire explained an additional 29 percent of the variance. Together, this shows that free will beliefs play a unique and significant role in explaining people's moral judgments. However, in this study, the psychological concepts of choice and desire demonstrate an effect seven times larger than free will beliefs, even after controlling for the strength of the beliefs. This finding is consistent with several recent research findings demonstrating the limited predictive value of free will beliefs on moral judgments (Monroe et al., 2014, 2017; Monroe & Malle, 2014), and suggests that future work testing how variations in people's belief in free will affect behavior must be grounded in an accurate view of the other agentic concepts that influence our moral beliefs and behaviors.

General Discussion

There is a commonplace assumption that free will and moral responsibility are foundational assumptions of the criminal law. But there is a surprising dearth of empirical research on the nature of the relationship. Our goal was to fill in this lacuna by exploring folk judgments about free will and moral responsibility in two legal contexts. On the one hand, we wanted to explore the role that judgments about free will play when it comes to legal excuses like automatism and duress. Our hypothesis was that to the extent that people judge that free will is compromised or undermined, they will judge that the offender isn't responsible (just as the law intends). In this way, free will serves as the bedrock of legal responsibility. If offenders are deemed to be unfree, they are deemed not to be morally and legally responsible. On the other hand, we wanted to explore the role that free will judgments play in cases involving the four *mens rea* elements—negligently, recklessly, knowingly, and purposely. Our hypothesis was that because the agents in these scenarios would be judged to be acting of their own free will, judgments about responsibility would track the *mens rea* elements instead— with offenders who negligently cause harm being less blameworthy than offenders to recklessly, knowingly, and purposely cause harm, respectively.

Our findings support our hypotheses by showing that free will serves as the minimal threshold for legal responsibility—that is, if an offender acted of their own free will, they are an apt target of moral and legal blame. But once offenders are in the "blameworthy" category, figuring out how much blame they deserve is a matter of other salient mental states. Judgments about these mental states are then used to fine-tune how deserving offenders are of disapprobation and punishment. Because our goal was to explore judgments about free will and responsibility in a more pedestrian and ecologically valid way than the scenarios more commonly used in the literature on folk intuitions about free will and responsibility, we purposely tried to keep things as simple as possible. Figuring out whether determinism, reductive physicalism, or epiphenomenalism also serve as excusing conditions in a legal context is a task for another day.

Notes

1. There is an ongoing debate about what kind of responsibility is at stake in the free will debate. Some philosophers claim that the key issue is basic desert—which is both retributive and non-consequentialist (Caruso & Morris, 2017; Clarke, 2005; Pereboom, 2001; Smilansky, 2000; Strawson, 1986). Others develop accounts of moral responsibility that do not take basic desert as foundational (Dennett, 2003; McKenna, 2019; Scanlon, 1998; Wallace, 1994).
2. Some philosophers argue that free will can and should be analyzed independently of moral responsibility (e.g., Clarke 2013; Ginet 1990; van Inwagen 2008; Vihvelin 2013).
3. There is an ongoing debate when it comes to what kind of free will is operative in the law—that is, compatibilist free will vs. libertarian free will. Both types of free will share a suite of cognitive, conative, and volitional capacities. The main difference between the two is whether free will requires something above and beyond these core capacities—for example, the unconditional ability to do otherwise. Given our focus, we need not take a stand on this issue. We are only committed to the weak claim that the shared capacities associated with both types of free will are operative in the folk jurisprudence. For more on the background debate, see Greene & Cohen (2004) and Morse (2007).
4. *Morissette v. United States*, 342 U.S. 246, 250 (1952).
5. *Steward Machine Co. v. Davis*, 301 U.S. 548, 590 (1937).
6. This is especially true for crimes that are *mala in se* (both immoral and illegal—e.g., murder) rather than *mala prohibita* (merely illegal—e.g., jaywalking).
7. Studies 1 and 2 were approved by the Institutional Review Board at College of Charleston.
8. MTurk is an online survey service that enables researchers to recruit and pay for participants for completing surveys of studies. For findings concerning the benefits of using MTurk—including the quality of the data and the improved diversity of the participant pool—see Burhmester, Kwang, & Gosling (2011); Paolacci, Chandler, & Ipeirotis (2010); Rand (2012).
9. See the Supplemental Material on our OSF page for the full details for The Free Will Inventory and The Vengeance Scale.

10 All patterns hold for judgments of blame, moral responsibility, and deserved punishment if examined independently.
11 Forty-three participants were omitted from the analyses for failing study attention checks leaving a final sample of 557 participants.
12 All patterns hold for individual judgments of blame, moral responsibility, and punishment, badness, and wrongness if examined independently.

References

Appelbaum, P.S., Scurich, N., & Raad, R. (2015). Effects of behavioral genetic evidence of perceptions of criminal responsibility and appropriate punishment. *Psychology, Public Policy, and Law*, 21(2), 134–44.

Burhmester, M., Kwang, T., & Gosling, S. (2011). Amazon's Mechanical Turk: A new source of inexpensive, yet high-quality data? *Perspectives on Psychological Science*, 6, 3–5.

Caruso, G.D., & Morris, S.G. (2017). Compatibilism and retributive desert moral responsibility: On what is of central philosophical and practical importance. *Erkenntnis, 82*: 837–55.

Clark, C. J., Luguri, J. B., Ditto, P. H., Knobe, J., Shariff, A. F., & Baumeister, R. F. (2014). Free to punish: A motivated account of free will belief. *Journal of Personality and Social Psychology*, 106, 501–13.

Clark, C. J., Baumeister, R. F., & Ditto, P. H. (2017). Making punishment palatable: Belief in free will alleviates punitive distress. *Consciousness and Cognition*, 51, 193–211.

Clark, C. J., Winegard, B. M., & Baumeister, R. F. (2019). Forget the Folk: Moral Responsibility Preservation Motives and Other Conditions for Compatibilism. *Frontiers in Psychology*, 10, 215.

Clarke, R. (2005). On an Argument for the Impossibility of Moral Responsibility. *Midwest Studies in Philosophy, 29*, 13–24.

Clarke, R. (2013). Some Theses on Desert. *Philosophical Explorations, 16*: 153–64.

Dennett, D. (2003). *Freedom Evolves*. New York: Viking Penguin.

Double, R. (1991). *The Non-Reality of Free Will*. New York: Oxford University Press.

Ekstrom, L. (2000). *Free Will: A Philosophical Study*. Boulder, CO: Westview Press.

Feinberg, Joel. 1970. *Doing and Deserving*. Princeton: Princeton University Press.

Feltz, A., & Cova, F. (2014). Moral responsibility and free will: A meta-analysis. *Consciousness and Cognition*, 30, 234–46.

Feltz, A., & Millan, M. (2013). An error theory for compatibilist intuitions. *Philosophical Psychology*, 28, 529–55.

Fischer, J. M. (1994). *The Metaphysics of Free Will: An Essay on Control*. Oxford: Blackwell Publishers.

Fischer, J. M., & Ravizza, M. (1998). *Responsibility and Control: An Essay on Moral Responsibility*. Cambridge: Cambridge University Press.

Ginet, C. (1990). *On Action*. Cambridge: Cambridge University Press.

Greene, J., & Cohen, J. (2004). For the law, neuroscience changes nothing and everything. *Philosophical Transactions of the Royal Society B.*, 359, 1775–85.

Haji, I. (1998). *Moral Appraisability*. New York: Oxford University Press.

Haynes, S.D., Rojas, D., & Viney, W. (2003). Free will, determinism, and punishment. *Psychological Reports*, 93(3f), 1013–21.

Knobe, J. (2014). Free will and the scientific vision. In E. Machery & E. O'Neill (Eds.), *Current Controversies in Experimental Philosophy* (pp. 69–85). New York: Routledge.

Levy, N. (2011). *Hard Luck: How Luck Undermines Free Will and Moral Responsibility.* New York: Oxford University Press.

Malle, B. F., Guglielmo, S., & Monroe, A. E. (2014). A theory of blame. *Psychological Inquiry*, 25(2), 147–86. https://doi.org/10.1080/1047840X.2014.877340

McKenna, M. (2013). Reasons-Responsiveness, Agents, and Mechanisms. In David Shoemaker (Ed.), *Oxford Studies in Agency and Responsibility* (Vol. 1, pp. 151–84). New York: Oxford University Press.

McKenna, M. (2019). The free will debate and basic desert. *The Journal of Ethics*, 23, 241–55.

Mele, A. (2006). *Free Will and Luck*. Oxford: Oxford University Press.

Monroe, A., & Malle, B. (2010). From uncaused will to conscious choice: The need to study, not speculate about people's folk concept of free will. *Review of Philosophy and Psychology*, 1, 211–24.

Monroe, A. E., & Malle, B. F. (2014). Free will without metaphysics. In A. R. Mele (Ed.), *Surrounding Free Will* (pp. 25–48). New York: Oxford University Press.

Monroe, A. E., Dillon, K. D., & Malle, B. F. (2014). Bringing free will down to Earth: People's psychological concept of free will and its role in moral judgment. *Consciousness and Cognition*, 27, 100–8.

Monroe, A. E., Brady, G. L., & Malle, B. F. (2017). This isn't the free will worth looking for. *Social Psychological and Personality Science*, 8, 191–9. https://doi.org/10.1177/1948550616667616

Morse, S. J. (2007). The non-problem of free will in forensic psychiatry and psychology, 25, *Behavioral Sciences & The Law*, 25, 203–20.

Murray, D., & Nahmias, E. (2014). Explaining away incompatibilist intuitions. *Philosophy and Phenomenological Research*, 88, 434–67.

Nadelhoffer, T., Gromet, D., Goodwin, G., Nahmias, E., Sripada, C., & Sinnott-Armstrong, W. (2013). The mind, the brain, and the criminal law. In T. Nadelhoffer (Ed.), *The Future of Punishment* (pp. 193–211). New York: Oxford University Press.

Nadelhoffer, T., Shepard, J., Nahmias, E., Sripada, C., & Ross, L. (2014). The Free Will Inventory: Measuring beliefs about agency and responsibility. *Consciousness and Cognition*, 25, 27–41.

Nadelhoffer, T., Yin, S., & Graves, R. (2020). Folk intuitions and the conditional ability to do otherwise. *Philosophical Psychology* (online first).

Nadelhoffer, T., Wright, J., Goya-Tocchetto, D., & McGuire, Q. (2020). Folk jurisprudence and neurointervention: An interdisciplinary investigation. In N. Vincent, T. Nadelhoffer, & A. McCay (Eds.), *Neurointerventions and the Law: Regulating Human Mental Capacity* (pp. 193–222). New York: Oxford University Press.

Nadelhoffer, T., Rose, D., Buckwalter, W., & Nichols, S. (2020). Natural compatibilism, indeterminism, and intrusive metaphysics. *Cognitive Science*, 44(8), e12873.

Nahmias, E., & Murray, D. (2011). Experimental philosophy on free will: An error theory for incompatibilist intuitions. In J. Aguilar, A. Buckareff, & K. Frankish (Eds.), New Waves in Philosophy of Action (pp. 189–216). New York: Palgrave MacMillan.

Nahmias, E., Morris, S., Nadelhoffer, T., & Turner, J. (2004). The phenomenology of free will. *The Journal of Consciousness Studies*, 11, 162–79.

Nahmias, E., Morris, S., Nadelhoffer, T., & Turner, J. (2005). Surveying free will: Folk intuitions about free will and moral responsibility. *Philosophical Psychology, 18,* 561–84.

Nahmias, E., Morris, S., Nadelhoffer, T., & Turner, J. (2006). Is incompatibilism intuitive? *Philosophy and Phenomenological Research, 73,* 28–53.

Nelkin, D.K. (2011). *Making Sense of Freedom and Responsibility.* New York: Oxford University Press.

Nichols, S. (2006). Folk intuitions on free will. *Journal of Cognition and Culture, 6,* 57–86.

Nichols, S., & Knobe, J. (2007). Moral responsibility and determinism: The Cognitive science of folk intuition. *Noûs, 41,* 663–85.

Packer, H. L. (1968). *The Limits of the Criminal Sanction.* Stanford, CA: Stanford University Press.

Paolacci, G., Chandler, J., & Ipeirotis, P. (2010). Running experiments on Amazon Mechanical Turk. *Judgment and Decision Making, 5,* 411–19.

Pereboom, D. (2001). *Living without Free Will.* New York: Cambridge University Press.

Rand, G. (2012). The promise of Mechanical Turk: How online labor markets can help theorists run behavioral experiments. *Journal of Theoretical Biology, 299,* 172–9.

Rose, D., Buckwalter, W., & Nichols. (2017). Neuroscientific prediction and the intrusion of intuitive metaphysics. *Cognitive Science, 41,* 482–502.

Rychlak, R., & Rychlak, J. (1997). Mental health experts on trial: Free will and determinism in the courtroom. *West Virginia Law Review, 100,* 193.

Sartorio, C. (2016). *Causation and Free Will.* Oxford: Oxford University Press.

Scanlon, T.M. (1998). *What We Owe to Each Other.* Cambridge: Harvard University Press.

Scurich, N., & Appelbaum, P.S. (2015). The blunt-edged sword: Genetic explanations of misbehavior neither mitigate nor aggravate punishment. *Journal of Law and the Biosciences, 3*(1), 140–57.

Shariff, A. F., Greene, J. D., Karremans, J. C., Luguri, J., Clark, C. J., Schooler, J. W., et al.(2014). Free will and punishment: A mechanistic view of human nature reduces retribution. *Psychological Science, 25*(8), 1563–70.

Simmons, J. P., Nelson, L. D., & Simonsohn, U. (2012). A 21 word solution. Dialogue: The Official Newsletter of the Society for Personality and Social Psychology, *26,* 4–7.

Smilansky, S. (2000). *Free Will and Illusion.* Oxford: Oxford University Press.

Sripada, C. (2012). What makes a manipulated agent unfree? *Philosophy and Phenomenological Research, LXXXV*(3), 563–93.

Stillman, T. F., Baumeister, R., & Mele, A. R. (2011). Free will in everyday life: Autobiographical accounts of free and unfree actions. *Philosophical Psychology, 24*(3), 381–94.

Strawson, G. (1986). *Freedom and Belief.* Oxford: Oxford University Press.

Stroessner, S. J., & Green, C. W. (1990). Effect of belief in free will or determinism on attitudes toward punishment and locus of control. *Journal of Social Psychology, 130,* 789–99.

Stuckless, N. (1992). The Vengeance Scale: Development of a measure of attitudes toward revenge. *Journal of Social Behavior and Personality, 7*(1), 25–42.

Tygart, C. E. (1994). Respondents' "free will" view of criminal behavior and support for capital punishment. *International Journal of Public Opinion Research, 6*(4), 371–4.

Van Inwagen, P. (2008). How to think about the problem of free will. *Journal of Ethics 12*(3–4): 327–41.

Vargas, M. (2013). *Building Better Beings: A Theory of Moral Responsibility*. New York: Oxford University Press.
Vihvelin, K. (2013). *Causes, Laws, & Free Will: Why Determinism Doesn't Matter*. New York: Oxford University Press.
Viney, W., Waldman, D., & Barchilon, J. (1982). Attitudes towards punishment in relation to beliefs in free will and determinism. *Human Relations, 35*, 939–50.
Viney, W., Parker-Martin, P., & Dotten, S. (1988). Beliefs in free will and determinism and lack of relation to punishment rational and magnitude. *Journal of General Psychology, 115*, 15–23.
Wallace, R. Jay. (1994). *Responsibility and the Moral Sentiments*. Cambridge: Harvard University Press.
Waller, B. (2015). *The Stubborn System of Moral Responsibility*. Cambridge, MA: MIT Press.
Wolf, S. (1990). *Freedom within Reason*. New York: Oxford University Press.

7

Moral Responsibility, Manipulation, and Experimental Philosophy

Alfred R. Mele

Introduction

Externalists and internalists disagree about the bearing of agents' histories on their moral responsibility for their actions. An efficient way to introduce the specific issue on which they disagree begins with a couple of quotations from Harry Frankfurt.

> To the extent that a person identifies himself with the springs of his actions, he takes responsibility for those actions and acquires moral responsibility for them; moreover, the questions of how the actions and his identifications with their springs are caused are irrelevant to the questions of whether he performs the actions freely or is morally responsible for performing them.
> (Frankfurt, 1988, p. 54)

> If someone does something because he wants to do it, and if he has no reservations about that desire but is wholeheartedly behind it, then—so far as his moral responsibility for doing it is concerned—it really does not matter how he got that way. One further requirement must be added …. the person's desires and attitudes have to be relatively well integrated into his general psychic condition. Otherwise they are not genuinely his …. As long as their interrelations imply that they are unequivocally attributable to him … it makes no difference—so far as evaluating his moral responsibility is concerned—how he came to have them.
> (Frankfurt, 2002, p. 27)

Frankfurt's internalistic thesis about moral responsibility here may be expressed as follows: as long as an agent is in a certain internal condition when he A-s, a condition characterized in these quotations, he is morally responsible for A-ing, no matter how he came to be in that internal condition.[1] For present purposes, an agent's *internal condition* at a time may be understood as something specified by the collection of all psychological truths about the agent at the time that are silent on how he came to be as he is at that time.[2]

Externalists reject Frankfurt's internalist thesis (and related internalist theses). To support their rejection of these theses they appeal to an array of cases featuring manipulation. For one such case, see Section 2. What I have called "conditional externalism" about direct moral responsibility (Mele, 2019, p. 14) is the following thesis:

> Even if some conditional internalist thesis is true, agents sometimes are [directly] morally responsible for *A* partly because of how they came to be in the internal condition that issues in their *A*-ing; and, more specifically, in these cases, there is another possible way of having come to be in that internal condition such that if they had come to be in that condition in that way, then, holding everything else fixed (except what is entailed by the difference, of course), including the fact that they *A*-ed, they would not have been morally responsible for *A*.
>
> (Mele, 2019, pp. 13–14)

As I understand *direct* moral responsibility, to say that an agent is *directly* morally responsible for *A*-ing is to say that "he is morally responsible for *A*-ing and that moral responsibility is not wholly inherited from his moral responsibility for other things" (Mele, 2019, p. 11).

I have long been on the externalist side of things, and my arguments for externalism have featured cases of manipulation (Mele, 1995, 2006, 2019). Recently, I put my intuitions about such cases to the test in an experimental philosophy study (Mele, 2019, Appendix). I turn to experimental philosophy in Section 3.

Moral Responsibility: Background

The conception of moral responsibility that has guided my work on moral responsibility is wholly backward-looking. This is how I put it in a recent book:

> As I understand moral responsibility, an agent's being morally responsible for performing good or bad intentional actions of the sort featured in the stories presented in this book entails that he deserves some moral credit or moral blame for those actions. I take no position on exactly how moral credit and moral blame are to be understood. But I follow Derk Pereboom, [2014, p. 2] when I report that the desert I have in mind does not derive from consequentialist or contractualist considerations.
>
> (Mele, 2019, p. 4)

I grant, of course, that there are alternative conceptions of moral responsibility, and I certainly do not claim that my conception is the only legitimate one. What I am doing in the passage I quoted is informing my readers about what I mean by "moral responsibility" in that book.[3]

Another feature of my conception of moral responsibility merits mention here as background. As I see it, "agents are not morally responsible for actions that fall outside the sphere of morality—or, more precisely, actions that morality is not in the business of prohibiting, requiring, or encouraging" (Mele, 2019, p. 4). (I owe this way of putting things to Josh Gert.)

Stories

Consider the following stories.[4]

Sweet Jane. Jane is one of the kindest, most generous people on Earth. For years, she has devoted a great deal of time and energy to helping needy people in her community and the local Girl Scouts. Her system of values plays a major role in generating her generous behavior, of course.[5] Jane was not always kind and generous, however. When she was a teenager, Jane came to view herself, with some justification, as self-centered, petty, and somewhat cruel. She worked hard to improve her character, and she succeeded.

Pre-manipulation Chuck. Chuck enjoys killing people. When he was much younger, Chuck took pleasure in torturing animals, but he was not wholeheartedly behind this. These activities sometimes caused him to feel guilty, he experienced bouts of squeamishness, and he occasionally considered abandoning animal torture. However, Chuck valued being the sort of person who does as he pleases and who unambiguously rejects conventional morality as a system designed for and by weaklings. He freely set out to ensure that he would be wholeheartedly behind his torturing of animals and related activities, including his merciless bullying of vulnerable people, and he was morally responsible for so doing. One strand of his strategy was to perform cruel actions with increased frequency in order to harden himself against feelings of guilt and squeamishness and eventually to extinguish the source of those feelings. Chuck strove to ensure that his psyche left no room for mercy. His strategy worked. In hardening his heart as he did, Chuck also ensured that he had no values at all that could motivate a charitable deed. To be sure, he might buy some Girl Scout cookies to lure an innocent child away for evil purposes; but a cookie-buying motivated in that way is not a charitable deed.

One Good Day. Chuck awakes with a strong desire to devote his day to helping homeless people and Girl Scouts. He is, of course, very surprised by this desire. What happened is that, while Chuck slept, a team of psychologists that had discovered the system of values that make Jane tick implanted those values in Chuck after erasing his competing values. They did this while leaving his memory intact, which helps account for his surprise. Chuck reflects on his new desire. Among other things, he judges, rightly, that it is utterly in line with his system of values. He also judges that he finally sees the light about life: its point and purpose is to make the world a better place. Upon reflection, Chuck "has no reservations about" his desire to devote the day to charitable deeds and "is wholeheartedly behind it" (Frankfurt, 2002, p. 27). Furthermore, the desire is "well integrated into his general psychic condition" (Frankfurt, 2002, p. 27). Seeing nothing that he regards as a good reason to refrain from spending the day as he wants to, he comes up with a plan for the day. Chuck works for eight hours with a local Habitat for Humanity crew in his neighborhood. When the work day ends, he drives around town for an hour and buys several boxes of Girl Scout cookies from every Girl Scout he sees—about fifty boxes in all. Then he delivers the cookies to a local homeless shelter. His motives are pure, as Jane's are when she does her charitable deeds. Chuck's view of things as he goes about executing his plan for the day is utterly predictable, given the content of the values that ultimately ground his reflection. Chuck "identifies himself with the springs of his action" (Frankfurt, 1988, p. 54), and he does his good deeds "because he wants to" do them (Frankfurt, 2002, p. 27). When Chuck falls asleep that night, the brainwashing is undone and he returns to normal (for him); the manipulators were conducting a one-day experiment.

As I understand moral responsibility (see section 1), if Chuck is morally responsible for his good deeds, he deserves some credit for them from a moral point of view. In my opinion, he deserves no credit at all for them, and I infer that he is not morally responsible for these deeds in *One Good Day*. If Chuck's good deeds are free actions, it is difficult to see what would stand in the way of his being morally responsible for them. In my opinion, Chuck performs these deeds unfreely. Some conditions that some compatibilists[6] have deemed sufficient for free and morally responsible action (for example, Frankfurt's conditions, as quoted earlier) are satisfied by Chuck's good deeds in this story.[7] But it is open to compatibilists to reject the claim that these conditions are indeed sufficient and to add a historical condition to their compatibilist mix. Elsewhere, I have argued for a negative historical condition—a condition requiring that the agent lack a history of a certain kind (Mele, 1995, pp. 172–3, 2019). (A negative historical condition leaves it open that a so-called "instant agent" might act freely and morally responsibly in the first moment of its existence.)[8] Chuck's history includes a radical reversal of a kind that, according to my negative historical condition, precludes Chuck's being morally responsible for his good deeds in *One Good Day*.

I predict that some readers will regard my claims that Chuck deserves no credit for his good deeds and does not freely perform them as obviously true whereas others will regard these claims as false. I have argued for these claims of mine elsewhere (most recently in Mele, 2019). My concern in the present article is how nonspecialists may respond to claims such as mine.

A Study: Toning it Down

In the appendix of my 2019 book, *Manipulated Agents: A Window to Moral Responsibility*, I reported the results of an experimental philosophy study I conducted on toned-down versions of *One Good Day* and a counterpart story about an agent like sweet Jane who was manipulated into being very much like evil Chuck for a day. I did this, as I put it there, "largely to check on whether my own intuitions about certain stories are out of line with judgments nonspecialists make about relevant cases" (p. 145). Here are the stories I tested.[9]

Good to Bad

For a long time, Jones has enjoyed helping people. When he was much younger, Jones came to view himself, with some justification, as self-centered, petty, and somewhat cruel. However, Jones wanted to be the sort of person who does the right thing and helps others. He worked hard to improve his character, and he succeeded. Part of his strategy was to perform kind and generous actions with increased frequency in order to develop his sensitivity to others and his willingness to help. His strategy worked. He came to want to help people whenever he can, without any reluctance at all.

A team of scientists invented a machine that can duplicate one person's desires and values in another person. The scientists decide to use this machine to duplicate the desires and values of a very bad man, Smith, in Jones. When Jones went to bed last night, he was very kind and generous. But while Jones slept, the scientists duplicated Smith's desires and values in Jones. They also erased all of Jones's desires and values that would have conflicted with those duplicated from Smith. The scientists made all of these changes to Jones's desires and values while leaving Jones's memory completely intact.

Jones wakes up with a desire to hurt people in his community by causing trouble for Girl Scouts and homeless people. Jones reflects on this desire and finds that it fits very well with his system of values. He also concludes that he finally sees the light about morality: morality is a system designed by and for weaklings. Upon reflection, Jones has no reservations about his desire to hurt people in his community; and given his values, Jones sees no good reason to refrain from hurting people. Jones devises a plan for what to do with his day: First, he finds a newly built Habitat for Humanity house in his neighborhood and vandalizes it. Then he drives around town for an hour and steals several boxes of Girl Scout cookies from helpless Girl Scouts—about fifty boxes in all. Finally, he steals all of the food and blankets from a local homeless shelter, and then destroys all of the food, blankets, and Girl Scout cookies in a giant bonfire. Jones identifies with his desire to hurt people and he hurts people because he wants to. When Jones falls asleep that night, the scientists undo everything they had done to him. When he wakes up the next day, he is just as kind and generous as ever.

Bad to Good

For a long time, Smith has enjoyed hurting people. When he was much younger, Smith enjoyed bullying other children, but he was uneasy about that. His cruel actions sometimes caused him to feel guilty. He experienced bouts of squeamishness, and he occasionally considered abandoning his cruel ways. However, Smith valued being the sort of person who does as he pleases and who rejects conventional morality as a system designed for and by weaklings. He set out to ensure that he would be wholeheartedly behind his merciless bullying of vulnerable people. Part of his strategy was to perform cruel actions with increased frequency in order to harden himself against feelings of guilt and squeamishness and eventually to extinguish those feelings. His strategy worked. He came to lack any feelings of guilt or squeamishness about bullying people.

A team of scientists invented a machine that can duplicate one person's desires and values in another person. The scientists decide to use this machine to duplicate the desires and values of a very good man, Jones, in Smith. When Smith went to bed last night, he was very cruel and sadistic. But while Smith slept, the scientists duplicated Jones's desires and values in Smith. They also erased all of Smith's desires and values that would have conflicted with those duplicated from Jones. The scientists made all of these changes to Smith's desires and values while leaving Smith's memory completely intact.

Smith wakes up with a desire to help people in his community by doing volunteer work and making charitable donations. Smith reflects on this desire and finds that it fits very well with his system of values. He also concludes that he finally sees the light about morality, and he wants to be the sort of person who does the right thing and helps others. Upon reflection, Smith has no reservations about his desire to help people in his community; and given his values, Smith sees no good reason to refrain from helping people. Smith devises a plan for what to do with his day: in the morning, he starts working with a local Habitat for Humanity crew in his neighborhood. When the workday ends, he drives around town for an hour and buys several boxes of Girl Scout cookies from every Girl Scout he sees—about fifty boxes in all. Then he delivers the cookies to a local homeless shelter. Smith identifies with his desire to help people and he helps people because he wants to. When Smith falls asleep that night, the scientists undo everything they had done to him. When he awakes the next day, he is just as cruel and sadistic as ever.

Participants each read one story and four statements about it. They responded on a seven-point scale ranging from 1 (strongly disagree) to 7 (strongly agree). Two of the four statements were comprehension checks. One concerned whether the agent worked on himself to become a person of a certain sort, and the other was about how he spent his day. Here are the other statements:

J1. Jones is morally responsible for the bad things he does on the day described in the story above.
J2. Jones deserves blame for the bad things he does on the day described in the story above.
S1. Smith is morally responsible for the good things he does on the day described in the story above.
S2. Smith deserves credit for the good things he does on the day described in the story above.

I discarded responses from participants who failed either comprehension check. The table represents results for the remaining participants, with responses of 5 or higher counted as representing agreement and responses of 3 or lower as representing disagreement.

Table 7.1 Moral Responsibility and Desert Results

	Good to Bad	Bad to Good
Moral Responsibility		
No	59.0%	56.9%
Yes	23.1%	26.4%
Mean (SE)	3.18 (0.22)	3.32 (0.23)
N	78	72

Dessert		
No	64.1%	59.7%
Yes	20.5%	23.6%
Mean	3.05 (0.20)	3.22 (0.21)
N	78	72

As readers can see, most participants agree with my verdicts about these two stories. As I reported in Mele, 2019, "I do not offer that fact in support of my externalist position; but if things had turned out otherwise, I would have been concerned" (pp. 147–8).

Another Study: Changing the Number of Changes

In a new study, Jay Spitzley (2021) tested stories like *Good to Bad* and *Bad to Good* along with some variants thereof. Spitzley tested four types of story:

1. Manipulation stories like mine, in which the manipulation is undone at the end of a day of good or bad deeds.
2. Manipulation stories that differ from stories of type 1 only in that the manipulation is *not* undone.
3. Manipulation stories in which the only manipulation happens at the end of a day of good or bad activity.
4. Stories about good or bad behavior in which there is no manipulation at all

In stories of type 1, he found mean responses (on a seven-point scale) for moral responsibility and desert that were very similar to the ones I reported in the table. (Because his moral responsibility and desert ratings did not differ significantly from each other, he merged them into a single score.) In stories of type 4, he found high means, as expected (6.1 for good and 6.65 for bad). In stories of type 3, the means did not significantly differ from those of unmanipulated agents (type 4). However, in stories of type 2, something interesting emerged. For a type 1 story in which a bad person was made good for a day, the mean rating was 3.7; but for a type 2 story in which the only difference was that the manipulation was not undone at the end of the day, the mean rating was much higher: 4.95. Additionally, Spitzley's type 1 story about a good person who was made bad for a day received a rating of 2.98, whereas his type 2 version of this story yielded a rating of 3.85.

What accounts for the difference in reactions to type 1 and type 2 stories? And is that difference a problem for me?

When I told my earliest "radical reversal" manipulation stories years ago (Mele, 1995, ch. 9), there was no undoing of the heavy-duty manipulation. Those early stories were spun in the context of a defense of an externalist view of psychological autonomy.

What I primarily wanted to illustrate was that two agents in very similar internal psychological conditions at a time may be such that one autonomously possesses a value of his whereas the other nonautonomously possesses a matching value because of a difference in the way the two persons came to be in the internal condition they are in at that time. I also went on in that chapter to use these stories to support some claims about *actions* performed shortly after the manipulation. I claimed that, owing to a difference in their histories, one of the agents at issue might A autonomously and freely and be morally responsible for A-ing whereas the other A-s nonautonously and unfreely and is not morally responsible for A-ing.

When it came to moral responsibility in particular, people would sometimes suggest, in conversation, that an agent in a bad-to-good story of mine deserves praise for his good deeds, and therefore is morally responsible for them, because praise would encourage him to keep up the good work. (I heard similar things about agents in good-to-bad stories.) In Section 1, I mentioned my backward-looking conception of moral responsibility. That same conception was at work in Mele, 1995. So I endeavored to preempt this forward-looking line of thought by simply building it into my stories that the manipulation is undone at the end of the day and the agent is back to normal (see Mele, 2009a, p. 170, 2009b, p. 465, 2013, p. 174, and several of the stories in Mele, 2019). Praise after his good day has ended would do the agent at issue no good.

Spitzley's type 2 cases open the door to a discussion that I tried to close. My reason for trying to close it was not that I regarded the discussion as uninteresting but instead that the discussion would be about a conception of moral responsibility that was not at issue in my work on manipulation. Although Spitzley's type 2 case featuring bad actions comes in just under 4, a neutral response, his type 2 story about good actions gets a 4.95 rating. So perhaps people are thinking that because the formerly bad guy is still good after his day of good deeds and might be encouraged to continue being good by some moral praise for those good deeds, he deserves praise for them. I myself, as I said, am working with a purely backward-looking conception of moral responsibility. From that perspective, I cannot endorse the claim that this agent deserves praise because of the effect praise might have on his character. (The same goes for the claim that the agent deserves praise because of the effect the praise might have on other people; they might be encouraged to do good as a consequence of observing the praise.) But, as I also said, I do not take my conception of moral responsibility to be the only legitimate one. Even Derk Pereboom, cited in this connection earlier, develops a forward-looking conception of moral responsibility to place alongside his backward-looking one (2014, ch. 6). The different conceptions may be used for different purposes, as Pereboom reports.

I asked whether the interesting difference in Spitzley's findings for type 1 and type 2 stories is a problem for me. My answer is no. If I were to claim that all conceptions of moral responsibility are purely backward-looking, the difference at issue would be something for me to worry about. But that is not a claim I endorse. The difference would also be something to worry about if Frankfurt's internalist view, to which I have opposed my externalist view, were to rest on a forward-looking conception of moral responsibility; for then we would be talking past each other. But, as far as I can tell, Frankfurt's conception of moral responsibility is no more forward-looking than mine is. On the positive side, Spitzley's findings about type 1 stories reinforce mine.

8

Direct and Derivative Moral Responsibility: An Overlooked Distinction in Experimental Philosophy

Pascale Willemsen

Introduction

Consider the following scenario: Jim is a lorry driver on his way home from a long drive. He has been on the road for hours, with two hours still to go. Jim realizes that he is getting more and more tired and that it would be wise to take a break. However, the thought of getting home as soon as possible and finishing the day in his own bed is too tempting. Jim keeps driving. A few minutes later, Jim falls asleep for just a few seconds. When he wakes up, he notices that he is only meters away from a car parked next to the road. Even though he hits the brakes immediately and as hard as he can, it is impossible for Jim to avoid the collision. Jim hits the car, and both the car and his lorry are severely damaged. *Is Jim morally responsible for the damage?*

If your intuitions are anything like mine, you believe that Jim is morally responsible for the damage, deserving of blame and punishment, and liable for compensations. But why do we believe that Jim is morally responsible? What is it by virtue of which Jim deserves blame and punishment? Note that Jim never intended to cause the damage. The accident was just that—an accident. Additionally, Jim was unable to avoid causing it. Since the braking distance was longer than the distance to the car when he woke up, it was physically impossible to avoid the accident. So why would we hold him responsible for something he could not have avoided?[1]

The case of Jim exemplifies a situation in which an agent is considered morally responsible for something which, at the time of the action, he could not have avoided. Cases in which an agent is deemed morally responsible despite not being able to act otherwise are used to argue against the Principle of Alternative Possibilities (PAP). Experimental philosophers have examined whether the folk make moral judgments in accordance with PAP. Arguing that philosophical thought experiments cannot suffice to substantiate the adequacy of PAP, they have conducted experimental studies which are inspired by those philosophical thought experiments and aim to provide additional, empirical, and more systematic evidence on whether moral responsibility is dependent on the agent's ability to act otherwise. Among others, John Turri (2017a) argued that the folk seem to be "natural compatibilists".[2] In six original experiments, Turri demonstrated that laypeople are willing to ascribe moral responsibility and blame to an agent who could not have acted otherwise. His empirical results also supported previous experimental findings (e.g., Buckwalter, 2017; Miller & Feltz, 2011; Murray & Lombrozo, 2017; Willemsen, 2018, 2020; Woolfolk et al., 2006).

In this paper, I will take three steps toward demonstrating that this experimental evidence should be considered with caution. First, I will introduce a conceptual distinction between two kinds of moral responsibility, namely *direct* and *derivative moral responsibility*—a distinction which I believe has been overlooked by experimental philosophers. Derivative moral responsibility refers to an agent's moral responsibility for an action or the outcome of an action by virtue of something else they did.[3] Non-derivative, or "direct" (as it is alternatively termed), moral responsibility denotes an agent's moral responsibility without any intermediate, responsibility-transmitting element. Second, I argue that the stories used in John Turri's original studies allow for the attribution of both direct and derivative moral responsibility. While the attribution of direct moral responsibility would indeed demonstrate that the folk reject PAP, the attribution of derivative moral responsibility would not allow for this conclusion and is compatible with both the acceptance and rejection of PAP. However, which kind of moral responsibility is actually ascribed is unclear. Third, I conducted three experiments to demonstrate that my reservations are not simply theoretical possibilities. Participants' judgments only seem to violate PAP as long as the attribution of derivative moral responsibility is an option. If derivative moral responsibility is less likely to be ascribed, the results no longer support the compatibilist conclusion Turri wished to draw.

I close with the audacious and troublesome claim that much of the experimental evidence to date also fails to draw this conceptual distinction and, more critically, to control for the possibility that laypeople's seemingly compatibilist intuitions are in fact moral judgments about derivative moral responsibility.

The Principle of Alternative Possibilities, Direct and Derivative Moral Responsibility

Philosophers typically believe two conditions to be necessary and only jointly sufficient for moral responsibility (Rudy-Hiller, 2018). First, the agent needs some sort of control over what they are doing—the *control condition* of moral responsibility. Following Frankfurt (1969), one popular way to spell out this control condition is the Principle of Alternative Possibilities:

(PAP): An agent is morally responsible for what she has done only if she could have done otherwise.

But what does it mean to be responsible for something *one has done*, and what does it mean that an agent *could have done otherwise* (see Miller & Feltz, 2011 for a similar discussion)? According to one understanding of PAP, moral responsibility requires that an agent's action results from her own choice among a variety of options. Consequently, an agent is morally responsible for the action she chose if there were alternative courses of actions the agent could have chosen instead.[4] Note that this understanding focuses on the agent's *action* and the *situational circumstances when initiating the action*—the *Principle of Alternative Actions* (see Willemsen, 2020, for a discussion). A different understanding of PAP does not focus on the circumstances under which the action was initiated, but rather takes the action to be defined by its *consequences* (for such an understanding of PAP, see, among others: van Inwagen, 1983, 1999; Sartorio, 2005). An agent is morally responsible for *killing* a man, for example, if the consequence of her action is the death of a person, and if this death could have been prevented. If the victim would have died no matter what, the agent is not morally responsible for the death. This is the *Principle of Alternative Outcomes* or, as Miller and Feltz (2011) termed it, the *Principle of Possible Prevention*.[5]

A second necessary condition for moral responsibility is the *epistemic condition*. An agent requires some relevant sort of awareness of what they are doing. Suppose that Tom pushes a button in his new office which he believes will turn on the light. In fact, the button administers severe electric shocks to a person in another room—something that Tom could not have possibly known. Even though Tom has full control over pushing the button, he is not sufficiently aware of what he is doing by pushing it to qualify as morally responsible. Relatedly, we typically consider young children blameless for hurting others, as we believe they lack sufficient understanding of the moral relevance of their actions.[6]

Only if both the control condition and the epistemic condition are met can the agent be morally responsible for their actions. This kind of responsibility is often referred to as *ultimate, true,* or *direct moral responsibility* (e.g., Levy, 2017; Matheson, 2019; Mele, 2020; Strawson, 1994). In the following, I will use the term "*direct moral responsibility*."

Consider the example from the beginning of this paper: Jim is tired, continues driving, falls asleep, and wakes up only to realize that hitting a parked car is unavoidable. Is Jim morally responsible for the accident and the damage he caused? On the face of it, Jim does not fulfill the control condition at the time of the accident. When he wakes up, only a few meters away from the parked car, Jim cannot decide to bring his own car to an earlier stop and thus not to hit the parked car. Nevertheless, it is intuitively plausible that Jim *is* morally responsible. What should we make of this? First, it might be argued that our moral intuitions clearly suggest that we implicitly reject PAP as incorrect and that a lack of alternative possibilities is considered compatible with moral responsibility. Alternatively, one could maintain the (conceptual or metaphysical) truth of PAP by discarding our intuition as somehow flawed or biased.

Here is a third way to explain our intuitions: Philosophers such as Zimmerman (1997), Pereboom (2012), Rosen (2003), and others have distinguished between direct moral responsibility and what they call "derivative" moral responsibility.[7] An agent is *derivatively* morally responsible for X if they are considered morally responsible for X at t_0. While one might agree that Jim cannot be *directly* morally responsible for the accident, he can be *derivatively morally responsible* for the accident in virtue of being directly responsible for something else, namely for driving in an impaired state. Appropriate responses to his tiredness would have been to take a break, get some fresh air, take a short nap, and then continue the drive. The reason we feel that Jim is morally responsible for the accident is that we ascribe responsibility for something over which, in our estimation, he had control. Jim is directly morally responsible for driving even though he was too tired, and thus he is derivatively morally responsible for the accident and the damage he caused by virtue of being directly responsible for driving in his impaired state.

Suppose that this explanation is a psychologically adequate description of why Jim is considered morally responsible. Can we conclude that by judging Jim derivatively morally responsible for the accident, we reject PAP? Not at all. A violation of PAP requires an agent to be considered directly morally responsible for X at t_0 and also unable to avoid performing X at t_0 However, if my premise is correct, Jim is derivatively morally responsible for X at t_0 in virtue of what he did at t_{-1}, a time during which we have no reason to assume that Jim was not in control of his actions. Thus, at no point are our intuitions in conflict with PAP.

Distinguishing direct and derivate moral responsibility can explain why we sometimes blame an agent even though the necessary conditions for (direct) moral responsibility are violated. It may further help us to be more specific as to why or by virtue of what we consider an agent responsible, and to better understand where the wrongness of an agent's behavior lies. In the following, I argue that this conceptual clarity is indispensable, especially when designing experimental studies on folk morality and interpreting their results.

Experimental Findings: Direct or Derivative Moral Responsibility?

While moral responsibility is a key topic of traditional moral philosophy, it has also attracted the attention of experimental philosophers. The control condition in particular has been subject to experimental studies because of its role in the compatibilism of moral responsibility and free will, as well as related issues such as moral luck and the so-called ought-implies-can principle.

When investigating the folk's intuitions, the usual strategy is to present participants with an experimental stimulus in which an agent cannot do other than they actually do and, therefore, the control condition is violated. Quite often, these experimental stimuli are adapted from a philosophical thought experiment, such as versions of Frankfurt cases (Miller & Feltz, 2011; Murray & Lombrozo, 2017; Nahmias et al., 2005; Turri, 2017b; Willemsen, 2020). Participants read the stimulus and are subsequently asked whether the agent is morally responsible or to blame. If participants agree that the agent is responsible despite their inability to act otherwise, this is taken as support for folk compatibilism.[8]

In the following, I focus on a recent paper by John Turri (2017a) entitled "Compatibilism can be natural." Turri presented participants with one of the following two stories:

Evaluation: A woman is evaluating her employee's performance. The employee performed excellently. Given the current condition of the woman's brain, it is physically impossible that she can give the employee a positive evaluation. As a matter of brain chemistry, it is literally impossible that she can give the employee a positive evaluation. She will give the employee a negative evaluation.

Delivery: A man promised to deliver a package by 4pm. He just got on the freeway. Given current traffic conditions, it is physically impossible that he can deliver the package by 4pm. As a matter of physics, it is literally impossible that he can make it by 4pm. He will arrive late.

In both stories, the agent is described as violating the control condition. The woman is no longer in control over whether she gives her employee a positive or negative evaluation due to the current condition of her brain; the delivery man is not in control over the time at which he delivers the parcel, as he got stuck in traffic. To lend support to the claim that the folk reject PAP, Turri needs to show two things:

1. Participants say that the agent could not have acted other than performing X at t.
2. Those participants who believe that the agent could not have acted otherwise still ascribe moral responsibility for X at t.

Turri (2017a, p. 79) does find this evidence across a variety of experiments, and concludes:

> The present experiments provide the best evidence to date for natural compatibilism, completely avoiding weaknesses of prior work on the topic [...] I used brief, plain, tightly matched, and anodyne stimuli, tested multiple narrative contexts, and included multiple measures to assess how participants understood key variables. Participants understood the stimuli in the relevant way. The manipulations were credible and effective.

Turri is correct that he managed to avoid many of the methodological shortcomings that have plagued other studies.[9] Given the superiority of his approach, his paper does have the potential to provide excellent evidence in favor of the position that the folk reject PAP. However, at least one further condition must be added:

3. The moral responsibility that participants ascribe is *direct* moral responsibility.

To provide any evidence that can speak to whether the folk accept or reject PAP, we need to make sure that when participants hold the agent morally responsible, they ascribe direct moral responsibility for the action that is described as unavoidable. Why? To tests whether the folk reject PAP, we need a situation in which the control condition is violated, and the agent's behavior was without alternatives. Only if participants ascribe moral responsibility in violation of the control condition is there evidence that PAP is rejected. However, if participants ascribe derivative moral responsibility instead, they have shifted their attention away from the situation that violates the control condition.

Therefore, we cannot make any inferences as to whether PAP is rejected, because PAP is no longer under investigation.

The demand I wish to make here is a methodological one, requiring us as experimental researchers to clearly show that we have tested the relevant moral intuition. While thorough research and the exclusion of all potential confounds are certainly what we do and should aim for, one might wonder whether I exaggerate a minor fluke that is unlikely to cause any actual trouble. Should we really expect that in a design as simple as Turri's, people misunderstood what they were supposed to do?

Despite the importance of the distinction between direct and derivative moral responsibility in the philosophical literature, there is no natural way to express the two different kinds of moral responsibilities in ordinary language. We typically ascribe blame to agents, hold them responsible, and punish or condemn them for causing harm to others. Usually, we do not specify whether this moral responsibility is direct or derivative in nature. This lack of conceptual clarity can cause problems in two ways. Firstly, a lack of discriminating vocabulary might cause the participants confusion as to what kind of moral responsibility they are being asked to ascribe. Participants might assume that there are various things for which we could blame the agent, all of which are somehow connected to the outcome. For some things the agent is directly responsible, while for others the agent is responsible only by virtue of something else. However, participants might wonder on what basis moral responsibility should be ascribed, perhaps in the following sense:

1. The agent could not have acted other than they actually did when they performed X at t_0.
2. Hence, the agent is not morally responsible for X at t_0, as they could not have acted otherwise (*a judgment in line with PAP*).
3. However, the agent performed some other blameworthy action Y at t_{-1} that led them to perform X at t_0.
4. Therefore, the agent is morally responsible for X at t_0 *by virtue of* being responsible for Y at t_{-1}, despite not being able to do otherwise at t_0 (*a judgment seemingly in violation of PAP*).[10] In an experimental setting, such a line of reasoning will lead to judgments that seem as if participants reject PAP and attribute moral responsibility despite a recognition of a lack of alternative possibilities. However, since the moral responsibility judgment is a derivative one, it is not incompatible with PAP at all.

Alternatively, participants might not possess this level of self-reflection, and lack access to the reasons for which they blame others. The fact that there is no discriminatory vocabulary available could be taken as direct evidence that, while *philosophically* relevant, the distinction is irrelevant in our everyday lives. As a consequence, upon reading the test query, participants may have ascribed moral responsibility without wondering (or caring) what it is they ascribed moral responsibility for—they had the intuition that the agent was blameworthy for something, and that is the response they provided.

Let us examine Turri's vignettes to see if they leave room for derivate moral responsibility attribution. In *Evaluation*, a woman is described as unable to act other than to give her employee a negative evaluation as a matter of her brain chemistry.

It is unclear whether participants are familiar with the science underlying the test vignette, or are aware of the implications of the current conditions of a person's brain chemistry. If they are not, participants might have tried to make sense of this information by making additional assumptions. For instance, they might have believed that the woman caused her own inhibition by not sleeping enough or by taking drugs which now impair her judgment and proper brain function. Since Turri does not specify why the woman's brain is in this state, the woman might be considered morally blameworthy because she could and should have avoided whatever has caused this brain state—or so participants might have reasoned. The woman is, therefore, considered derivatively morally responsible for not giving the employee a positive evaluation by virtue of causing or allowing her brain to be in this malfunctioning state. Such results, though, do not test PAP, and therefore do not allow any inferences as to whether the folk reject it.

Similarly, in *Delivery*, a man is described as unable to deliver a parcel by 4 pm due to being stuck in traffic. Turri succeeds in telling a story with which people are familiar, just as he claims is necessary for reliable experimental results. However, people might be *too* familiar with the story. We usually know very well why we are late for an appointment, and it is usually poor planning. Participants might have believed that the man should have foreseen the possibility of a traffic jam, and that he simply left too late. They might also have believed that he should have checked the route in advance, been more alert to the traffic news on the radio, or taken other preparatory measures. Again, if participants enrich the story in this way, it is only reasonable to ascribe derivative moral responsibility. Unfortunately, nothing in the original vignette rules out these (mis)interpretations. Turri's results, thus, would not suggest that the folk reject PAP.[11]

Turri himself seems to have been aware of the possibility that his vignettes could be interpreted in this way. In the general discussion (Turri, 2017a, p. 79), he voices what I take to be a variation of my worry:

> It might be wondered whether people attribute the relevant moral status because they believe that at some point in time, not described in the scenario, the agent could have done something that would have prevented his subsequent inability. If so, the objection continues, none of the results would support natural compatibilism.

Turri does not believe this objection to be powerful, and argues that "if natural incompatibilism was true, then it seems unlikely that participants would respond as the objection envisions." I believe this response is mistaken. The worry his critic (in this case, me) has is not that the folk are natural *in*compatibilists or, as I have reframed the problem, that they accept PAP. The worry is that, be the folk as they may, the experimental design is unable to provide evidence in either direction. Nevertheless, I am sympathetic to his concluding remark that if an objection like mine is correct and participants do trace back moral responsibility, then "ordinary social cognition might never confront the issue of compatibilism or incompatibilism." I believe this is in fact a possibility worth exploring in future research and should be taken seriously, as it would raise serious questions about whether experimental studies on folk compatibilism are a worthwhile endeavor. While I cannot provide a satisfactory investigation of social cognition more generally, I assume for the sake of argument that ordinary social cognition at least sometimes confronts issues related to PAP, and I hope to offer some evidence supporting the need for a reservation which Turri discards much too quickly.

To test whether this alternative interpretation can account for Turri's results, I conducted three experiments. In Studies 1 A and B, I tested whether the agent is held morally responsible in a derivative sense. In these studies, I manipulated two things. First, I replicated Turri's original design and added a follow-up question. Participants who indicated that the agent could not act other than they did *and* that the agent is responsible (a judgment in potential violation of PAP) were asked to explain their moral judgment. If my reasoning is correct, participants would explain their judgments through additional assumptions about how the agent could have prevented their own inability. Second, I created an additional test condition with a manipulation of the original vignettes. These manipulated versions provided information that the agent is not (or is less obviously) to blame for causing their inability (see Table 8.1 for details). If causing an inability to act otherwise is required for people to blame the agents in the original vignettes, describing the agents' inabilities as not self-induced, and therefore blameless, should significantly reduce blame judgments. I tested these manipulations for two different morality queries that can be found in the literature, namely for the agent's blameworthiness for the outcome (Study 1 A) and for the agent being morally responsible (Study 1 B). In deference to the concern that my results in Studies 1 A and B might have been due to the stimuli doubling in length or the introduction of new factors to the stories, I address this possibility in Study 2 by comparing participants' responses to more closely matched vignettes.

Studies 1 A and B

The experimental design for Study 1 built on Turri's original design. The experimental design and all prediction and statistical analyses were pre-registered with the Open Science Framework:

(*https://osf.io/82ems/?view_only=c229aede0d19439b83bcddb31ad938da*).

Since there is no general consensus as to whether "blame" or "moral responsibility" provides a more adequate measure for moral responsibility, I tested two responsibility questions. I followed Turri in this decision. In Study 1 A, the responsibility query asked whether the agent is *to blame*; in Study 1 B, the responsibility query asked whether the agent is *morally responsible*. The experiments were identical in all other respects.

The experiment was motivated by the following predictions:

1. I expected to replicate Turri's original results when using the original vignettes.
2. Most participants who give seemingly compatibilist responses will explain their judgment by indicating that there was something the agent could have done to ensure that they would keep their promise or provide an adequate evaluation.

3. For both vignettes, people will blame the agent under No Self-Induced Inability conditions significantly less compared to the original vignettes.
4. For both vignettes, people will still judge the agent under No Self-Induced Inability conditions as unable to perform the action.

Methods for Studies A and B

I utilized a 2 (vignette: Delivery vs. Evaluation) x 2 (condition: Original vs. No Self-Induced Inability) between-subjects design. The Original condition was identical to Turri's original design for both vignettes (Section 4). In the No Self-Induced Inability condition, I added information which made it clear that the agent's inability was not the result of his or her own recklessness (see Table 8.1).

The questions that I used were identical to Turri's original ones and were answered on a rating scale from 1 ("strongly disagree") to 7 ("strongly agree"):

1. *Ability*: The man could still deliver the package by 4 pm
2. *Responsibility*: The man is to blame (*is morally responsible*) for the time he delivers the package.
3. *Likelihood*: On a scale of 0 to 100 percent, how likely is it that the man will deliver the package by 4 pm?

Table 8.1 Modified vignettes used in the experiment. Underlined sections represent additions made to the original vignettes.

	Delivery	Evaluation
No Self-Induced Inability	A man promised to deliver a package by 4 pm. He planned his route carefully and left very early, so that he would have plenty of time to get to his destination.	A woman is evaluating her employee's performance. The employee performed excellently and the woman is resolved to and about to give her employee a very good evaluation.
	He just got on the freeway, when two trucks collide before him. The freeway is blocked, and the police inform everyone that it will take at least until late in the night to clear the freeway. Unfortunately, this freeway is the only street that leads to the destination of the package.	Unfortunately and unbeknownst to her, the woman suffered a minor stroke before she began the crucial part of the evaluation. This stroke changed the current condition of the woman's brain.
	Given current traffic conditions, it is physically impossible that the man can deliver the package by 4 pm. As a matter of physics, it is literally impossible that he can make it by 4 pm. He will arrive late.	Given the current condition of the woman's brain, it is physically impossible that she can give the employee a positive evaluation. As a matter of brain chemistry, it is literally impossible that she can give the employee a positive evaluation. She will give the employee a negative evaluation.

When subjects gave an answer to the ability question of 4 or below (indicating indifference or disagreement, respectively), and at the same time gave an answer to the responsibility question of 4 or above (indicating indifference or agreement, respectively), I presented them with the following additional questions (with Time only shown for *Delivery*):

4. *Explanation*: Your judgment indicates that you believe the man is to blame for the time he delivers the package. Please explain your judgment by choosing the option that best expresses your intuition:
   The man is to blame for the time he delivers the package ...
   A. ... although there was nothing he could have done to ensure he would deliver the package in time.
   B. ... because there was something he could have done to ensure he would deliver the package in time.
5. *Time*: Please tell us your best guess of the time the man got on the freeway. Please use the following format: 11:32 pm (hour:minutes am/pm) (do not forget am/pm!)

Study 1 A

Participants

773 participants were recruited through the UK-based internet platform *Prolific* (https://www.prolific.ac). All participants were compensated for their participation (0.25 GBP, estimated 7.50 GBP per hour). All participants were native speakers of English and had not previously participated in an experiment using the same vignettes. I excluded fifty-seven participants from the analysis for either failing the attention check, not completing the survey, or finishing the survey in less than 40 seconds (please see pre-registration for further details). Results are reported for 716 participants ($M = 34.37$, $SD = 12.17$, 56% female, 44% male).

Results

Ability and Responsibility Ratings

I conducted t-tests against the midpoint of the scale (4) for ability ratings. Replicating Turri's original results, participants' ability ratings were significantly below the midpoint of the scale for both Original conditions (Delivery: $M = 1.14$, $t = -61.16$, $p <.001$; Evaluation: $M = 2.19$, $t = 14.1$, $p <.001$), indicating that they judged the agent unable to perform their obligation. T-tests against the midpoint revealed that blame ratings did not significantly differ from the scale midpoint in the Original condition (Delivery: $M = 3.84$, $t = -1.18$, $p =.24$; Evaluation: $M = 4.08$, $t = 0.52$, $p =.06$) (see Figure 8.1).

In contrast, for the No Self-Induced Inability condition, t-test against the midpoint of the scale (4) revealed that both ability (Delivery: $M = 1.35$, $t = -30.28$, $p <.001$; Evaluation: $M = 2.42$, $t = -9.98.1$, $p <.001$) and blame ratings (Delivery: $M = 1.31$, $t = -38.37$, $p <.001$; Evaluation: $M = 3.03$, $t = -5.53.1$, $p <.001$) were significantly below the midpoint. This lends support to the prediction that participants would not consider the agents blameworthy when the vignette clearly states that the agents were not at fault for their inabilities.

Ability ratings were further analyzed using a 2 (Vignette: Delivery vs. Evaluation) x 2 (Original of Inability: Original vs. No Self-Induced Inability) between-subjects Anova. As predicted, ability ratings did not differ between Original and No Self-Induced Inability, as neither the main effect of Origin of Inability ($F(1, 712) = 3.29, p =.07$) nor the interaction of Origin of Inability and Vignette was significant ($F(1, 712) = 0.01, p =.09$) (see Table 8.3). A second 2 x 2 Anova for blame ratings confirmed the prediction that blame ratings were significantly reduced in the No Self-Induced Inability condition, as demonstrated by the significant main effect of Origin of Inability ($F(1, 712) = 154.75, p <.001, \eta^2 =.18$). The main effect of Vignette was significant ($F(1, 712) = 46.29, p <.001, \eta^2 =.06$), and the interaction of Origin of Inability and Vignette was also significant ($F(1, 712) = 26.88, p <.001, \eta^2 = 0.04.$).

Additionally, the analyses revealed differences between vignettes, confirmed by planned contrasts. In the Original condition, ability ratings were higher for *Evaluation* than for *Delivery*, while there was no significant difference between vignettes for blame ratings. In the No Self-Induced Inability condition, however, both types of ratings were significantly higher for *Evaluation* than for *Delivery*.

These results indicate that making it explicit that the agents did not recklessly or negligently cause their own inabilities (the No Self-Induced Inability condition) reduces people's willingness to blame the agent. This finding supports an alternative interpretation of Turri's data—that people in the original design believed the agent to be at fault for their own inability, and that they blamed the agents for that instead of for not doing as they were supposed to. This, by extension, indicates that participants ascribed derivative, not the required direct, moral responsibility.[12]

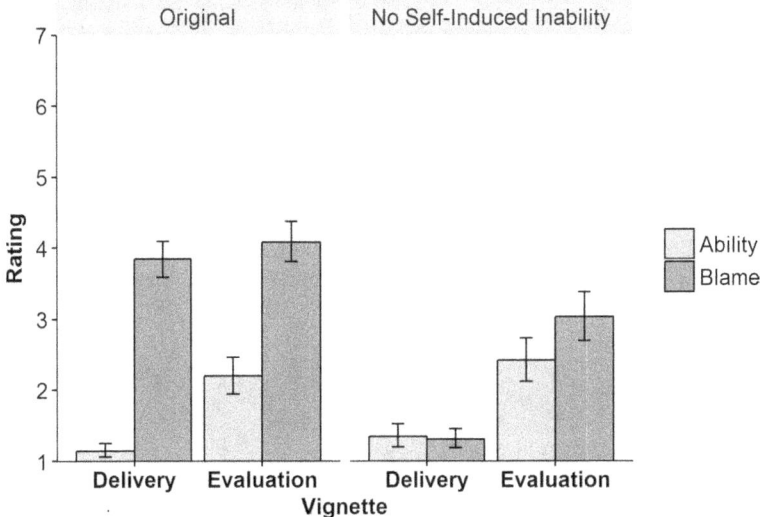

Figure 8.1 Participant's mean agreement with ability and blame questions in both conditions and vignettes. Error bars indicate 95% confidence intervals.

Likelihood Ratings

In all four conditions, participants judged it rather unlikely that the agent could still do as they were supposed to (Original Delivery: $M = 3.55$, $SD = 12.87$, Original Evaluation $M = 9.42$, $SD = 22.21$; No Self-Induced Inability Delivery: $M = 3.68$, $SD = 12.44$, No-Self Induced Inability Evaluation: $M = 10.97$, $SD = 20.05$). An Anova including the factors vignette and origin of inability revealed that they were higher in the *Evaluation* vignettes compared to *Delivery*—$F(1,712) = 23.57$, $p <.001$, $\eta^2 = 0.03$. These estimates correspond to the generally low (yet higher for *Evaluation*) ability ratings.

Explaining Intuitions in Violation of PAP

In the two Original conditions, 210 out of 304 participants indicated that the agent could not have acted otherwise (agreement to the ability question lower than or equal to 4), but that they were to blame for the consequences of their actions (agreement to the blame question above or equal to 4).[13] Thus, more than two-thirds of all participants give answers that seem to conflict with PAP. When asked to justify their judgment, 140 participants indicated that the agent was to blame *because* they could have done something to prevent the outcome. In contrast, only a third (seventy) of all participants who seem to reject PAP (210 out of 304 participants) indicated that the agent was to blame *although* there was nothing they could have done to prevent it.

For *Delivery*, 88% of participants said that the agent was to blame *because* there was something he could have done to prevent the outcome; 45% of participants stated the same for *Evaluation* (see Figure 8.2). More people agreed that there was something the agent could have done in *Delivery*, as compared to *Evaluation* ($\chi^2 = 49.62$, $p <.001$). Thus, more people gave a response incompatible with PAP for *Evaluation*. Following this specific study, I cannot offer empirical evidence which can explain this difference. However, as previously mentioned, *Delivery* and *Evaluation* differ in a series of potentially important respects, such as familiarity with the situation, relevant background knowledge about brain chemistry, and how external or internal to the agent the inability is. I submit that the most likely explanation is that we all know that when we are running late, there was usually something we could have done to prevent it.

To sum up: The Original version of the experiments allowed for the attribution of derivative moral responsibility. The results suggest that the agents are not held directly morally responsible, but that participants hold them responsible by virtue of failing to take adequate precautions to avoid their own inabilities.

Study 1 B

Study 1 B tested the same experimental design as Study 1 A, but for moral responsibility instead of blame ratings.

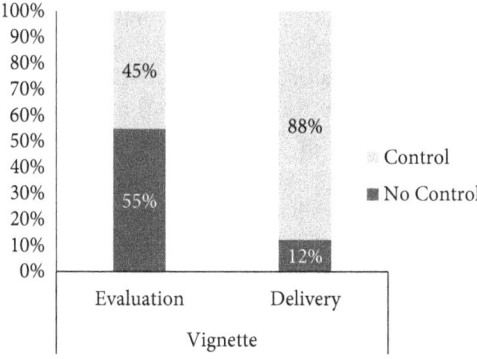

Figure 8.2 Percentages of people indicating that the agents were to blame although they had no control or because they had control in the Original condition.

Participants

710 participants were recruited on the UK-based internet platform *Prolific* (https://www.prolific.ac). All participants were compensated for their participation (0.25 GBP, estimated 7.50 GBP per hour). All participants were native speakers of English and had not previously participated in an experiment using the same vignettes. I excluded eighty participants from the analysis for either failing the attention check, not completing the survey, or finishing the survey in less than 40 seconds. Results are reported for 630 participants ($M = 33.84$, $SD = 10.97$, 61% female, 49% male).

Results

Ability and Moral Responsibility

As in Study 1A, I conducted t-tests against the midpoint of the scale for ability ratings. As predicted, I replicated Turri's results for the Original condition. Participants' ability ratings were significantly below the midpoint for both vignettes (Delivery: $M = 1.47$, $t = -24.99$, $p < .001$; Evaluation: $M = 2.52$, $t = -9.83$, $p < .001$), indicating that they judged the agent unable to do as they were supposed to. Further t-tests against the midpoint for responsibility ratings revealed that responsibility ratings were not significantly different from the midpoint in the case of *Delivery* (Delivery: $M = 4.17$, $t = 1.19$, $p = .2$), while they were significantly above the midpoint in the case of *Evaluation* (Evaluation: $M = 5.04$, $t = 6.98$, $p < .001$) (see Figure 8.3).

For the No Self-Induced Inability condition, a t-test against the midpoint of the scale (4) revealed that ability ratings (Delivery: $M = 1.33$, $t = -31.85$, $p < .001$; Evaluation: $M = 2.87$, $t = -5.71$, $p < .001$) were significantly below the midpoint. Moral responsibility ratings for *Delivery* were significantly below the midpoint ($M = 2.89$, $t = -6.75$, $p < .001$), while for *Evaluation* they were significantly above the midpoint ($M = 4.43$, $t = 2.37$, $p < .05$)

Ability ratings were further analyzed using a 2 (Vignette: Delivery vs. Evaluation) x 2 (Original of Inability: Original vs. No Self-Induced Inability) Anova. Ability ratings did not differ between Original and No Self-Induced Inability, as neither the main effect of Origin of Inability ($F(1, 626) = 0.52$, $p = .47$) nor the interaction of Origin of Inability and Vignette was significant ($F(1, 626) = 0.01$, $p = .08$). I conducted a second 2 x 2 Anova for responsibility ratings. As predicted, there was a significant main effect of Origin of Inability ($F(1, 626) = 34.72$, $p < .001$, $\eta^2 = 0.05$), as in the No Self-Induced Inability condition responsibility ratings were significantly lower compared to Original. Against my predictions, the manipulation had different strong effects on the two stories, as indicated by the significant two-way interaction ($F(1, 626) = 4.61$, $p < .05$, $\eta^2 = 0.05$). Responsibility ratings decreased significantly below the midpoint for the *Delivery* vignette. In *Evaluation*, responsibility ratings were still significantly above the scale midpoint, indicating that participants still judged the woman to be morally responsible for not meeting her obligation, even though the vignette clearly stated that she was not at fault.

The analyses revealed differences between vignettes, as confirmed by planned contrasts. In the Original condition, ability ratings were again higher for *Evaluation* than for *Delivery*. Moral responsibility ratings differed between vignettes, such that they were higher for *Evaluation* than for *Delivery* across both conditions. In addition, making it clear that the agent was blameless for actions before becoming unable to complete their obligations had a greater effect on moral responsibility ratings for *Delivery* than for *Evaluation*. This lends further support to the claim that the vignettes differ in important theoretical respects.

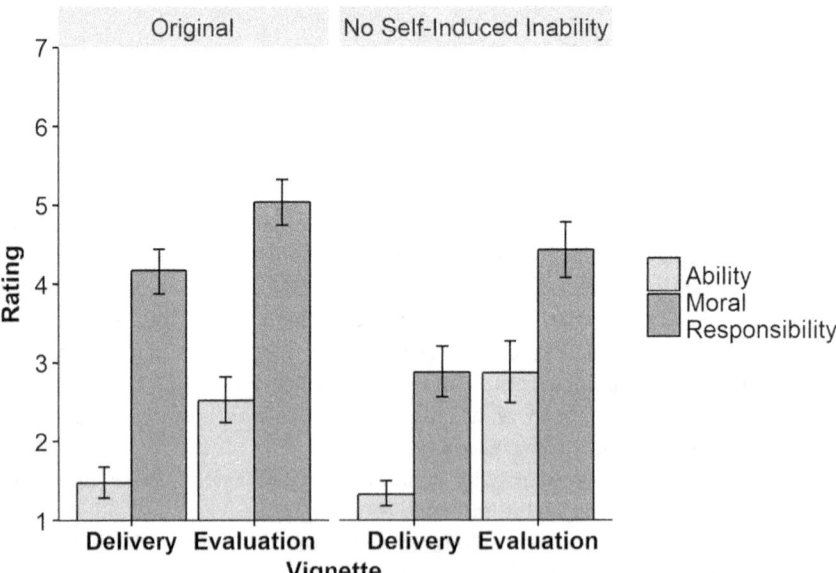

Figure 8.3 Participants' mean agreement with ability and moral responsibility questions in both conditions and vignettes. Error bars indicate 95% confidence intervals.

Likelihood

In all four conditions, participants judged it rather unlikely that the agent could still do as they were supposed to (Original Delivery: $M = 4.38$, $SD = 11.22$, Original Evaluation: $M = 16.61$, $SD = 27.89$; No Self-Induced Inability Delivery: $M = 6.26$, $SD = 17.43$, No Self-Induced Inability Evaluation: $M = 19.48$, $SD = 25.94$). Confirming the findings of Study 1 A, an Anova which included the factors vignette and origin of inability revealed that estimates were higher for the *Evaluation* vignettes than the *Delivery* ones, $F(1,626) = 52.25$, $p < .001$, $\eta^2 = .08$).

Explaining Intuitions in Violation of PAP

For the two Original conditions, 213 out of 630 participants indicated that the agent could not have acted otherwise (agreement to the ability question lower than or equal to 4), but that they were to blame for the consequences of their actions (agreement to the blame question above or equal to 4). When asked to justify their judgments in violation of PAP, 105 participants indicated that the agent was to blame *because* they could have done something to prevent the outcome. 108 participants who seemed to reject PAP indicated that the agents were to blame *although* there was nothing they could have done to prevent it.

This time, answers in the Original condition did not differ between vignettes ($\chi^2 = 0.04$, $p = 0.83$, n.s.). Both in *Evaluation* and in *Delivery*, participants' choices were distributed equally between the claim that the agent was to blame *because* there was something they could have done to prevent the outcome and the claim that they were to blame *although* there was nothing they could have done (see Figure 8.4).

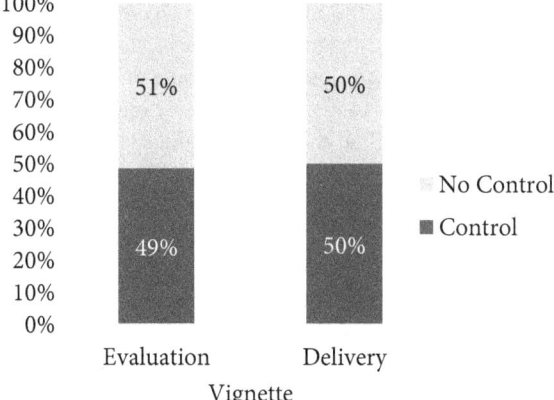

Figure 8.4 Percentages of people indicating that the agents were to blame although they had no control or because they had control in the Original condition.

Discussion

Studies 1 A and B challenge the reliability of Turri's compatibilist conclusion in two ways. First, the results lend support to the view that participants did not ascribe direct moral responsibility to the agent for their actions, but instead ascribed derivative moral responsibility. Excluding some of the potentially most obvious things that they should have done differently, such as leaving earlier or paying better attention to the traffic news, significantly reduced moral responsibility attribution. This effect occurred for both moral responsibility measures. In contrast, manipulating the origin of the agents' inabilities did not affect ability ratings. Adding information that the agents did not cause their own inabilities therefore only and directly affected the agents' moral status. These results are compatible with the idea that the moral responsibility that was measured was derivative, not direct, moral responsibility, and they put severe pressure on the validity of Turri's original interpretation in favor of folk compatibilism.

Second, the results also indicate more directly that participants did not buy into the necessary premise to test the acceptance of PAP, namely the agent's inability to act otherwise. More specifically, it seems that a large portion of the responses which seem to stand in conflict with PAP can be explained by participants' beliefs that there was something the agent could have done to avoid delivering the package late or writing a bad evaluation. As these results demonstrate, asking participants to explain their seemingly PAP-violating judgments can serve as a control for whether a judgment is actually in violation of PAP or not.

Study 2

The experimental manipulation described in Studies 1 A and B could raise potential concerns. Between the original and the manipulated conditions, vignettes do not differ only in the extent to which the agent could be considered blameworthy for something before the inability manifested. The manipulated vignettes are also, as a necessary consequence of the manipulation, significantly longer, and entail additional factors such as the police announcing the closure of the route or the stroke from which the woman suffers. As an alternative to my suggestion, one might believe that what really explains the effects between Original and No Self-Induced Inability vignettes is not the agents' recklessness, but the length of the vignettes (which has now doubled) or the introduction of additional agents or other variables.

Thus, in this second experiment, I directly tested this possibility. To reach a comparable length, I extended Turri's original *Delivery* vignette by adding irrelevant information with respect to the agent's blameworthiness. I predicted that making the Original conditions longer would not result in blame being significantly reduced. The experimental design and all predictions and analyses were again pre-registered with the Open Science Framework

(*https://osf.io/82ems/?view_only=c229aede0d19439b83bcddb31ad938da*).[14]

Methods

Participants

343 participants were recruited on the UK-based internet platform *Prolific* (https://www.prolific.ac). All participants were compensated for their participation (0.25 GBP, estimated 7.50 GBP per hour). All participants were native speakers of English and had not previously participated in an experiment using the same vignettes. I excluded forty-six participants from the analysis for either failing the attention check, not completing the survey, or finishing the survey in less than 40 seconds. Results are reported for 297 participants ($M = 36.10$, $SD = 10.95$, 66% female, 34% male).

Design and Procedure

I tested three between-subjects conditions, namely Original vs. No Self-Induced Inability vs. Original Long for the *Delivery* vignette. The Original and the No Self-Induced Inability conditions were identical to those used in Studies 1 A and B. In Original Long, I took the Original version and added irrelevant information in those places in which the No Self-Induced Inability condition contains information about the agent not being blameworthy for his inability.

The new modified Original Long vignette now reads:

> A man promised to deliver a package by 4 pm. <u>Before he leaves, he checks the results of yesterday night's football games and how his favourite player performed.</u>
>
> He just got on the freeway, <u>when he hears on the radio that the police announce an open day at the local police station next week Sunday. Young people interested in becoming a police officer can visit and ask questions about the job and the entry conditions. There will also be music and a bouncy castle for children.</u>
>
> Given current traffic conditions, it is physically impossible that the man can deliver the package by 4 pm. As a matter of physics, it is literally impossible that he can make it by 4 pm. He will arrive late.

After reading one of the three vignettes, participants answered the ability, responsibility, and likelihood questions from Study 1. Unlike in Studies 1 A and B, participants did not answer the time estimate question for *Delivery*, and neither were participants with seemingly PAP-violating intuitions asked to explain their judgments.

Results and Discussion

As Figure 8.5 shows, making the vignettes longer did not reduce blame ratings. In the No Self-Induced Inability Condition, blame was significantly lower compared to Original ($M = 3.58$, $SD = 2.0$ for Original, $M = 1.49$, $SD = 1.18$ for Not Self-Induced, $t = 8.9$, $p < .001$, $r = .58$) or to Original Long ($M = 4.68$, $SD = 1.79$, $t = 14.98$, $r = .75$).

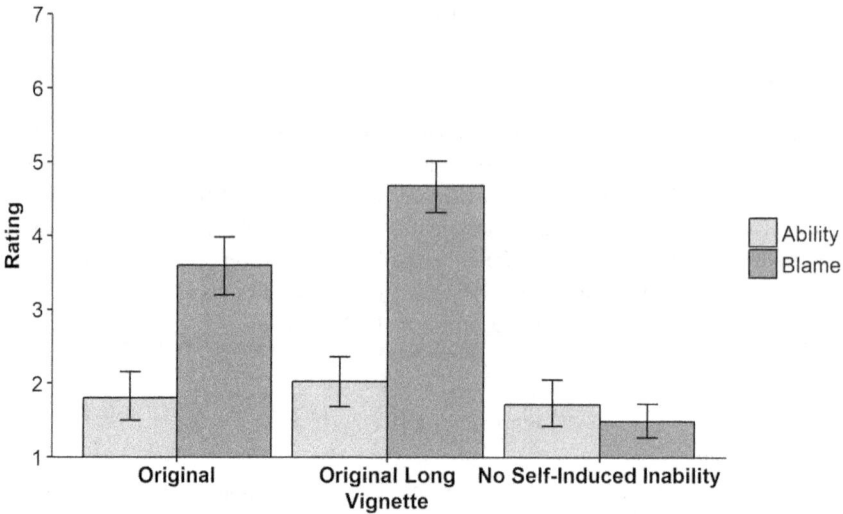

Figure 8.5 Participants' mean agreement with ability and moral responsibility questions in all three conditions. Error bars indicate 95% confidence intervals.

In line with my explanation for the effect found in Study 1, making the original vignettes longer (Original Long condition) did not by itself decrease blame ratings. Only when I provided blame-relevant information (No Self-Induced Inability) did blame ratings drop. These results provide evidence that the manipulation was successful, and that making it explicit that the agent is blameless for their inability reduces blame ratings.

Against my initial prediction, blame ratings for Original Long were not equally as high as blame ratings for Original, but were significantly higher ($t = 4.0, p < .001, r = .28$). However, I believe that this effect should not be overstated, as the effect might have been driven largely by participants assuming a connection between checking football results and not delivering the package in time. A reasonable assumption is that the delivery man left too late *because* he checked football results before leaving. However, the fact that introducing (arguably) irrelevant information to the Original Delivery vignette *increased* blame ascriptions instead of *decreasing* them only strengthens my argument that it is actually the content of the additional information that matters.

General Discussion

Do the folk accept or reject the Principle of Alternative Possibilities? Experimental philosophers have attempted to provide an empirical answer to this question and, thereby, to inform the traditional, non-empirical debate. I argue that in order to provide evidence for the folk rejecting PAP, three things must be demonstrated:

1. Participants say that the agent could not have acted otherwise than performing X at t.

2. Those participants who believe that the agent could not have acted otherwise still ascribe moral responsibility for X at t.
3. Participants ascribe direct moral responsibility.

Discussing and examining Turri (2017a), I argue that his experiments indeed show 1 and 2. The goal of this paper was to show that 1 and 2 alone do not suffice to make the point that the folk reject PAP, let alone that they are compatibilists. Rather, one also has to show that 3 is the case. I raised the concern that condition 3 is has not been justified, and that people in fact ascribe derivative (rather than direct) moral responsibility. I conducted three experiments to put this hypothesis to the test. Supporting my suspicion that participants tend to ascribe derivative moral responsibility, I demonstrated that revising the original vignettes by adding information specifying that the agent did not negligently or intentionally cause their own inability (something that might provide the grounds for derivative moral responsibility) significantly reduced moral responsibility ratings. Adding this information did not alter participants' ability or likelihood ratings, but only had an effect on moral responsibility ratings. The same effects occurred for blame as an alternative measure for moral responsibility. Additional questions asking for an explanation of judgments which seem to reject PAP revealed that people believed that there was something the agent could have done to prevent their own inability. These explanations strongly support the view that the kind of moral responsibility that participants ascribed was derived moral responsibility, not the direct moral responsibility we should require.

The effect found in this paper has far-reaching implications, as it points to a general methodological issue with many studies in experimental philosophy. Variations of the vignettes discussed in this paper and in Turri (2017) feature also in other publications that are often cited in the experimental literature, such as Turri (2017b, ten citations[15]), Buckwalter and Turri (2015, cited fifty times), Henne et al. (2016, cited twenty-seven times), and Chituc et al. (2016, cited fifty-five times). While many authors have been critical of this evidence, it continues to have a significant impact on the philosophical debate (Kissinger-Knox et al., 2018; Kurthy et al., 2017; Streumer, 2003; Willemsen & Wiegmann, 2017). In addition, most experimental studies rely on experimental stimuli that resemble the two vignettes described in this study, in that an agent is described as determined in conducting and acting in a specific situation (Buckwalter, 2017; Miller & Feltz, 2011; Murray & Lombrozo, 2017; Willemsen, 2018, 2020; Woolfolk et al., 2006).

As no experiment that I am aware of has tested for the possibility that participants ascribe derivative moral responsibility instead of direct moral responsibility,[16] we should be careful when drawing any philosophical conclusions from this evidence until follow-up studies confirm that participants ascribe direct moral responsibility. While the experimental stimuli are explicitly reported in these papers, they are often omitted in summary articles (which solely focus on the results of these studies) on the advances in experimental philosophy of compatibilism and PAP (Semler & Henne, 2019). Thus, experimental stimuli that are prone to triggering the attribution of derivative instead of direct moral responsibility are repeatedly used in experimental studies and their results are summarized in overview articles, hindering critical reflection on the stimuli and test queries.[17]

Notes

1. We might come closer to the answer if we consider a different scenario in which the agent did not intend the outcome and is unable to avoid causing it. Suppose that John is also a lorry driver on his way home. Despite no known history of any health issues, John suddenly has a heart attack and becomes unconscious. Because he is unconscious, he cannot bring his lorry to a stop. In such a case, I believe that most people do not have the intuition that John is morally responsible for the damage. In the rest of this paper, we will discuss the important differences between Jim and John.
2. The jump from a violation of PAP to compatibilism is much more complicated than my formulations suggest. For the time being, let us assume that moral intuitions in violation of PAP suggest a compatibilist stance.
3. In the philosophical literature, derivative moral responsibility is discussed as the result of a tracing strategy. This strategy plays a major role in many theories of responsibility (see, e.g., Khoury 2012, King 2014, Shabo 2015, and Timpe 2011).
4. Please note that this clarification is still not sufficiently sharp. For instance, according to an unconditional reading, "could have chosen instead" means that the agent could have chosen otherwise even if all antecedent conditions had been the same. Defenders of a conditional reading, usually compatibilists, understand "could have chosen otherwise" as saying "if the something leading to the decision had been different." In a recent paper, Huber et al. (forthcoming) provide empirical evidence that this distinction matters for research on folk intuitions.
5. Typically, having alternative courses of action available goes hand in hand with being able to bring about alternative outcomes. Choosing a different course of action usually leads to different outcomes. However, it is possible for an outcome to be determined in a way that, no matter what an agent does, the same outcome will occur. Suppose that a patient is very ill and suffers from an incurable disease. No matter what the physicians do, the patient will die. Here, the physicians can act differently without being able to bring about alternative outcomes. Alternatively, think of a case in which a person can only act she actually does, but whether or not she brings about a certain outcome largely depends on other factors beyond her control. Such cases are critical to discussions about the moral significance of luck.
6. Both the control and the epistemic conditions are subject to intense philosophical debate, and various specifications of them have been offered. It is beyond the scope of this paper to do justice to this debate. For an overview, see Rudy-Hiller, 2018.
7. The distinction also plays a key role in explaining how an agent can be morally responsible for unwitting omissions (e.g., Nelkin & Rickless, 2017; Rosen, 2003, 2004; Sartorio, 2007). Suppose that I promise to buy groceries on my way home from work. When I come to the crossing at which I am supposed to turn left to the supermarket, I take a right turn as I would otherwise usually do. I forget to go to the supermarket. In this case, it seems that I was not aware of what I was doing—I was not aware that I was breaking my promise to buy groceries. Yet, it seems reasonable to hold me responsible for the missing groceries. The moral responsibility here ascribed is, again, derivative and can be traced back to an earlier point in time at which I fulfilled all necessary conditions for moral responsibility. Knowing how forgetful I am, I should have made myself a reminder or paid more attention to my duties (see e.g., King, 2009 and Robichaud & Wieland, 2017 for critical positions; see Rudy-Hiller, 2018 for an overview).

8   Please note that this interpretation is in fact inadequate. Compatibilism is a thesis about the compatibility of moral responsibility or free will with determinism. While some philosophers believe that determinism is the most systematic violation of the ability to act otherwise, not all do. Many compatibilists argue that the ability to do otherwise is a necessary precondition for moral responsibility (and, thus, that PAP is true); they also argue that determinism is compatible with having this ability. Thus, they are compatibilists and they maintain the truth of PAP.

   In the following, I will try to avoid such misleading formulations. I believe that Turri's paper is much more adequately framed as addressing the equally interesting question of whether the folk reject PAP.

9   It is beyond the scope of this paper to discuss these methodological flaws in detail. To name a few, some papers were criticized for having used experimental stimuli and descriptions of causal determinism that laypeople did not fully understand in the relevant way. Other studies failed to test whether participants actually believed that the agent could not have done otherwise. In yet other studies, vignettes were confounded and not sufficiently tightly matched (see Turri, 2017a for a more detailed discussion).

10 Members of the Lund-Gothenburg Moral Philosophy Group pointed out to me that this explanation, while convincing, might make too charitable an assumption about laypeople's moral cognition. The story I offer here assumes that people go through a rational reasoning process in which they make assumptions about what most probably led to the agent's situation. Alternatively, one would have to think that people are just mean, unreflective blaming machines searching for validation of their outcome-triggered desire to blame.

11 Note that these two stories are asymmetric with respect to the two version of PAP. *Evaluation* creates a scenario in which the Principle of Possible Prevention of an unfortunate outcome is at issue. The woman can only give the employee a negative evaluation—neither a positive nor a neutral one. She therefore cannot prevent the outcome. At the same time, it seems that the Principle of Alternative is at issue as well. She cannot act other than to give the employee a negative evaluation, and one doubts that she is in control over this action in a relevant sense. Since she believes that the employee performed excellently, her actions stand in conflict with her mental state. In *Delivery*, such a conflict is not described, and the delivery man seems to be in perfect control over his behavior. It also seems that his inability to deliver in time is external to him. All of these asymmetries might have an effect on participants' interpretations of the story (see Willemsen, 2020 for a discussion).

12 These results are in line with some more general observations discussed in Walter Sinnott-Armstrong's chapter in this volume.

13 One might wonder why I chose to include the neutral midpoint. A rating right in the middle between "strongly disagree" and "strongly agree" is most likely to express indecisiveness and cannot be interpreted either in favor or disfavor of PAP. I believe that including the neutral midpoint tips the scale in favor of intuitions in violation of PAP and thus makes it easier for Turri to argue in favor of what he calls "folk compatibilism." However, I decided to follow Turri in this decision. At the end, the aim of this paper is to examine the validity of Turri's given his premises.

14 In this experiment, I only used the *Delivery* vignette and did not also test the *Evaluation* vignette. There are several reasons for this decision. First, as mentioned in Section 3, it is unclear whether participants even understand the connection between brains, chemistry, and an agent's behavior. The *Delivery* vignette seems sufficiently

intelligible. Second, the *Evaluation* vignette further leaves room for several interpretations according to which the agent does have alternative possibilities when performing the action in question. One might think, for instance, that the negative evaluation is conditional on the woman writing the evaluation right now. However, so participants might reason, she does not have to write the evaluation *now*. The vignette only specifies that the woman is going to write a negative evaluation, as opposed to a positive one; it does not specify that she has to write the evaluation now, as opposed to writing it later. What is worse, it remains unclear whether the woman is aware of her own neurological status. If participants think that she might be and that she could write the evaluation at a later point, it is clear that the woman is directly responsible for the bad evaluation and should not have written it in the first place.

15 All citations are based on GoogleScholar and were last checked on March 23, 2021.
16 It might be argued that all studies on omissions, negligence, and recklessness necessarily deal with derivative rather than direct moral responsibility. In a case of negligence, to say that the agent was negligently responsible is to say that the agent is derivatively morally responsible for the outcome in virtue of failing to anticipate the risks involved in acted the way they did and failing to take adequate precautions. I fully agree that in these studies, derivative moral responsibility is likely to be investigated. The point I wish to make is that the question of whether direct or derivative responsibility is ascribed in these cases has not been empirically addressed.
17 This research was funded by the Swiss National Science Foundation (SNSF), grant number PCEFP1_181082. I would like to express my gratitude to Sabrina Coninx, Neele Engelmann, Lena Kaestner, Beate Krickel, Matthew Lindauer, Judith Martens, Thomas Nadelhoffer, Kevin Reuter, Simon Stephan, and Alex Wiegmann for providing invaluable feedback on earlier versions of this paper.

References

Buckwalter, W. (2017). Ability, responsibility, and global justice. *Journal of Indian Council of Philosophical Research*, 34(3), 577–90.

Buckwalter, W., & Turri, J. (2015). Inability and obligation in moral judgment. *PLOS ONE*, 10(8), e0136589.

Chituc, V., Henne, P., Sinnott-Armstrong, W., & De Brigard, F. (2016). Blame, not ability, impacts moral "ought" judgments for impossible actions: Toward an empirical refutation of "ought" implies "can." *Cognition*, 150, 20–5.

Fischer, J. M., & Ravizza, M. (1998). *Responsibility and Control: A Theory of Moral Responsibility*, 1st Edition. Cambridge: Cambridge University Press.

Frankfurt, H. G. (1969). Alternate possibilities and moral responsibility. *The Journal of Philosophy*, 66(23), 829–39.

Ginet, C. (2000). The epistemic requirements for moral responsibility. *Nous*, 34(s14), 267–77.

Henne, P., Chituc, V., De Brigard, F., & Sinnott-Armstrong, W. (2016). An empirical refutation of "ought" implies "can." *Analysis*, 76(3), 283–90.

Huber, L., Reuter, K., & Cacchione, T. (forthcoming). Children and adults don't think they are free: A skeptical look at agent causationism. In P. Willemsen & A. Wiegmann (Eds.), *Advances in Experimental Philosophy of Causation*. London: Bloomsbury Press.

Kane, R. (1999). Responsibility, luck, and chance: Reflections on free will and indeterminism. *The Journal of Philosophy, 96*(5), 217–40.

Khoury, A. C. (2012). Responsibility, tracing, and consequences. *Canadian Journal of Philosophy, 42*(3–4), 187–207.

King, M. (2009). The problem with negligence. *Social Theory and Practice, 35*, 577–95.

King, M. (2014). Traction without tracing: A (partial) solution for control-based accounts of moral responsibility. *European Journal of Philosophy, 22*(3), 463–82.

Kissinger-Knox, A., Aragon, P., & Mizrahi, M. (2018). "Ought implies can," framing effects, and "empirical refutations." *Philosophia, 46*(1), 165–82.

Kurthy, M., Lawford-Smith, H., & Sousa, P. (2017). Does ought imply can? *PLOS ONE, 12*(4), e0175206.

Levy, N. (2017). The good, the bad, and the blameworthy. *Journal of Ethics and Social Philosophy, 1*(2), 1–16.

Lycan, W. G. (2003). Free will and the burden of proof. *Royal Institute of Philosophy Supplement, 53*, 107–22.

Matheson, B. (2019). Towards a structural ownership condition on moral responsibility. *Canadian Journal of Philosophy, 49*(4), 458–80.

Mele, A. R. (2020). Direct versus indirect: Control, moral responsibility, and free action. *Philosophy and Phenomenological Research*, phpr.12680. https://doi.org/10.1111/phpr.12680

Miller, J. S., & Feltz, A. (2011). Frankfurt and the folk: An experimental investigation of Frankfurt-style cases. *Consciousness and Cognition, 20*(2), 401–14.

Murray, D., & Lombrozo, T. (2017). Effects of manipulation on attributions of causation, free will, and moral responsibility. *Cognitive Science, 41*(2), 447–81.

Nahmias, E., Morris, S., Nadelhoffer, T., & Turner, J. (2005). Surveying freedom: Folk intuitions about free will and moral responsibility. *Philosophical Psychology, 18*(5), 561–84.

Nelkin, D. K., & Rickless, S. C. (2017). Moral responsibility for unwitting omissions: A new tracing view. In D. Nelkin & S. Rickless (Eds.), *The Ethics and Law of Omissions* (pp. 106–30). Oxford: Oxford University Press.

Pereboom, D. (2012). Frankfurt examples, derivative responsibility, and the timing objection. *Philosophical Issues, 22*, 298–315.

Robichaud, P., & Wieland, J. W. (2017). *Responsibility: The Epistemic Condition*. New York: Oxford University Press.

Rosen, G. (2003). Culpability and ignorance. *Proceedings of the Aristotelian Society, 103*(1), 61–84.

Rosen, G. (2004). Skepticism about moral responsibility. *Philosophical Perspectives, 18*(1), 295–313.

Rudy-Hiller, F. (2018). The Epistemic condition for moral responsibility. *The Stanford Encyclopedia of Philosophy*. https://plato.stanford.edu/archives/fall2018/entries/moral-responsibility-epistemic/

Sartorio, C. (2007). Causation and responsibility. *Philosophy Compass, 2*(5), 749–65.

Shabo, S. (2015). More trouble with tracing. *Erkenntnis, 80*(5), 987–1011.

Semler, J., & Henne, P. (2019). Recent experimental work on "ought" implies "can." *Philosophy Compass, 14*(9).

Sommers, T. (2010). Experimental philosophy and free will. *Philosophy Compass, 5*(2), 199–212.

Strawson, G. (1994). The impossibility of moral responsibility. *Philosophical Studies, 75*(1–2), 5–24.

Streumer, B. (2003). Does "ought" conversationally implicate "can"? *European Journal of Philosophy*, *11*(2), 219–28.

Timpe, K. (2011). Tracing and the epistemic condition on moral responsibility. *The Modern Schoolman*, *88*(1–2): 5–28.

Turri, J. (2017a). Compatibilism can be natural. *Consciousness and Cognition*, *51*, 68–81.

Turri, J. (2017b). How "ought" exceeds but implies "can": Description and encouragement in moral judgment. *Cognition*, *168*, 267–75.

Van Inwagen, P. (1975). The incompatibility of free will and determinism. *Philosophical Studies*, *27*(3), 185–99.

Vargas, M. (2006). On the importance of history for responsible agency. *Philosophical Studies*, *127*(3), 351–82.

Willemsen, P. (2018). Omissions and expectations: A new approach to the things we failed to do. *Synthese*, *195*(4), 1587–614.

Willemsen, P. (2020). The relevance of alternate possibilities for moral responsibility for actions and omissions. In T. Lombrozo, J. Knobe, & S. Nichols (Eds.), *Oxford Studies in Experimental Philosophy Volume 3* (pp. 232–74). New York: Oxford University Press.

Willemsen, P., & Wiegmann, A. (July 23, 2017). I must although I can't!? Suggestions for a two-level theory of "ought implies can." https://doi.org/10.31234/osf.io/hyq9u

Woolfolk, R. L., Doris, J. M., & Darley, J. M. (2006). Identification, situational constraint, and social cognition: Studies in the attribution of moral responsibility. *Cognition*, *100*(2), 283–301.

Zimmerman, M. J. (1997). Moral responsibility and ignorance. *Ethics*, *107*(3), 410–26.

Victim Omissions: How Doing Nothing Affects Judgments of Cause and Blame

Laura Niemi and Paul Henne

Introduction

Suppose that Suzy is at the grocery store. When the cashier turns around, Suzy sees that the cash drawer is open, so she quickly steals $50. Suzy walks out with it, and the cashier is later penalized for the drawer coming up $50 short. Now, consider a slightly different case where Suzy is at the grocery store and the cashier mistakenly hands Suzy $50 extra. Suzy notices it but walks out anyway, and the cashier is later penalized for the drawer coming up $50 short. In the first case, Suzy's *action* seems to be the cause of the cashier's problem, more so than Suzy's *inaction* in the second case. This is an example of what we will refer to as the *action effect for causal judgment*: people consistently judge that actions like these are more causal than inactions (Cushman & Young, 2011; Henne et al., 2019; Jamison et al., 2020; Spranca et al., 1991; Walsh & Sloman, 2011; Willemsen & Reuter, 2016). It also seems like Suzy is more blameworthy when she actively takes the money instead of when she just does not give the money back to the cashier. This difference in judgment is what we will refer to as the *action effect for blame* (Bostyn & Roets, 2016; Siegel et al., 2017).

Researchers have primarily investigated causal judgments and blame judgments about the actions or inactions of *agents*, the doers of actions, rather than *patients*, the individuals affected by agents' actions (e.g., Siegel, et al., 2017). In a criminal context, where the doers of concern were involved in some kind of harmful or illegal activity, the agent-patient dichotomy maps onto the perpetrator-victim dyad. Victims, however, also perform actions and inactions that are necessary for the bad outcome to occur, for instance, when the cashier left the drawer open and turned away, or when they mistakenly handed Suzy the money. Here, the cashier being scammed was only possible because of those actions or inactions performed by the victim.

People, however, judge the perpetrator and the victim differently, so a victim's causal contribution to the outcome or judgments of victim blame might deviate from what would be expected based on the action effect. The present research investigates the following question: do people judge victims' actions as more causal and blameworthy than their inactions? In other words, does the action effect apply to victims (i.e., patients)? This question is important for moral psychology because previous work has examined judgment of agents' morally relevant actions and inactions but not the actions and inactions of victims in morally relevant events. However, people can and do allocate blame and attribute causation to victims (Anderson et al., 1997; Harber et al., 2015; Malle et al., 2014; Niemi & Young, 2016; Van Prooijen & Van Den Bos, 2009). Herein, we report the results of four experiments showing that people do *not* exhibit the typical willingness to say that actions are more causal and more blameworthy than inactions in the case of victims. We discuss what explains this lack of evidence for an action effect for victims and why people seem to think victim inactions are more causal than their actions.

Actions and Inactions

Researchers have consistently found the action effect for causal judgment (e.g., Henne et al., 2019; Jamison et al., 2020). In one classic experiment on this effect, Cushman and Young (2011) gave participants the following action and inaction versions of a vignette (among some others):

Action
Ed is driving five sick people to the hospital with a cord hanging out the side of his car. He approaches a rock climber resting by the side of the road. If he does not slow down, the climber will be knocked off the road by the cord and fall down a steep cliff. If he does slow down, the five sick people will die before they reach the hospital. Ed keeps driving quickly and knocks the rock climber off the side of the road.

Inaction
Jack is driving five sick people to the hospital with a cord hanging out the side of his car. He approaches a rock climber who is about to fall off the side of the road and down a steep cliff. If he slows down, the rock climber can use the cord to prevent himself from falling, but the five sick people will die before they reach the hospital. Jack keeps driving quickly and the climber falls off the side of the road.

In cases like these, the outcome is fixed: the sick people live, and the climber falls from the cliff. The researchers varied the action or inaction of the driver: the driver actively knocks the climber off the road (action), or the climber falls when the driver does not stop to prevent him from falling (inaction). Participants attributed more causation to the agents who acted, relative to those who failed to act for both moral and non-moral scenarios (Cushman & Young, 2011; Willemsen & Reuter, 2016).

Researchers disagree on what explains the action effect for causal judgment. But there are a few plausible explanations explored in recent literature. Some researchers argue that actions in cases like these are more causal because they are more norm-violating than inactions (Willemsen & Reuter, 2016), and norm-violating events are generally understood to be more causal than norm-conforming events (e.g., Henne et al., 2021). In research investigating this view, Willemsen and Reuter gave participants the above vignettes from Cushman and Young (2011), and they asked participants to identify the rule the agents violated in the vignette and then rate the importance of the rule that they identified. Critically, participants judged that the rule that Ed broke in the action case above was more important than the rule that Jack broke in the inaction case above, so participants perceived the broken rule in the action case as more norm-violating, relative to the inaction case (Willemsen & Reuter, 2016). Moreover, when Willemsen and Reuter controlled for norms by designing a vignette that made the rules explicit and matched them across action and inaction conditions, participants showed no difference in causal judgments between the action and inaction conditions (Willemsen & Reuter, 2016).

Another alternative hypothesis is that the perceived transference of force between the potential causal factor and the outcome accounts for this action effect in causal judgment (for discussion, see Henne et al., 2019). That people find it intuitive that contact and physical force factor into the ordinary concept of causation—especially in morally relevant matters like crimes—is unsurprising. Some recent work in cognitive science also supports this view. Wolff and colleagues argue that causal reasoning involves the simulation of interacting entities and their perceived vectors (Wolff, 2007; Wolff, et al., 2010). On this view, the perception of force dynamic explains the action effect. Ed's action, for instance, is more causal than Jack's inaction because Ed's action transfers force onto the outcome while Jack's inaction does not transfer any force at all to the outcome; it simply fails to prevent it from not occurring.

Recent research, however, supports a different account: counterfactual thinking explains why people attribute more causation to actions than to inactions (Henne et al., 2019). This view makes two assumptions. First, it assumes that causal judgment depends in some way on counterfactual thinking (e.g., Gerstenberg et al., 2017; Lewis, 1974; Mackie, 1974). On counterfactual accounts, when people reason about the cause of an outcome, they do this by thinking about a counterfactual alternative to that event and asking if the outcome would still occur in that alternative possibility. So, to determine if Ed knocking the climber off of the road caused the climber to fall off the cliff, people imagine a possibility where Ed did not continue driving quickly, and then they ask if the climber still would have fallen from the cliff. If Ed did not continue driving, the climber would not have fallen, so people should judge that Ed's action made a difference—it caused the climber to fall. Second, this account assumes that people tend to consider the counterfactuals to actions more frequently than inactions (Byrne, 2016; Byrne & McEleney, 2000; Kahneman & Tversky, 1982). When they do this, it highlights that the action made a difference to the outcome—it caused the outcome to occur (Henne et al., 2019).

To see how this account explains the action effect, consider again the example above. On this new counterfactual account, people are more inclined to imagine the counterfactual to Ed's action—the possible situation where he does not keep driving—and when they do, they see that the outcome would not occur in that situation. As such, it is clear that Ed's action made a difference to the climber's fall. In the inaction case, people are not more inclined to imagine the counterfactual where Jack actively slows down and the climber survives. As such, people are less inclined to see Jack's inaction as making a difference to the outcome. While there is compelling evidence for each of these explanations for the action effect for causal judgment, there is some evidence that it is related to counterfactual thinking (Henne et al., 2019).

Many researchers assume that the action effect for causal judgments is related to the action effect for judgments of blame (e.g., Cushman & Young, 2011; Bostyn & Roets, 2016; Siegel et al., 2017). Some studies, in fact, have found that people judge actions as more blameworthy than inactions, and they have investigated the relationship between causal judgments and judgments of blame (e.g., Bostyn & Roets, 2016). In one novel study, Siegel and colleagues presented participants with a series of fictional agents who made moral decisions (2017). Participants observed the agents making a series of choices between taking a certain amount of money and shocking another anonymous agent. Among the authors' many interesting manipulations, they manipulated action and inaction; before participants saw each choice the agents made, Siegel and colleagues showed participants what the default number of shocks and amount of money an agent would receive if that agent *did nothing* (inaction) and then an alternative number of shocks and amount of money that the agent would receive if the agent decided to *switch* (action). Siegel and colleagues then revealed the agents' choice to act (switch) or not act at all (and take the default), and participants then judged the agents' decision on a scale from "blameworthy" to "praiseworthy" (Siegel et al., 2017). For both blameworthy and praiseworthy choices, participants judged that actions were more blameworthy and praiseworthy than inactions (Siegel et al., 2017). Consistent with a lot of earlier work (Cushman & Young, 2011), the authors concluded that people's moral judgments for the action effect for blame (and for praise) were influenced by people's causal judgments (Siegel et al., 2017).

Counterfactuals, Causation, and Blame of Victims

So far, we have discussed evidence suggesting that to understand some features of blame, we can look, in part, to causal judgments. And, to understand causal judgments, we can look to counterfactual thinking. In this research on the causal influence and blameworthiness of victims' actions and inactions, we consider all of these factors. Recent work has taught us a lot about victim blame attribution. Spotlighting victims' roles in counterfactual events by making their pre-victimization behaviors salient intensifies moral judgment (e.g., Branscombe et al., 1996; Roese, 1997). Furthermore, in line with research on normality and causal judgments (Hitchcock & Knobe, 2009), the normality of victim-related counterfactuals seems to matter for blame. Victim blame has been found to depend in part on whether a victim's pre-victimization actions or inactions were apparently atypical (Branscombe et al., 1996)—that is, when what the victim *could have* done differently to change the outcome was just not to do anything unusual. Those actions or inactions that violated social (including gender) norms (e.g., accepting a lift from a stranger) were more likely to be viewed as causal factors for the victimization event by way of making a difference to the outcome. Moreover, the victim may appear more blameworthy, despite the fact that those counterfactual possibilities are not relevant to the perpetrator's intentional act (Pickard, 2021).

This connection between counterfactual thinking, blame, and the focus on the victim versus perpetrator has been directly investigated in prior research (Niemi & Young, 2016). In a series of studies, participants read vignettes with perpetrators and victims in sexual misconduct scenarios. In one condition, the perpetrator was in the sentential subject position for the majority of sentences; in the other condition, the victim occupied the subject position, in which the structural details of what occurred remained the same. Participants morally evaluated the scenarios and those involved. Those who read about the scenarios that focused on the victim attributed more responsibility to victims, and they reported more ways that victims could have changed the outcome (i.e., counterfactual statements). These causation-relevant representations—responsibility and counterfactual possibilities—mediated the effect of the victim-perpetrator focus on blame. That is, being perceived as an *agent* in the event (by being in the sentential subject position) had the effect of being perceived as more responsible and as someone who could have done more to change the outcome.

In the current studies, we build on these findings by investigating how participants judge cause and blame for victims—the individuals in the *patient* position—when they act or do not act before being victimized. As prior work showed that focusing on victims made them seem like agents and increased their perceived causal contribution and blameworthiness (Niemi & Young, 2016), it was possible that the action effect (where people judge action as more causal and blameworthy than inaction) would be maintained for victims. Alternatively, people may not view victims like agents, even when they are the protagonists of vignettes. Instead, they may judge victims' actions and inactions differently, compared to agents', in line with inferences about the normality of inaction for moral patients.

Research Questions

This research investigates whether the action effect extends to a victim-perpetrator situation. Dyadic morality (Gray et al., 2012) indicates that the action effect should only apply to perpetrators—the doers of the actions. On this account, which attempts to explain dyadic morally relevant situations, victims are the recipients of actions, or the affected patients—*inaction* is apt in this case. So, if we find no evidence for the action effect for victims, this would suggest that higher-level individual roles (e.g., agents-patients roles) powerfully influence perception of behaviors observed within isolated events (like acting or inaction).

Why study inaction? Doing so will shed light on *when* doing nothing may be considered worse than doing something: in our studies below, people judge victims' pre-victimization behaviors. The results will indicate the plausibility of studying in future work a counterfactual explanation of victim blame, namely, that people allocate causation and blame to victims by considering victim-related counterfactuals unique to the victim role (i.e., "Victims who did not act *could have acted* to prevent their victimization").

If the action effect does not hold for victims, this will also suggest that accounts of causal cognition and moral judgment must make room for the possibility that what we know about the psychological processing of actions and omissions is fundamentally incomplete. One way victims' behaviors leading up to the victimization event are evaluated is in terms of normative expectations about taking action or opting not to, which shape attributions of cause and blame.

Preview of the Studies

The four studies presented here investigate people's judgments of victims' actions and inactions that are necessary for a victimization event. In all studies, we used vignettes, and we manipulated whether the victim performed an action or an inaction. Participants read vignettes involving a victim and a perpetrator, and the victim either acted in a way that enabled the bad outcome (action), or did nothing, failing to prevent the bad outcome (inaction). In all experiments, the vignettes described an event involving burglary, theft, or hacking. We collected ratings of the extent to which the protagonist who was affected by a bad outcome causally contributed to the outcome, and how much they should be blamed for its occurrence. We found no difference in ratings of cause and blame across actions and inactions in Experiment 1. So, in Experiment 2, we revised the vignettes to emphasize the outcome as a jointly caused event in order to emphasize that the outcome depended on factors related to both the victim and the perpetrator. We again found no difference in ratings of cause and blame across actions and inactions, suggesting once again that, unlike prior findings, the action effect did not occur for judgments of victims. Because we did not see the action effect with victims in Experiments 1 and 2 even when we made joint causation clearer, we approached Experiment 3 with the aim of making not only the joint causal structure clear but also the victim and perpetrator equally concrete, so their dependency on each other would be more salient to participants. To do this, we gave both the victim and perpetrator names in the vignettes used in Experiment 3: for instance, a victim (e.g., "Jack") was victimized by a burglar with a name (e.g., "Kevin"), rather than "a burglar." Increasing the concreteness of the perpetrator to better match the victim produced a *reverse* action effect: people saw victims' inactions as *more* causal and blameworthy than their actions. We aimed to replicate these results in Experiment 4 with three vignettes. While the finding was not statistically significant ($p = .05$), the pattern of results was similar to our findings in Experiment 3 for causation but not for blame.

This collection of studies indicates the following: (i) there is no evidence that the action effect obtains when judging causal contribution and blame of victims, (ii) the absent action effect is not dependent on the explicit causal structure, and (iii) there is some evidence that a small reverse action effect obtains when both individuals involved in the jointly caused event (victim and perpetrator) are made concrete.

Experiment 1

There were two aims of this experiment. First, we investigated whether people judged victims' actions as more causal than victims' inactions when these events causally contribute to a bad outcome. Second, we investigated whether there is an action effect for judgments of blame for victims, that is, whether people judge victims' actions as more blameworthy than victims' inactions when these events causally contribute to the bad outcome. To investigate these issues, we developed three vignettes that involved a perpetrator and a victim of a crime. We manipulated event type (action or inaction), and we measured participants' agreement with a causal statement and a statement about blame.

Participants

All participants were US nationals, were born in and resided in the United States, spoke English as their first language, and had a 99 percent approval rating on *Prolific*. A total of 1061 participants completed the experiment that was programmed in Qualtrics. Five participants reported not paying attention, so they were excluded. We analyzed data from the remaining 1056 participants (M_{age} = 34, SD = 11.6, $Range_{age}$ = [18–75], 45 percent female).

Materials and Procedure

We advertised the experiment as "A Study About Your Judgments" and included the description: "Participants will be asked to read a short passage and then answer some questions about it." Before participants entered the experiment, they read a consent form.

After consenting to participate, participants were randomly assigned to 1 of 6 conditions in a 2 (Event Type: action, inaction) × 3 (Vignette: burglary, theft, hack) between-participants design. Each participant read one vignette (example in Table 9.1; see Appendix for all vignettes and dependent measures). On the following page, they were asked for their level of agreement with a causal statement about the agent's action or inaction on a -50-50 scale [-50 = strongly disagree, 0 = neutral, 50 = strongly agree]. On the following page, they were asked for their level of agreement with a statement about the agent's blame for their action or inaction on a -50-50 scale [-50 = strongly disagree, 0 = neutral, 50 = strongly agree]. Participants were then asked for basic demographic information and to respond to one explicit attention check (See Appendix). All data and analysis code as well as an online appendix are available at https://osf.io/5s6g3/

Table 9.1 Burglary vignette used in Experiment 1 and the dependent variables.

Action:	Inaction:
Jack lives in a blue single-family house located on the south side of a city. The south side implemented a crime ordinance recently, and residents are supposed to have their front windows closed during the daytime hours.	Jack lives in a blue single-family house located on the south side of a city. The south side implemented a crime ordinance recently, and residents are supposed to have their front windows closed during the daytime hours.
Every day, Jack leaves around 8:30 AM to go to work. One day, he got ready for work, grabbed his keys and lunch, and saw that the front window was closed. It was hot and stuffy in the house, and he wanted to let in some fresh air during the day. Even though the ordinance said the front windows should be closed during the day, he opened the window and went to work.	Every day, Jack leaves around 8:30 AM to go to work. One day, he got ready for work, grabbed his keys and lunch, and saw that the front window was open. It was hot and stuffy in the house, and he wanted to let in some fresh air during the day. Even though the ordinance said the front windows should be closed during the day, he left the window open and went to work.
While Jack was at work, a burglar entered his house through the front window. The burglar took many of Jack's belongings and damaged his property.	While Jack is at work, a burglar entered his house through the front window. The burglar took many of Jack's belongings and damaged his property.

Causal Question, Action:	Causal Question, Inaction:
To what extent do you agree with the following statement about the passage you just read?	To what extent do you agree with the following statement about the passage you just read?
Jack's house was burglarized because Jack opened his window.	Jack's house was burglarized because Jack left the window open.
Blame Question: To what extent do you agree with the following statement about the passage you just read? Jack is to blame for Jack's house being burglarized.	

Results

For this experiment, we fitted data to linear mixed-effects models, and we included vignette as a random effect (random intercepts only) in all models. We assessed significance for fixed effects via Satterthwaite's degrees of freedom method. We report the means and standard deviations causal judgments and judgments of blame in Table A3.

For the causal question, there was no evidence that participants judged the victims actions ($M = 32.23$, $SD = 21.51$, $n = 527$) as more causal than the victims inactions ($M = 32.85$, $SD = 23.00$, $n = 529$) ($b =.61$, $SE = 1.33$, $t =.46$ $p =.64$, CI [-1.99, 3.22]) (Figure 1A).

For the blame question, there was no evidence that participants judged the victims who performed actions ($M = 25.19$, $SD = 26.30$, $n = 527$) as more blameworthy than the victims who performed inactions ($M = 25.37$, $SD = 26.99$, $n = 529$) ($b =.17$, $SE = 1.54$, $t =.11$, $p =.90$, CI [-2.85, 3.21]) (Figure 1B).

Discussion

In Experiment 1, we found no evidence of an action effect for causal judgment or for judgments of blame. Researchers have found the action effect for causal judgment in many domains (Cushman & Young, 2011; Henne et al., 2019; Jamison et al., 2020; Spranca et al., 1991; Walsh & Sloman, 2011; Willemsen & Reuter, 2016), yet we did not find it for ratings of victims' causal contributions, nor for ratings of victims' blameworthiness, in a range of crimes.

One concern about our study is that the causal structure could have been ambiguous. In previous work that found the action effect, researchers have made the causal structure explicit (Henne et al., 2019). The action effect comes about in joint-causation structures, but it reverses—such that inactions are more causal than actions—in cases of overdetermination (Henne et al., 2019). Since we did not make the causal structure clear, participants in our study may have failed to see the victims' action or inaction as jointly sufficient for the outcome. For example, some participants may have believed that the perpetrator would have committed the crime no matter what the victim did, so people might have seen victims' action or inaction as not jointly causing the bad outcome. For instance, people might have thought that the burglar would have burgled Jack's house no matter what, so Jack's action or inaction was not seen as necessary for the burglary at all—similar to overdetermination causal structures. We aimed to avoid this possible reading by making the causal structure explicit in Experiment 2.

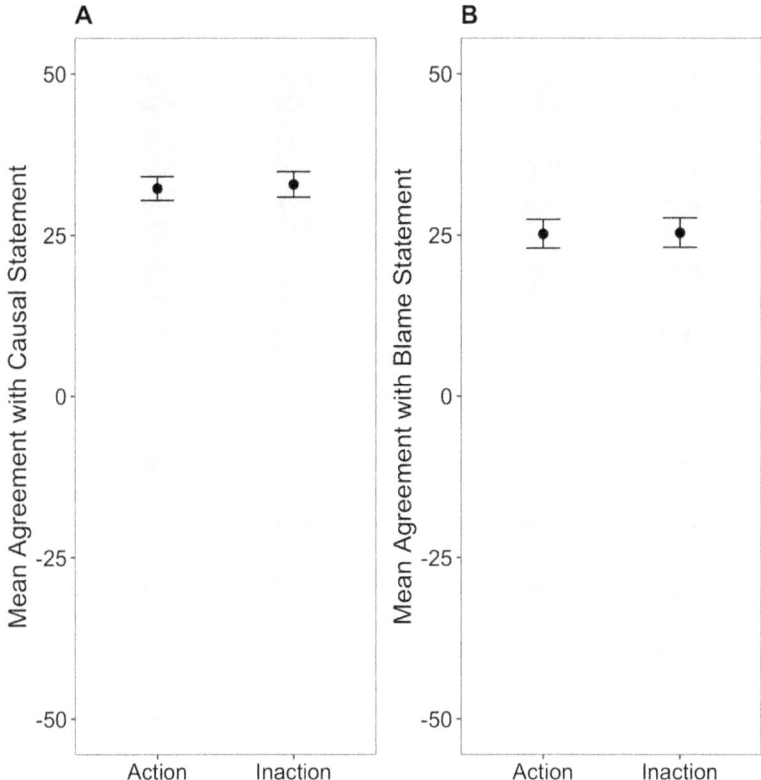

Figure 9.1 Mean agreement with the causal (A) and blame (B) statements in Experiment 1. Error bars indicate 95 percent confidence intervals. Light grey points represent individual participant responses evenly jittered.

Experiment 2

This experiment had the same aims as Experiment 1. We modified one vignette from Experiment 1 to emphasize a joint-causation structure, and we used the same measures.

Participants

All participants were US nationals, were born in and resided in the United States, spoke English as their first language, had a 99 percent approval rating on *Prolific*, and had not participated in Experiment 1. A total of 350 participants completed the experiment that was programmed in Qualtrics. One participant reported not paying attention, so they were excluded. We analyzed data from the remaining 349 participants (M_{age} = 32, SD = 12.1, $Range_{age}$ = [18–72], 57 percent female).

Materials and Procedure

The procedure was identical to that in Experiment 1—only participants read our revised vignette. After consenting to participate, participants were randomly assigned to 1 of 2 conditions (Event Type: action, inaction) in a between-participants design. Each participant read one vignette just like that in Table 9.1 (see Table A4). The only difference was that the following sentence was added just before the last sentence in the vignette: "Jack's house was secure, so the front window was the only way the burglar could have gained entry." This addition clarified the joint-causation structure of the scenario. The dependent measures were identical to those used in Experiment 1. Participants were then asked for basic demographic information and to respond to the same explicit attention check used in Experiment 1.

Results

For the causal question, there was no evidence that participants judged the victims' actions ($M = 25.25$, $SD = 24.98$, $n = 174$) as more causal than the victims' inactions ($M = 24.70$, $SD = 27.67$, $n = 175$) ($t(343.82) =.19$, $p =.84$, $d =.02$, CI [-.19,.23]) (Figure 2A).

For the blame question, there was no evidence that participants judged the victims who performed actions ($M = 6.02$, $SD = 32.37$, $n = 174$) as more blameworthy than the victims who performed inactions ($M = 4.57$, $SD = 22.52$, $n = 175$) ($t(346.7) =.41$, $p =.68$, $d =.04$, CI [-.17,.25]) (Figure 2B).

Discussion

Again, we found no evidence of an action effect for causal judgments about victims or for judgments of victim blame.

At this point, we wondered if there was another issue with our materials. Some work suggests that the extent to which people see some event as concrete or abstract affects people's causal explanations (Bechlivanidis et al., 2017). The degree of abstraction could have been an issue for our vignettes, because the materials used in previous work on the action effect have used concrete scenarios. Our vignettes, however, describe the perpetrators abstractly; for instance, they were described as nameless thieves or hackers who could have been challenging for participants to imagine. We aimed to correct this issue in Experiment 3.

Experiment 3

We had the same aims in this experiment as in Experiments 1 and 2. We modified the burglary vignette from Experiment 2 such that the perpetrator is more concretely described. To do this, we gave the perpetrator a name (Kogut & Ritov, 2005).

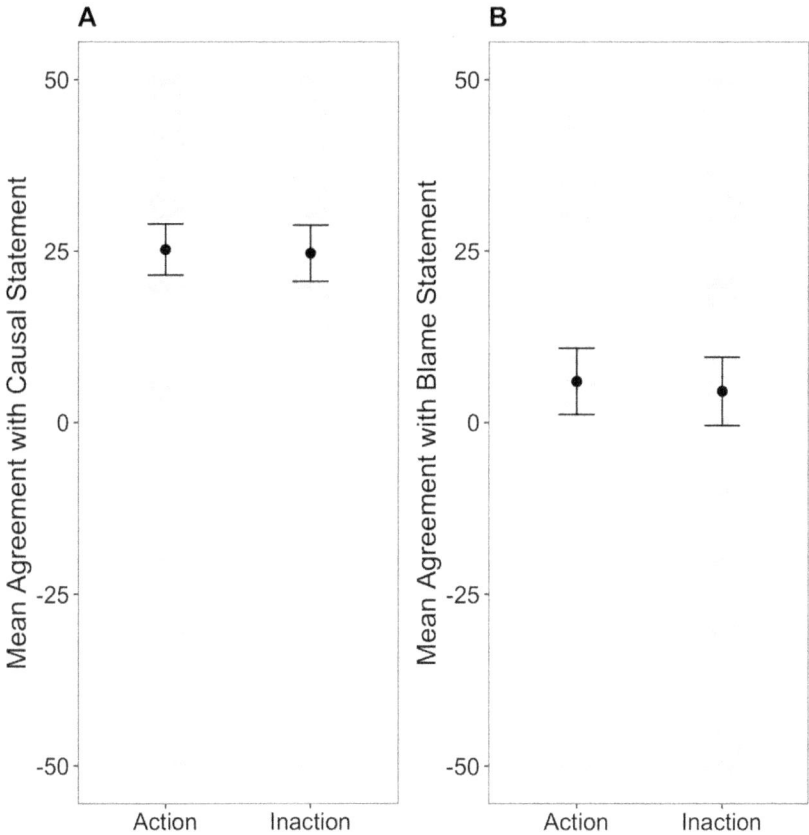

Figure 9.2 Mean agreement with the causal (A) and blame (B) statements in Experiment 2. Error bars indicate 95 percent confidence intervals. Light grey points represent individual participant responses evenly jittered.

Participants

All participants were US nationals, were born in and resided in the United States, spoke English as their first language, had a 99 percent approval rating on *Prolific*, and had not participated in Experiments 1 or 2. A total of 351 participants completed the experiment that was programmed in Qualtrics. Two participants reported not paying attention, so they were excluded. We analyzed data from the remaining 349 participants (M_{age} = 34, SD = 12.3, $Range_{age}$ = [18–74], 57 percent female).

Materials and Procedure

The procedure was identical to that in Experiment 1 and 2—only participants read our revised vignette. After consenting to participate, participants were randomly assigned to 1 of 2 conditions (Event Type: action, inaction) in a between-participants design. Each participant read one vignette just like that in Table 9.1 (see Table A5). The only difference was that we added concrete details like names for the agents and specific items that were stolen so that people could better imagine the scenario and any counterfactual alternatives. The dependent measures were on the same scales as those used in Experiment 1. Participants were then asked for basic demographic information and to respond to the same explicit attention check used in Experiments 1 and 2.

Results

For the causal question, participants judged the victims' actions ($M = 16.98$, $SD = 31.89$, $n = 174$) as less causal than the victims' inactions ($M = 26.81$, $SD = 26.39$, $n = 175$) ($t(334.55) = -3.13$, $p = .001$, $d = -.34$, CI [$-.56, -.13$]) (Figure 3A).

For the blame question, participants judged the victims who performed actions ($M = -1.62$, $SD = 34.57$, $n = 174$) as less blameworthy than the victims who performed inactions ($M = 6.58$, $SD = 33.17$, $n = 175$) ($t(346.23) = -2.26$, $p = .02$, $d = -.24$, CI [$-.45, -.03$]) (Figure 3B).

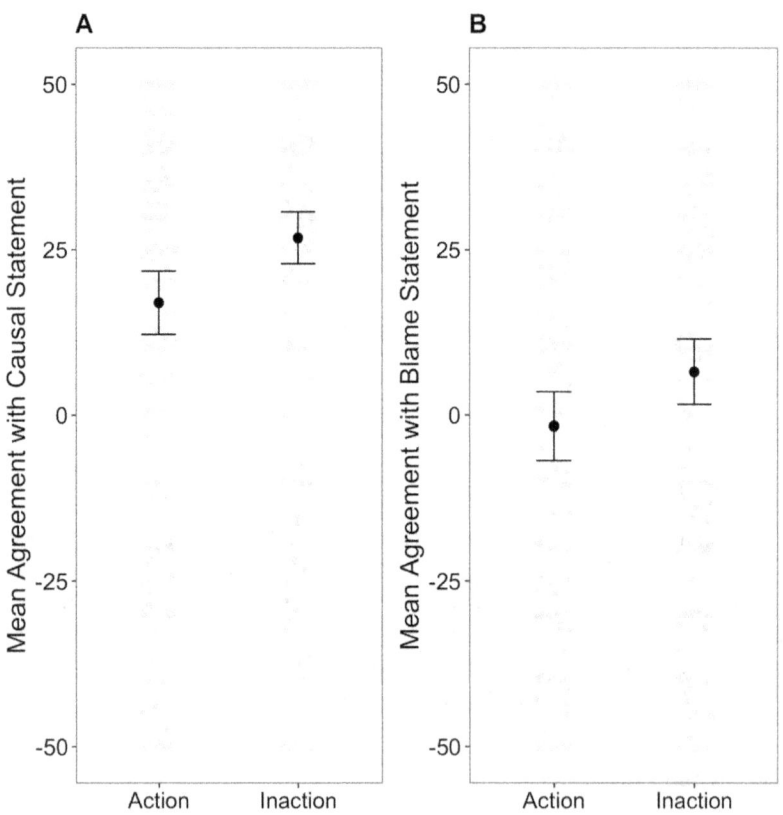

Figure 9.3 Mean agreement with the causal (A) and blame (B) statements in Experiment 3. Error bars indicate 95 percent confidence intervals. Light grey points represent individual participant responses evenly jittered.

Discussion

Surprisingly, in Experiment 3, we observed a reverse action effect both for causal judgments and judgments of blame. In other words, participants judged victims' inactions as *more* causal and blameworthy than their actions. It seems describing the perpetrator in concrete terms facilitated a reversal of participants' action effect—even when the causal structure was clearly emphasized by specifying how the victim's action or inaction was necessary for the outcome. Because of this striking result, we aimed to replicate it in Experiment 4 using a variety of vignettes.

Experiment 4

In this experiment, we aimed to replicate the reverse action effect for victims that we found in Experiment 3. To do so, we modified the vignettes from Experiment 1 such that they clearly described the causal structure and clearly described the perpetrator and crime concretely as in the vignette in Experiment 3.

Participants

All participants were US nationals, were born in and resided in the United States, spoke English as their first language, had a 99 percent approval rating on *Prolific*, and had not participated in any other experiments in this manuscript. A total of 943 participants completed the experiment that was programmed in Qualtrics. Eleven participants reported not paying attention, and one participant [ID = R_12tGdMJJILPuQ3A] messaged us and reported a technical error, so they were excluded. We analyzed data from the remaining 931 participants (M_{age} = 35, SD = 13.3, $Range_{age}$ = [18–82], 51 percent female).

Materials and Procedure

The procedure was identical to that in Experiments 1–3—only participants read our revised vignettes. After consenting to participate, participants were randomly assigned to 1 of 6 conditions in a 2 (Event Type: action, inaction) × 3 (Vignette: burglary, theft, hack) between-participants design. Each participant read one vignette similar to that in Table 9.1 (see Table A6-8). The only difference was that we added concrete details about the perpetrators and the crimes committed so that people could better imagine the scenario. The dependent measures were on the same scales as those used in Experiments 1–3. Participants were then asked for basic demographic information and to respond to the same explicit attention check used in Experiments 1–3.

Results

We analyzed the data as we did in Experiment 1. For the causal question—while the trend indicated a reversed action effect—the difference between participants' judgments of the victims' actions (M = 24.11, SD = 28.93, n = 465) and the victims' inactions was not significant ($M = 27.32$, $SD = 26.81$, $n = 466$) ($b = 3.30$, $SE = 1.73$, $t = 1.90$, $p = .05$, CI [-0.10, 6.70]) (Figure 4A).

For the blame question, there was no evidence that participants judged the victims who performed actions ($M = 16.42$, $SD = 31.64$, $n = 465$) as more blameworthy than the victims who performed inactions ($M = 15.41$, $SD = 30.59$, $n = 466$) ($b = -.86$, $SE = 1.84$, $t = -.47$, $p = .63$, CI [-4.49, 2.75]) (Figure 4B).

Discussion

For causal judgments, the results of Experiment 4 trended in the direction of the results of Experiment 3, which demonstrated a reverse action effect. Both of these experiments used vignettes with a clear causal structure and equally concrete individuals in contrast with Experiments 1 and 2. For blame judgments, we found no evidence of an action effect.

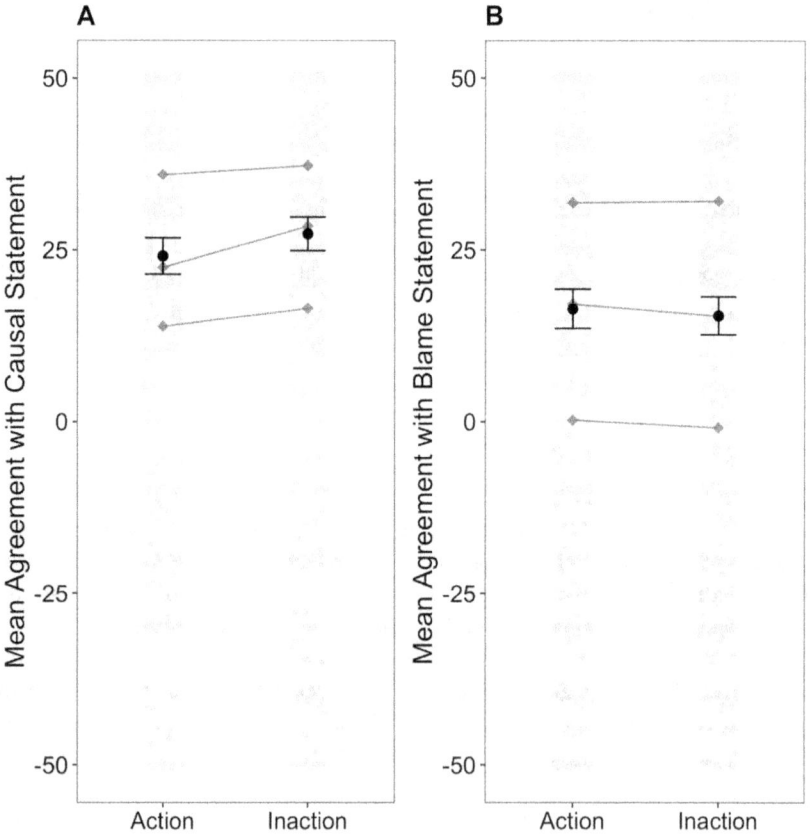

Figure 9.4 Mean agreement with the causal (A) and blame (B) statements in Experiment 4. Error bars indicate 95 percent confidence intervals. Red diamonds represent means for each vignette. Light grey points represent individual participant responses evenly jittered.

General Discussion

In four experiments, we found no evidence for an action effect for causal judgments or judgments of blame for victims. That is, we did not find evidence that people judged victims' actions that are necessary for harmful outcomes to be more causal or blameworthy than victims' inactions that are necessary for the harmful outcome. These results—for situations that focused on victims—differ drastically from the results found in previous work that focused on perpetrators.

Interestingly, for causal judgments we did find some evidence for a consistent *reverse* action effect. That is, in Experiment 3, participants judged victims' inactions to be more causal than their actions. While the trend was not significant in Experiment 4, participants—for each vignette—also tended to judge inactions as more causal than actions. That is, there is some evidence of a reverse action effect for victims.

There are a few possible explanations for why we found a reverse action effect rather than a standard action effect, and we hope that these explanations are explored in future work. One explanation relates to the causal structure that participants perceived in our vignettes. To understand this explanation, it might be helpful to introduce some details of previous work on the action effect for causal judgment. In one study on this effect, Henne and colleagues (2019) presented participants with vignettes, manipulated whether an agent performed an action or an inaction, and asked people for their causal judgments about the agents' action or inaction. In line with previous work, Henne and colleagues (2019) found that people judged actions as more causal than inactions in cases of joint-causation, where each action or inaction is necessary but only jointly sufficient for the outcome. Henne and colleagues (2019), however, also manipulated the causal structure of the situation such that it was either a case of joint-causation or one of overdetermination, where each action or inaction was individually sufficient for the outcome but not individually necessary. Surprisingly, in cases of overdetermination, participants judged that inactions were more causal than actions (Henne et al., 2019).

This previous work may help explain the tendency for people to show a reversal of the action effect for causal judgment in our experiments. In Experiments 2–4, we tried to emphasize the causal structure of our scenarios so that they were clearly cases of joint-causation. For instance, in the burglary vignette, we added the following sentence: "Jack's house was secure, so the front window was the only way the burglar could have gained entry." Here, we clarified that the victims' inaction or actions were necessary and jointly sufficient (with the perpetrator's action) for the bad outcome. Participants, however, might not be seeing the situation like this; they may have thought that the perpetrator would have performed their action regardless of what the victim did; for instance, participants might have thought that the burglar would have burgled the victim's home even if the victim had not opened or left the window open. If so, then participants might have seen the victims' action or inaction and the perpetrators' action as individually sufficient but not individually necessary for the outcome. For example, participants might have thought that Jack leaving the window open or opening the window was sufficient to get burgled. If people see the causal structure like this when they read the vignettes, then the fact that they see inactions as more causal than actions is consistent with previous work (Henne et al., 2019). However, what is different in the case of victims is that people might project different causal structures onto the situation than those that were intended. Future work could investigate this possibility by asking the degree to which people think each event is sufficient or necessary for the bad outcome.

Even if it is determined that crimes have unique causal structures that make them suitable for more or less attribution of causation and responsibility to victims via inferences about necessity and sufficiency, it is an empirical question whether the experience of victim blame for such crimes is psychologically different from blame of the perpetrator. Most likely, reflecting the corresponding agent-patient roles, they are different, and blame of victims regulates behaviors and enforces social norms relevant to victims in those scenarios in particular. In this research, unlike the prior work with agents (Henne et al., 2019) we found no evidence for the action effect for victims, some evidence for a reverse action effect, and no effect for blame, strongly suggesting that higher-level agent-patient roles differentially shape people's moral judgments. This important possibility has not been fully explored, and it is consequential to all models of moral judgment. For example, one model proposes a step-by-step process for blame: this involves a detection of a norm-violating event, attributions of causation and intentionality, assessments of capacity and obligation, then an attribution of blame (Malle et al., 2014). Some argue that the model cannot accommodate victim blame (Niemi & Young, 2014): victims cannot both fail to cause an event in the role of the patient yet end up blameworthy. Furthermore, the counterfactual questions one must ask to resolve each step seem to differ markedly for victims and perpetrators; they reflect different norms, expectations, and sometimes inactions or actions (Niemi & Young, 2014). For instance, in the case of intentionality, someone might ask the following about the perpetrator: "Did they mean to do it?" But they might also ask something different about the victim: "Was there anything they could have done?" Like with intentionality, the agent-patient role affects the perception of event-type effects on blame. More work needs to explore these differences.

People's reasoning about patients involves different expectations about causation by acting or not acting, as well as blameworthiness. The current results represent another piece of evidence that, while it might seem reasonable, we do not capture the full picture of causal and moral judgment by studying agents alone.

Conclusion

We investigated the action effect for causal judgments and for judgments of blame for victims of crimes. We found no evidence of these effects in the case of victims, which is radically different from the case of perpetrators. We found some evidence that people judge victims' inactions as *more* causal but not more blameworthy than their actions. Future work should explore these differences in judgments about victim blame.[1]

Note

1 This research was funded by a startup grant from Cornell University to Laura Niemi and the Applied Moral Psychology Lab at Cornell and a startup grant from Lake Forest College to Paul Henne and the Reasons and Decisions Lab at Lake Forest College.

References

Anderson, K. B., Cooper, H., & Okamura, L. (1997). Individual differences and attitudes toward rape: A meta-analytic review. *Personality and Social Psychology Bulletin*, 23(3), 295–315.

Bechlivanidis, C., Lagnado, D. A., Zemla, J. C., & Sloman, S. (2017). Concreteness and abstraction in everyday explanation. *Psychonomic Bulletin & Review*, 24(5), 1451–64. https://doi.org/10.3758/s13423-017-1299-3

Bostyn, D. H., & Roets, A. (2016). The morality of action: The asymmetry between judgments of praise and blame in the action–omission effect. *Journal of Experimental Social Psychology*, 63, 19–25.

Branscombe, N. R., Owen, S., Garstka, T. A., & Coleman, J. (1996). Rape and accident counterfactuals: Who might have done otherwise and would it have changed the outcome? *Journal of Applied Social Psychology*, 26(12), 1042–67.

Byrne, R. M. J. (2016). Counterfactual thought. *Annual Review of Psychology*, 67(1), 135–57. https://doi.org/10.1146/annurev-psych-122414-033249

Byrne, R. M. J., & McEleney, A. (2000). Counterfactual thinking about actions and failures to act. *Journal of Experimental Psychology: Learning, Memory, and Cognition*, 26(5), 1318–31. https://doi.org/10.1037/0278-7393.26.5.1318

Cushman, F., & Young, L. (2011). Patterns of moral judgment derive from nonmoral psychological representations. *Cognitive Science*, 35(6), 1052–75. https://doi.org/10.1111/j.1551-6709.2010.01167.x

Gerstenberg, T., Peterson, M. F., Goodman, N. D., Lagnado, D. A., & Tenenbaum, J. B. (2017). Eye-tracking causality. *Psychological Science*, 28(12), 1731–44

Gray, K., Young, L., & Waytz, A. (2012). Mind perception is the essence of morality. *Psychological Inquiry*, 23, 101–24.

Harber, K. D., Podolski, P., & Williams, C. H. (2015). Emotional disclosure and victim blaming. *Emotion*, 15(5), 603.

Henne, P., Pinillos, Á., & De Brigard, F. (2017). Cause by omission and norm: Not watering plants. *Australasian Journal of Philosophy*, 95(2), 270–83.

Henne, P., Niemi, L., Pinillos, Á., De Brigard, F., & Knobe, J. (2019). A counterfactual explanation for the action effect in causal judgment. *Cognition*, 190, 157–64. https://doi.org/10.1016/j.cognition.2019.05.006

Henne, P., Kulesza, A., Perez, K., & Houcek, A. (2021). Counterfactual thinking and recency effects in causal judgment. *Cognition, 212*, 104708.

Henne, P., O'Neill, K., Bello, P., Khemlani, S., & De Brigard, F. (2021). Norms affect prospective causal judgments. *Cognitive Science*, 45(1), e12931.

Hitchcock, C., & Knobe, J. (2009). Cause and norm. *The Journal of Philosophy*, 106(11), 587–612.

Icard, T. F., Kominsky, J. F., & Knobe, J. (2017). Normality and actual causal strength. *Cognition, 161*, 80–93. https://doi.org/10.1016/j.cognition.2017.01.010

Jamison, J., Yay, T., & Feldman, G. (2020). Action-inaction asymmetries in moral scenarios: Replication of the omission bias examining morality and blame with extensions linking to causality, intent, and regret. *Journal of Experimental Social Psychology, 89,* 103977. https://doi.org/10.1016/j.jesp.2020.103977

Kahneman, D., & Tversky, A. (1982). The Psychology of Preferences. *Scientific American, 246*(1), 160–73.

Kogut, T., & Ritov, I. (2005). The "identified victim" effect: An identified group, or just a single individual? *Journal of Behavioral Decision Making, 18*(3), 157–67.

Lewis, D. (1974). Causation. *The Journal of Philosophy, 70*(17), 556–67.

Mackie, J. L. (1974). The cement of the universe: A study of causation. Oxford: Clarendon Press.

Malle, B. F., Guglielmo, S., & Monroe, A. E. (2014). A theory of blame. *Psychological Inquiry, 25*(2), 147–86.

Niemi, L., & Young, L. (2014). Blaming the victim in the case of rape. *Psychological Inquiry, 25*(2), 230–3.

Niemi, L., & Young, L. (2016). When and why we see victims as responsible: The impact of ideology on attitudes toward victims. *Personality and Social Psychology Bulletin, 42*(9), 1227–42.

Pickard, H. (2021). Responsibility and explanations of rape. *On Crime, Society, and Responsibility in the Work of Nicola Lacey,* 95.

Roese, N. J. (1997). Counterfactual thinking. *Psychological Bulletin, 121*(1), 133.

Siegel, J. Z., Crockett, M. J., & Dolan, R. J. (2017). Inferences about moral character moderate the impact of consequences on blame and praise. *Cognition, 167,* 201–11.

Spranca, M., Minsk, E., & Baron, J. (1991). Omission and commission in judgment and choice. *Journal of Experimental Social Psychology, 27*(1), 76–105. https://doi.org/10.1016/0022-1031(91)90011-T

Van Prooijen, J. W., & Van Den Bos, K. (2009). We blame innocent victims more than I do: Self-construal level moderates responses to just-world threats. *Personality and Social Psychology Bulletin, 35*(11), 1528–39.

Walsh, C. R., & Sloman, S. A. (2011). The meaning of cause and prevent: The role of causal mechanism. *Mind & Language, 26*(1), 21–52. https://doi.org/10.1111/j.1468-0017.2010.01409.x

Willemsen, P., & Reuter, K. (2016). Is there really an omission effect? *Philosophical Psychology, 29*(8), 1142–59. https://doi.org/10.1080/09515089.2016.1225194

Wolff, P. (2007). Representing causation. *Journal of Experimental Psychology: General, 136*(1), 82.

Wolff, P., Barbey, A. K., & Hausknecht, M. (2010). For want of a nail: How absences cause events. *Journal of Experimental Psychology: General, 139*(2), 191.

10

Free Will and Skilled Decision Theory

Adam Feltz, Braden Tanner, Gwen Hoang,
Jenna Holt and Asif Muhammad

Introduction

In this chapter, we provide evidence for a new individual difference with respect to free will and moral responsibility—statistical numeracy. We provide evidence that those who are more statistically numerate understand key features of determinism better than those who are not statistically numerate. We also show that some features of scenarios (e.g., concreteness) used to measure compatibilist judgments might interfere with people's understanding of those key features. We conclude by suggesting some ways that these individual differences might be used to argue that the folk, at least those who understand key elements of deterministic scenarios, are more likely to be incompatibilist about freedom and moral responsibility than those who understand less.

Individual Differences in Free Will Intuitions

More than a decade of research has suggested that folk intuitions[1] about freedom and moral responsibility are complicated and multiply determined. Some of the initial research suggested that some people can have compatibilist intuitions (i.e., that free will and moral responsibility are compatible with determinism). For example, Nahmias, Morris, Nadelhoffer, and Turner (2005) found that in response to a vignette describing determinism, most people thought that the person in that scenario could be free and morally responsible for the actions that they perform. This basic effect has been replicated many times ((Feltz, 2015b; Nahmias, Coates, & Kvaran, 2007; Nahmias, Morris, Nadelhoffer, & Turner, 2006; Nahmias & Murray, 2010; Nichols, 2007) for a meta-analysis, see Feltz and Cova (2014)). Other research suggests that many factors can influence people's free will judgments including whether the scenarios are described concretely or abstractly (Nichols & Knobe, 2007), the affective components of the scenarios (Nichols & Knobe, 2007), whether a person is thought be bypassed in the scenario (Nahmias et al., 2007), whether the person acting is psychologically distanced from the participant (Weigel, 2013), and whether the person's acts are fated (Feltz, 2015b), just to name a few.

To be clear from the start: we want to emphasize that there is not likely any "the folk" view, any single mechanism responsible for all folk intuitions, or any single factor that influences all people's intuitions about freedom and moral responsibility (or many contentious philosophical issues). That is, for many philosophical issues, there is no univocal view that all people share. Rather, there are often stable individual differences with respect to those intuitions even if factors like the abstractness or concreteness of a scenario can influence "on average" judgments. One piece of evidence to support that claim comes from the fact that all of the studies that we are aware of concerning freedom and moral responsibility have substantial dissenting minorities. For example, the original studies by Nahmias et al. (2006) found that, overall, around 70 percent of people had compatibilist intuitions. However, that means that a sizable number of people (around 30 percent) did not have compatibilist intuitions. Consequently, there was no "the folk" judgment about freedom and moral responsibility even in these initial studies (to be fair, Nahmias et al. point this fact out, perhaps in an effort to treat the majoritarian view as the most prominent folk view). This same pattern of substantial dissenting minorities is generally found in empirical studies about freedom and moral responsibility (Feltz & Cova, 2014).

In some instances, we can predict *who* is likely to hold the dissenting view. For instance, there is a growing body of evidence that the personality trait extraversion predicts compatibilist intuitions. Extraversion is a global personality trait in most prominent models of personality (including the Big Five and HEXACO models). Extraversion is characterized by people who are warm, gregarious, and socially outgoing (John & Srivastava, 1999). Those who are extraverted tend to have compatibilist intuitions in at least some paradigmatic cases that have been used to measure free will and moral responsibility (Feltz & Cokely, 2009). In a recent meta-analysis, the overall correlation between extraversion and compatibilist judgments across twenty-five studies was estimated to be about .2 (95% CI =.15 -24.), equaling an estimated 17 percent of the explainable variance in high-affect cases (see Feltz and Cokely (2019) for a fuller discussion and meta-analysis).

These kinds of individual differences have been used to make various theoretical claims. For example, some factors related to intuitions are thought to be irrelevant to the truth of the content of an intuition. But many factors do appear to be related to or influence some people's intuitions, including order of presentation (Swain, Alexander, & Weinberg, 2008), perspective (Feltz, Harris, & Perez, 2012), and culture (Machery, Mallon, Nichols, & Stich, 2004). These factors have been argued to be irrelevant to the truth of the content of an intuition, thereby calling into question their use for evidence for some philosophical claims (Alexander & Weinberg, 2007; Horvarth, 2010; Sinnott-Armstrong, 2008; Weinberg, Nichols, & Stich, 2001). The personality trait extraversion is arguably like these extraneous features. To the extent that these free will judgments are caused by extraversion, then the use of those intuitions for some (but not for other) philosophical purposes could also be called into question. For example, these intuitions may not be good candidates for evidence for non-conceptual, non-linguistic truths about determinism's relation to free will (i.e., the Neo-Platonic truth about free will and determinism (Stich & Tobia, 2016)). Or, at a minimum, it is difficult to decide *which* intuitions should count as evidence given the current methods and standards in philosophy (Feltz & Cokely, 2012).

While extraversion is one feature that is likely to be related to compatibilist intuitions, there could be, and almost certainly are, other individual differences related to compatibilist judgments (i.e., compatibilist intuitions are likely to be multiply determined). One of these other individual differences is likely to be *expertise*. Expertise has been characterized as consistent, superior performance on paradigmatic tasks relevant to one's expertise (Ericsson, Prietula, & Cokely, 2007).

For example, Shaun Nichols (2007) has done some work concerning what positions concerning compatibilism historical free will experts occupy. The conceptual space surrounding compatibilist intuitions can be characterized by two dimensions: whether one thinks that determinism is true, and whether one thinks that determinism is compatible with determinism. Crossing these two dimensions generates four distinct positions that one could hold (e.g., determinism is true and compatible with determinism). However, according to Nichols, no historical figure in his review thinks that indeterminism is true and also holds a compatibilist position. However, the other three possible positions are occupied by historical experts on free will. Hence, at least for some experts, one potential philosophical position that one could take concerning compatibilism is not occupied.

Other work suggests that for contemporary experts on free and moral responsibility, incompatibilism is the preferred position.[2] In one set of studies, Schulz, Cokely, and Feltz (2011), developed and validated a Free Will Skill test. The test measured how much a person knows about contemporary debates on free will and moral responsibility. Rather than relying on self-reports of expertise or philosophical credentials, the Free Will Skill test measured actual knowledge about the free will debate with objectively true or false questions about free will. The performance on the Free Will Skill test predicted greater acceptance of incompatibilism. Hence, there is some reason to think that among skilled and knowledgeable experts in free will, incompatibilism is the preferred position (although, consistent with our general argument that there is no single set of intuitions, there were some experts who were compatibilist).

All of the work reviewed so far is consistent with the framework for Skilled Decision Theory (Figure 10.1). Skilled Decision Theory lays causal grounds that promote skilled decision making in both experts and non-experts through careful integration of deliberation and a representative understanding of the decision to be made (Cokely et al., 2018).

People generally make good decisions. What is considered a good decision is typically one in which an individual weighs and integrates their personal values with available evidence (Baron, 2008; Feltz & Cokely, 2016). A central element in the Framework is that people often must have a representative understanding of the decision stakes (e.g., risks and benefits associated with the decision; required knowledge to act on) in order to make a good decision (Feltz et al., 2016). Without understanding and subsequently having calibrated or appropriate affective reactions, personally oriented deliberation can lead to an array of costly mistakes, biases, and miscalibrated confidence (e.g., confirmation bias, anchoring, bias sampling; Cokely et al., 2018). Numeracy, which we will discuss in greater detail below, and associated meta-cognitive skills are often related to components of skilled decision-making.

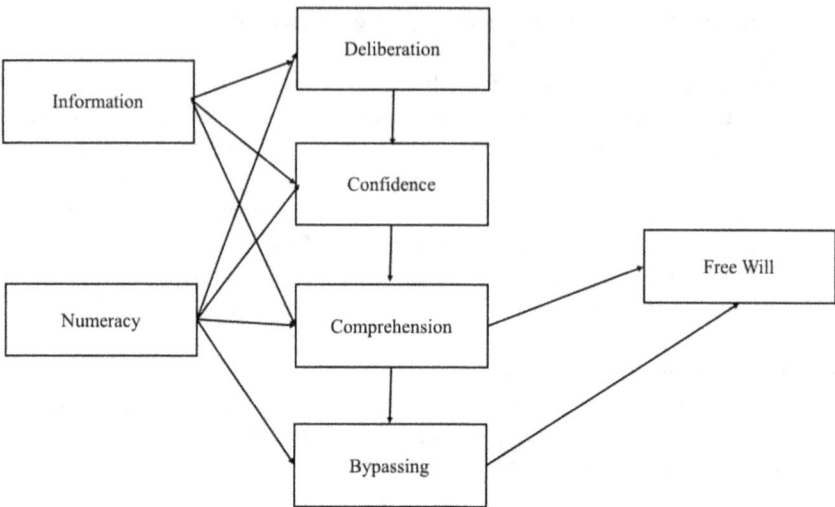

Figure 10.1 The Framework for Skilled Decision Making, taken from Cokely et al. (2018).

Numeracy has been defined in multiple ways (e.g., (Beazley, 1984; Bishop, 1992; Coben, 2000; Cockroft & Birtain, 1982; Gal, 1995; Ginsburg, Manly, & Schmitt, 2006; Golbeck, Ahlers-Schmidt, Paschal, & Dismuke, 2005; Steen, 1990, 2001). At a basic level, numeracy is considered to be an understanding of the real number line, time, measurement, and estimation, whereas at a higher level, numeracy is considered as an understanding of ratio, fractions, proportions, percentages, and probabilities (Reyna, Nelson, Han, & Dieckmann, 2009). According to (Steen, 1990), numeracy includes quantity, dimension, shape, pattern, uncertainty, and change. Another perspective concerning numeracy is that it is the ability to use mathematical knowledge and skills to effectively function in a societal context (i.e., in a group or community, (Beazley, 1984; Bishop, 1992). In other words, numeracy often helps people to make better decisions (Cokely et al., 2018; Cokely, Galesic, Schulz, Ghazal, & Garcia-Retamero, 2012; Peters, 2012; Peters et al., 2006). Numeracy has been found to be a powerful predictor in a number of decision-making domains such as medicine (Garcia-Retamero & Cokely, 2017; Garcia-Retamero & Cokely, 2013; Lipkus & Peters, 2009; Petrova, Garcia-Retamero, & Cokely, 2015; Reyna et al., 2009), finance (Banks & Oldfield, 2007; Lusardi, 2012), and climate change (Kahan et al., 2012).

In accord with the Framework for Skilled Decision theory, over the past decade we've observed an interesting, yet unreported, relation between free will judgments, understanding of elements of deterministic scenarios, and numeracy.[3] Nearly a decade ago, we started including numeracy in a battery of standard instruments in our lab's studies. Some of these studies were about determinism's relation to free will and moral responsibility. To foreshadow, numeracy was related to free will judgments and comprehension questions[4] and there was some evidence that the abstractness and the concreteness of the scenarios interacted with numeracy's relation to understanding the comprehension question and free will judgments. Below, we review two of these preliminary studies.

The first set of data comes from an unreported data set from a small sample study in our lab ($N = 36$). In this study, participants received a standard scenario in the experimental study of compatibilist intuitions based on scenarios used by Nahmias et al. (2007). Call this scenario the *concrete* scenario.

> Most respected psychologists are convinced that eventually we will figure out exactly how all of our decisions and actions are entirely caused. For instance, they think that whenever we are trying to decide what to do, the decision we end up making is completely caused by the specific thoughts, desires, and plans occurring in our minds. The psychologists are also convinced that these thoughts, desires, and plans are completely caused by our current situation and the earlier events in our lives, and that these earlier events were also completely caused by even earlier events, eventually going all the way back to events that occurred before we were born.
>
> So, once specific earlier events have occurred in a person's life, these events will definitely cause specific later events to occur. For example, please imagine that one day a person named John decides to kill his wife so that he can marry his lover, and he does it. Once the specific thoughts, desires, and plans occur in John's mind, they will definitely cause his decision to kill his wife.
>
> Assume the psychologists are right that events that occurred before John was born definitely caused his decision to kill his wife. Please rate to what degree you agree with the following statements.

After reading these paragraphs, participants were given the following comprehension question.

> If the psychologists are right, John would do the same thing if the world were recreated with the same events and circumstances.
>
> (Yes/No)

After answering the comprehension question, participants read the following instructions and responded to these free will prompts.

Assume the psychologists are right. Please indicate your agreement with the following statements (1 = strongly disagree, 7 = strongly agree):

1. John decided to kill his wife of his own free will.
2. John's killing of his wife was "up to him."
3. John is morally responsible for killing his wife.

Participants also responded to the seven-item Berlin Numeracy test (Cokely et al., 2012) (see also (Schwartz, Woloshin, Black, & Welch, 1997)). The three free will items had strong internal reliability (Cronbach's alpha = 92), so we used the mean of responses in all analyses ($M = 5.49$, $SD = 1.72$). Comprehension was negatively, but not significantly, related to free will judgments ($r = -.24$, $p = .16$). However, numeracy was negatively and significantly related to comprehension ($r = -.39$, $p = .02$) and positively, but not significantly, related to free will judgments ($r = .19$, $p = .26$).

The second set of data comes from a published study (Feltz, 2015b). In this instance, we used scenarios that involved both abstract and concrete cases. Concrete deterministic cases are like the scenario described above—people are asked to make judgments about specific actions (e.g., John killing his wife). For abstract deterministic cases, that kind of contextualizing information is omitted, and participants are only asked to judge whether a person could be free in a deterministic universe (e.g., they only receive the description in the first paragraph of the concrete case, and the questions are not about any specific individual). In the Feltz (2015b) study, participants were given the same concrete scenario above. A separate group of participants answered an *abstract* version of the concrete scenario. The abstract scenario was the same as concrete except that the second paragraph was deleted and all references to Jim killing his wife were moved from the third paragraph. Participants responded to similar prompts, except they were asked about whether "a person" could be free, morally responsible, or have actions up to them. Participants also completed a four-item measure of numeracy.

The purpose of the Feltz (2015b) study was to estimate how strongly related one's judgments are about whether one is actually free and morally responsible in our world versus whether one *would* be free and morally responsible if some conditions (e.g., determinism) were true. As such, Feltz (2015b) adapted items from the FAD-Plus scale that measures free will related beliefs (Paulhus & Carey, 2011). The FAD-Plus scale has four subscales—belief in free will, belief in scientific determinism, belief in fatalistic determinism, and belief in unpredictability. The subscales most relevant for our purposes were the free will and scientific determinism subscales. Higher scores on the free will subscale indicated a stronger belief that John in the concrete scenario or a person in the abstract scenario acted freely. Higher scores on the scientific determinism subscale indicated a stronger belief that the actions in the relevant universe were determined.

Replicating the basic relations in the unpublished study reported above, numeracy was negatively, but nonsignificantly, related to ratings of Scientific Determinism ($r = -.16$, $p = .12$) and Free Will ($r = -.08$, $p = .43$) in the Concrete Scenario ($N = 98$). For the Abstract Scenario ($N = 101$), numeracy was positively, but not significantly, related to Scientific Determinism ($r = .14$, $p = .18$), but negatively related to free will judgments ($r = -.27$, $p < .01$). Further analyses revealed that the concrete/abstract condition significantly interacted with numeracy with respect to the scientific determinism judgment, $t = 2.06$, $p = .04$, but no significant interaction for free will judgments was detected, $t = 1.08$, $p = .28$.

Each of these studies suggests that numeracy is related to compatibilist intuitions and judgments. However, neither of the studies was specifically designed to test relations with numeracy and each departed in important ways from the seminal cases used in the experimental philosophy of free will. The first study reported did not manipulate the abstract and concrete conditions and had limited power. The second study did not use traditional measures of free will and comprehension. In addition, both studies did not measure important aspects about compatibilist judgments, namely *bypassing* (Nahmias et al., 2007). Bypassing is the phenomenon where people misunderstand determinism as going around, or not involving, conscious agency. Most (if not all) compatibilists do not hold that determinism entails that one's conscious agency is bypassed. Rather, one's beliefs, desires, intentions are just one more element in the causal sequence that results in actions. If one understands determinism as precluding these types of mental states from playing a role in action, one misunderstands an important element of compatibilist approaches to free will's relation to determinism. To test whether people have incompatibilist intuitions, one needs to measure not only whether participants think the universe is determined but also that a person in that universe is not bypassed.

Rather than rely on existing data that are suggestive of the relations between numeracy and understanding key elements of compatibilist judgments, we set out to test our hypotheses in a sufficiently powered study. Here, we focus on the central theoretical constructs of the Framework for Skilled Decision Theory: numeracy, understanding, and free will judgments. First, based on past research and the Framework, we hypothesized the following model:

However, and critically, we hypothesized that the abstract and concrete scenarios would moderate these relations, consistent with patterns found in previous research. Namely, numeracy would be positively related to comprehension and negatively related to bypassing in the abstract case. However, in the concrete case, numeracy would be unrelated to comprehension, and positively related to free will judgments. We had no specific predictions about the relation of bypassing to numeracy since we did not have evidence for that relation in past studies. However, it stands to reason that numeracy would be negatively related to bypassing in the abstract but not in the concrete condition. We set out to test these relations.

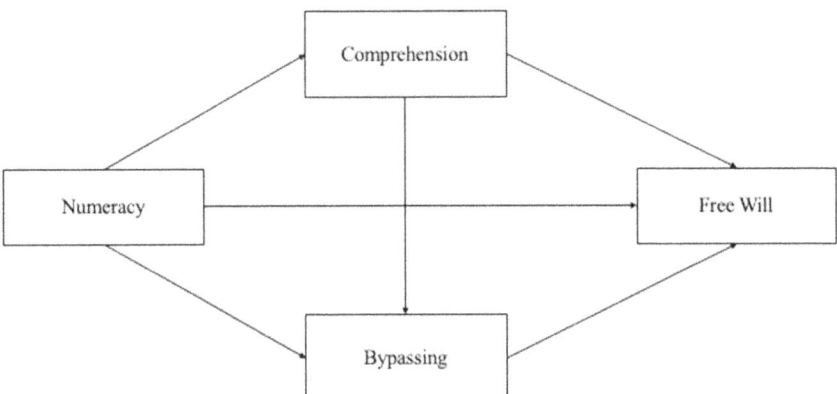

Figure 10.2 The hypothesized model for the understanding components of skilled decisions about free will.

Experiment

Participants

711 participants were recruited from a state university's undergraduate subjects pool. 570 were female (73 percent) and two declined to report sex. The average age was 18.68, ($SD = 1.74$, $range = 18\text{-}47$).

Materials

Participants were randomly assigned two one of two conditions: the abstract condition ($N = 354$) or the concrete condition ($N = 357$). Each condition adopted describing determinism in terms of complete causation. In the concrete condition, participants received the concrete scenario described above (Nahmias et al., 2007). Those in the abstract condition read the following abstract scenario adopted from (Nichols & Knobe, 2007):

> Imagine a universe (Universe A) in which everything that happens is completely caused by whatever happened before it. This is true from the very beginning of the universe, so what happened in the beginning of the universe caused what happened next, and so on right up until the present. For example, one day John decided to have French Fries at lunch. Like everything else, this decision was completely caused by what happened before it. So, if everything in this universe was exactly the same up until John made his decision, then it had to happen that John would decide to have French Fries.

After reading one of these scenarios, participants answered the following series of questions in order that were adopted from Nahmias et al. (2007). The questions were phrased concretely (asking specifically about John killing his wife) or abstractly (asking about some person who exists in that universe). We made substitutions to reflect the different descriptions in the scenarios to match up with the abstract and concrete differences. The differences are reflected by brackets indicating the language used in the abstract scenario.

Comprehension Questions. Participants answered the following questions by responding "yes," "no," or "don't know."

1. Do you personally think that all of our decisions are ultimately caused by events occurring before our birth?
2. Regardless of how you answered question 1, [in Universe A], is it accurate to say that if the universe were recreated in exactly the same way, people would make all the same decisions?
3. [In Universe A], all events are completely caused by what happens before them.

4. [In Universe A], all events in the universe could be perfectly predicted from events that happened in the past.
5. [In Universe A], once the events in the past happened, they completely caused all of John's actions.

Bypassing Questions. Participants responded to the following questions on a six-point scale (1 = strongly disagree, 6 = strongly agree). Substitutions had to be made in the abstract case to not reference any particular individual or action. Those changes are represented in brackets.

1. [In Universe A], John's [a person's] decision to steal the necklace has no effect on what he ends up doing.
2. [In Universe A], what John [a person] wants has no effect on what he ends up doing.
3. [In Universe A], what John [a person] believes has no effect on what he ends up doing.
4. [In Universe A], John [a person] has no control over what he does.

Free Will Questions. Participants answered the following questions on a six-point scale (1 = strongly disagree, 6 = strongly agree). Brackets indicate language used for the abstract scenario.

1. John is [In Universe A, it is possible for a person to be] fully morally responsible for killing his wife and children.
2. [In Universe A] It is possible for John [a person] to have free will.
3. [In Universe A], John [a person] deserves to be blamed for killing his wife and children.

Results

The primary goal was to test the hypothesized path model. First, a set of reliability analyses was conducted on the Comprehension, Bypassing, and Free will questions for the full data set. Each had strong internal reliability: Comprehension *Cronbach's alpha* = .84, Bypassing *Cronbach's alpha* = .81, Free Will *Cronbach's alpha* = 81. Because of the strong internal reliability, composite scores were calculated for each set of variables. The total correct answers for the comprehension questions were used (total of 2–5). The means were used for both Bypassing and Free Will questions.

Second, a set of *t-tests* were conducted to estimate differences with Bypassing, Free Will, and Comprehension questions as a function of the concrete/abstract condition. There was a moderately sized difference between the concrete ($M = 1.23$, $SD = 1.37$) and abstract ($M = 2.29$, $SD = 1.44$) conditions for the Comprehension questions $t(1, 709) = 10.1$, $p < .001$, $d = 0.76$. For the Bypassing question, there as a moderately sized difference between concrete ($M = 2.57$, $SD = 1.11$) and abstract ($M = 3.29$, $SD = 1.22$)

conditions, $t(1, 709) = 8.25$, $p < .001$, $d = 0.62$. There was a large difference between concrete ($M = 4.91$, $SD = 0.91$) and abstract ($M = 3.66$, $SD = 1.22$) conditions for free will judgments $t(1, 709) = 15.41$, $p < .01$, $d = 1.16$. Hence, the manipulation of concrete and abstract scenarios replicated previous research and had the predicted effects on judgments. Overall, there was moderate agreement that the person in the concrete scenario was free and morally responsible. However, there was ambivalence on average about whether a person in the abstract scenario was free and morally responsible.

Third, we wanted to estimate the relations among the dependent variables. We report zero-order correlations for the abstract and concrete conditions separately in Table 10.1.

The correlations suggested that there was an interaction among the variables as a function of being in the concrete and abstract conditions. We formally tested these interactions in a two-group path model. In this case, the two groups were those in the abstract and concrete condition. To estimate the interaction in a path model, two models are compared—a fully unconstrained model that allowed all paths to vary between the two groups and a constrained model that did not allow paths to vary as a function of being in different groups. The two models are compared with respect to model fit. If the two models' fit are significantly different between the two groups, that suggests there is an interaction with respect to some elements in the model (i.e., at least one of the paths varied as a function of the group membership). Given a significant difference between models, one can select which paths are likely to be invariant between the two groups and reassess model fit. Through this process, interactions can be identified with the paths that significantly vary between the two models—and lack of interactions indicated by those paths that do not vary significantly between the two models.

Path analyses were conducted with the Lavaan (Rosseel, 2012) and piecewiseSem (Lefcheck, 2016) packages in R (Team, 2018). To test for the interactions, we created saturated path models (all paths were identified). One model specified the paths to be constrained (i.e., the same in both models) and the other model allowed path estimates to vary. Then, the two models were compared to determine if the unconstrained model and constrained model fit the data differently. If they fit the data differently, that suggests that the grouping condition (i.e., abstract/concrete) interacted with at least some of the paths of in the model.

Table 10.1 Correlations for Comprehension, Bypassing, Free Will, and Numeracy separated by condition. Note: ^ $p < .1$, ** $p < .01$.

	Concrete			Abstract		
	Comprehend	Bypassing	Free Will	Comprehend	Bypassing	Free Will
Comprehend						
Bypassing	-.08			.18**		
Free Will	.03	-.25**		-.24**	-.45**	
Numeracy	.01	-.15**	.17**	.21**	-.04	-.09^

The two models were significantly different using the χ^2 difference test: χ^2 = 319.26, p <.01, suggesting that some of the path estimates in the model were different between concrete and abstract conditions. However, the overall difference in fit does not identify which paths varied between the grouping conditions. To explore the possible interactions, we used local estimation of each path to test for invariance in the relations (invariance would suggest no moderation). The only relation that was invariant between the two models was numeracy's relation to Bypassing (p = .48). Given this, we manually constrained that relation between the two conditions and allowed the other relations to vary as a function of abstract/concrete conditions. There was no observed difference between the newly constrained model and the unconstrained model (see Figure 10.3): χ^2 = 0.5, p =.48 suggesting that the only path that did not vary was the path from numeracy to bypassing. The overall model with the numeracy to bypassing relations constrained and abstract and concrete conditions as grouping variables had acceptable fit to the data: χ^2 (1) =.5, p = 48, $RMSEA$ = 0, 90% CI = 0 -.12, p =.64, CFI = 1, TLI = 1.

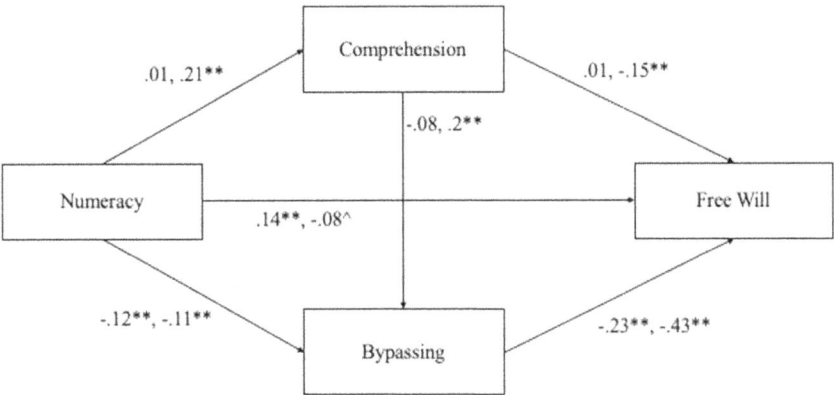

Figure 10.3 Path model representing the paths for the two groups. The first value represents the concrete standardized estimates, and the second value represents the abstract standardized estimate. ^ p <.1, ** p <.01.

Discussion

Replicating previous work, we found a large difference between concrete and abstract cases. Additionally, bypassing was consistently related to lowered free will and moral responsibility judgments, and this effect was consistent (even if moderated) between abstract and concrete conditions. Our focus was identifying individual differences for these scenarios based on numeracy, which we found. Those who were more numerate also thought there was less bypassing than those who were less numerate, and this relation was not significantly moderated by condition. Numeracy was related to increased comprehension of deterministic elements of the scenarios, but only in the abstract condition. There was also a qualitative shift in numeracy's relation to free will judgments—numeracy was positively related to free will judgment in the concrete condition but negatively related in the abstract condition. Finally, comprehension of deterministic elements of scenarios was only significantly related to bypassing and free will judgments in the concrete condition.

One implication of these data is that there is a new individual difference that seems to be important to free will related judgments—numeracy. Unlike previous individual differences (e.g., extraversion), numeracy was related to free will and comprehension and bypassing judgments in addition to free will judgments, at least in some conditions. These results add to the growing body of evidence of individual differences in free will judgments and highlight the potential risk of referring to "the folk" as a monolithic entity.

Beyond documenting that free will judgments are multiply determined by differences in general skills, domain specific understanding, and general attitudes, these data may allow some ways to determine which sets of intuitions are to be preferred. One limitation of previous research on individual differences in free will judgments is that it was difficult to make arguments about which sets of intuitions to prefer. For example, the large body of research suggesting that extraversion is related to compatibilist judgments does not in and of itself offer a way to prefer one set of intuitions over another. Extraversion appears to be an extraneous feature with respect to the truth of free will judgments (at least for some purposes). It is difficult, given the current technology and techniques in philosophy, to determine which sets of contents are true, or are more likely to be true (Feltz & Cokely, 2012).

However, numeracy could be importantly related to the truth of the content of intuitions. First, as we have already mentioned, numeracy is generally related to higher quality decisions across a host of different circumstances. For these reasons, we would have some justification to think that numeracy would be related to better judgments about free will, at least for those who are not free will experts. Those who are more numerate are better able to understand and process the information that they are provided and make higher quality judgments given that information. So, in general, we should expect that those nonexperts who are more numerate would pay attention to, process, and understand relevant information that would then produce a higher quality judgment.

In this case, we have some evidence that those who are more numerate understand relevant information better than those who are less numerate, at least in some instances. Those who were more numerate were less likely to think that people are bypassed in both the abstract and concrete conditions. This suggests that they are more likely to understand determinism in a way that is consistent with compatibilist understandings of determinism. Moreover, those who were more numerate understood the deterministic elements of the scenario better in the abstract case and not in the concrete case. While it is speculative, one can conjecture that there is something about the concrete case that is inhibiting some people (including some of the more numerate) from understanding those key aspects (see below). This raises important questions about how representative the concrete scenario is for measuring attitudes about free will and moral responsibility (Feltz & Cokely, 2019).[5] Addressing which measures are appropriate, and how we would know, are beyond the scope of this paper. However, as our study helps illustrate, more work needs to be done to understand the measurement properties of commonly used instruments in experimental philosophy.

While we have no direct evidence, these data are consistent with various views about the abstract/concrete effects on free will judgments. One view, the affective biasing view, suggests that people normally have an incompatibilist view of freedom and moral responsibility. However, in some instances, some contextual features can get in the way of the application of that normally incompatibilist view (Nichols & Knobe, 2007). In this case, we are not sure that affect is what interferes with the application of one's incompatibilist view. Rather, there is something about the concrete scenario that hinders people from *understanding* deterministic elements.[6] Perhaps participants given some contextualizing information feel as if they are supposed to do something with that additional information, or perhaps participants import indeterministic elements in evaluating those scenarios (Nadelhoffer et al., 2020). After all, participants might think that they are provided with all the contextualizing information *for a reason*. Those who are more numerate are often better at integrating that kind of contextualizing information to make decisions than those who are less numerate (Cokely & Feltz, 2014; Cokely et al., 2018; Petrova et al., 2017; Ybarra et al., 2018). This explanation could explain why the more numerate are better at the comprehension question in the abstract compared to the concrete case. Or, perhaps some participants do not think that the determined elements of the scenario are central to the task they are asked to complete. Our data are silent on these (and other) potential explanations for the data. Future work, potentially using different methodologies (e.g., talk aloud and protocol analysis), would be required to decide among them.

There are many shortcomings associated with these data—and many possible ways that a compatibilist could respond to these data suggesting that those who are most likely to interpret information correctly are less likely to be compatibilist. First, the data collected in the path model were only from US undergraduates. Second, we only used one set of materials to test these relations. Finally, some of the relations were relatively small. But the smallness of the effects should be contextualized since we know next to nothing about the reliability of the instruments used. Even given these shortcomings, these data reinforce that the general individual differences approach to free will judgments (and philosophical judgments in general) can be illuminating and hopefully point the way to a fuller understanding of everyday judgments about freedom and moral responsibility.

Notes

1   Intuitions have been defined in a number of different ways (Feltz & Bishop, 2010). Here, all we mean by intuitions are the kinds of reactions that people have to philosophically relevant scenarios like the ones reported in this chapter.
2   Some evidence to the contrary is the result from the PhilPapers survey project that suggested that about 60 percent of professional philosophers endorse compatibilism

(Bourget & Chalmers, 2014). Perhaps one explanation for some of the differences between the PhilPapers study and the Shulz et al study is the use of a verified test of free will expertise rather than credentials of being a philosopher. This difference could potentially be important, especially given the domain specialization in philosophy (see (Cokely & Feltz, 2014)).

3   Before using numeracy, we routinely included the cognitive reflection task (CRT) in our studies (Frederick, 2005). We rarely found reliable relations between CRT and free will related judgments and attitudes. However, the effect sizes are consistent with some other work suggesting CRT might be related to some free will judgments (Hannikainen et al., 2019).

4   With notable few exceptions, past research has largely treated comprehension questions for determinism as *screening* questions for compatibilist judgments (Feltz, Perez, & Harris, 2012). That is, those who did not answer those comprehension questions correctly were excluded from subsequent analyses. The justification is that the intuitions of those who did not think that the action in the scenarios were determined could not have compatibilist intuitions. However, some researchers have attempted to understand the role that comprehension plays in understanding the comprehension questions see (Cokely & Feltz, 2010; Nadelhoffer, Rose, Buckwalter, & Nichols, 2020).

5   Robert Kane (personal communication) once told us that he did not think that scenarios describing determinism were good, representative measures of determinism's relation to free will. He thought that any number of elements in those kinds of scenarios could interfere with pure measures of people's attitudes about determinism. Rather, he thought that the cleanest measurement would be simply to ask people if free will and moral responsibility are compatible with determinism. Our data support Kane's view to some extent.

6   This view is consistent with the general reporting of high comprehension failures for free will judgments set in deterministic universes (Feltz, Perez, et al., 2012). As we have studied elsewhere, understanding is often a necessary (and sometimes sufficient) element in better decisions (Cokely & Feltz, 2014; Feltz, 2015a; Feltz & Cokely, 2016, 2017; S. Feltz & Feltz, 2019a, 2019b; Mahmoud-Elhaj, Tanner, Sabatini, & Feltz, 2020; Offer-Westort, Feltz, Bruskotter, & Vucetich, 2020; Ybarra, Allan, Garcia-Retamero, Feltz, & Cokely, 2018).

References

Alexander, J., & Weinberg, J. M. (2007). Analytic epistemology and experimental philosophy. *Philosophy Compass, 2,* 56–80.

Banks, J., & Oldfield, Z. (2007). Understanding pensions: Cognitive function, numerical ability and retirement saving. *Fiscal Studies, 38,* 143–70.

Baron, J. (2008). *Thinking and Deciding,* 4th Edition. New York: Cambridge University Press.

Beazley, K. (1984). Education in Western Australia: Report of the committee of inquiry into education in Western Australia. *Education Department of Western Australia.* https://scpp.esrc.unimelb.edu.au/bib/P00001807.htm

Bishop, J. (1992). Removing cultural barriers to numeracy. In *Proceedings of the Australian Council for Adult Literacy Conference. The Right to Literacy: The Rhetoric, the Romance, the Reality* (pp. 147–58). Sydney: Australian Council for Adult Literacy.

Bourget, D., & Chalmers, D. (2014). What do philosophers believe? *Philosophical Studies, 170*, 465–500.

Coben, D. (2000). Numeracy, mathematics, and adult learning. In I. Gal (Ed.), *Adult Numeracy Development: Theory, Research, Practice* (pp. 33–50). Cresskill: Hampton Press.

Cockroft, W., & Birtain, G. (1982). *Mathematic Counts*: HM Stationary Office. http://www.educationengland.org.uk/documents/cockcroft/cockcroft1982.html

Cokely, E. T., & Feltz, A. (2010). Questioning the free will comprehension question. In S. Ohlsson & R. Catrambone (Eds.), *Proceedings of the 32nd Annual Conference of the Cognitive Science Society*. Austin, TX: Cognitive Science Society.

Cokely, E. T., & Feltz, A. (2014). Expert intuition. In L. Osbeck & B. Held (Eds.), *Rational Intuition* (pp. 213–38). Cambridge: Cambridge University Press.

Cokely, E. T., Galesic, M., Schulz, E., Ghazal, S., & Garcia-Retamero, R. (2012). Measuring risk literacy: The Berlin Numeracy Test. *Judgment and Decision Making, 7*(1), 25–47. Retrieved from <go to isi>://WOS:000300401900003

Cokely, E. T., Feltz, A., Ghazal, S., Allan, J., Petrova, D., & Garcia-Retamero, R. (2018). Skilled decision theory: From intelligence to numeracy and expertise. In A. Ericsson, R. Hoffman, A. Kozbelt, & A. Williams (Eds.), *Cambridge Handbook of Expertise and Expert Performance* (pp. 476–505). Cambridge: Cambridge University Press.

Ericsson, K. A., Prietula, M. J., & Cokely, E. T. (2007). The making of an expert. *Harvard Business Review, 85*(7–8), 114–193.

Feltz, A. (2015a). Ethical information transparency and sexually transmitted diseases. *Current HIV Research, 13*, 421–31.

Feltz, A. (2015b). Experimental philosophy of actual and counterfactual free will intuitions. *Consciousness and Cognition, 36*, 113–30.

Feltz, A., & Bishop, M. (2010). The proper role of intuitions in epistemology. In M. Milkowski & K. Talmont-Kaminiski (Eds.), *Beyond Description: Naturalism and Normativity* (pp. 101–22). London: College Publications.

Feltz, A., & Cokely, E. T. (2009). Do judgments about freedom and responsibility depend on who you are? Personality differences in intuitions about compatibilism and incompatibilism. *Consciousness and Cognition, 18*(1), 342–50.

Feltz, A., & Cokely, E. T. (2012). The philosophical personality argument. *Philosophical Studies, 161*(2), 227–46.

Feltz, A., & Cova, F. (2014). Moral responsibility and free will: A meta-analysis. *Consciousness and Cognition, 30*, 234–46. doi:10.1016/j.concog.2014.08.012

Feltz, A., & Cokely, E. T. (2016). Personality and philosophical bias. In J. Sytsma & W. Buckwalter (Eds.), *A Companion to Experimental Philosophy* (pp. 578–89). New York: Wiley-Blackwell.

Feltz, A., & Cokely, E. T. (2017). Informing ethical decision making. In K. Rommelfanger & L. S. Johnson (Eds.), *Handbook of Neuroethics* (pp. 314–27). New York: Routledge.

Feltz, A., & Cokely, E. T. (2019). Extraversion and compatibilist intuitions: A ten-year retrospective and meta-analysis. *Philosophical Psychology, 32*, 388–403.

Feltz, S., & Feltz, A. (2019a). Consumer accuracy at identifying plant-based and animal-based milk products. *Food Ethics, 4*, 85–112.

Feltz, S., & Feltz, A. (2019b). The Knowlege of Animal as Food Scale. *Human-animal Interaction Bulletin, 7*, 19–45.

Feltz, A., Harris, M., & Perez, A. (2012). Perspective in intentional action attribution. *Philosophical Psychology, 25*, 335–50.

Feltz, A., Perez, A., & Harris, M. (2012). Free will, causes, and decisions individual differences in written reports. *Journal of Consciousness Studies, 19* (9–10), 166–89.

Frederick, S. (2005). Cognitive reflection and decision making. *Journal of Economic Perspectives, 19*(4), 25–42.

Gal, I. (1995). Statistical tools and statistical literacy: The case of the average. *Teaching Statistics, 17,* 97–9.

Garcia-Retamero, R., & Cokely, E. T. (2013). Communicating health risks with visual aids. *Current Directions in Psychological Science, 22,* 392–9.

Garcia-Retamero, R., & Cokely, E. (2017). Designing visual aids that promote risk literacy: A systematic review of health research and evidence-based design heuristics. *Human Factors, 59,* 582–627.

Ginsburg, L., Manly, M., & Schmitt, M. (2006). The components of numeracy. In *NCSALL Occasional Paper.* Cambridge: National Center for the Study of Adult Literacy and Learning.

Golbeck, A., Ahlers-Schmidt, C., Paschal, A., & Dismuke, S. (2005). A definition and operational framework for health numeracy. *American Journal of Preventive Medicine, 29,* 375–6.

Hannikainen, I. R., Machery, E., Rose, D., Stich, S., Olivola, C. Y., Sousa, P., ... Zhu, J. (2019). For whom does determinism undermine moral responsibility? Surveying the conditions for free will across cultures. *Frontiers in Psychology, 10,* 2428. doi:10.3389/fpsyg.2019.02428

Horvarth, J. (2010). How (not) to react to experimental philosophy. *Philosophical Psychology, 23,* 448–80.

John, O. P., & Srivastava, S. (1999). The big five trait taxonomy: History, measurement, and theoretical perspectives. In L. A. Pervin & O. P. John (Eds.), *Handbook of Personality: Theory and Research* (pp. 102–38). Guilford Press.

Kahan, D. M., Peters, E., Wittlin, M., Slovic, P., Ouellette, L. L., Braman, D., & Mandel, G. (2012). The polarizing impact of science literacy and numeracy on perceived climate change risks. *Nature Climate Change, 2*(10), 732–5.

Lefcheck, J. (2016). PiecewiseSEM: Piecewise structural equation modeling in R for ecology, evolution, and systematics. *Methods in Ecology and Evolution, 7,* 573–9.

Lipkus, I. M., & Peters, E. (2009). Understanding the role of numeracy in health: Proposed theoretical framework and practical insights. *Health Education & Behavior, 36*(6), 1065–81.

Lusardi, A. (2012). Numeracy, financial literacy, and financial decision-making (No. w17821). *National Bureau of Economic Research.*

Machery, E., Mallon, R., Nichols, S., & Stich, S. P. (2004). Semantics, cross-cultural style. *Cognition, 92*(3), B1–B12.

Mahmoud-Elhaj, D., Tanner, B., Sabatini, D., & Feltz, A. (2020). Measuring objective knowledge of potable recycled water. *Journal of Community Psychology, 48*(6), 2033–52.

Nadelhoffer, T., Rose, D., Buckwalter, W., & Nichols, S. (2020) Natural compatibilism, indeterminism, and intrusive metaphysics. *Cognitive Science, 44*:8, e12873

Nahmias, E., Morris, S., Nadelhoffer, T., & Turner, J. (2005). Surveying freedom: Folk intuitions about free will and moral responsibility. *Philosophical Psychology, 18*(5), 561–84.

Nahmias, E., Morris, S., Nadelhoffer, T., & Turner, J. (2006). Is incompatibilism intuitive? *Philosophy and Phenomenological Research, 73*(1), 28–53.

Nahmias, E., Coates, D., & Kvaran, T. (2007). Free will, moral responsibility, and mechanism: Experiments on folk intuitions. *Philosophy and the Empirical*, *31*, 214–42.

Nahmias, E., & Murray, D. (2010). Experimental philosophy on free will: An error theory for incompatibilist intuitions. In J. A. Aguilar, A. Buckareff, & K. Frankish (Eds.), *New Waves in Philosophy of Action* (pp. 189–215). New York: Palgrave MacMillan.

Nichols, S. (2007). The rise of compatibilism: A case study in the quantitative history of philosophy. *Midwest Studies in Philosophy*, *31*, 260–70.

Nichols, S., & Knobe, J. (2007). Moral responsibility and determinism: The cognitive science of folk intuitions. *Nous*, *41*(4), 663–85.

Offer-Westort, T., Feltz, A., Bruskotter, J., & Vucetich, J. (2020). What is an endangered species? Judgments about acceptable risk. *Environmental Research Letters*, *15*, 014010.

Paulhus, D. L., & Carey, J. M. (2011). The FAD-Plus: Measuring lay beliefs regarding free will and related constructs. *Journal of Personality Assessment*, *93*(1), 96–104.

Peters, E. (2012). Beyond comprehension: The role of numeracy in judgments and decisions. *Current Directions in Psychological Science*, *21*, 31–5.

Peters, E., Vastfjall, D., Slovic, P., Mertz, C. K., Mazzocco, K., & Dickert, S. (2006). Numeracy and decision making. *Psychological Science*, *17*(5), 407–13. doi:10.1111/j.1467-9280.2006.01720.x

Petrova, D., Garcia-Retamero, R., & Cokely, E. T. (2015). Understanding the harms and benefits of cancer screening: A model of factors that shape informed decision making. *Medical Decision Making*, *35*(7), 847–58.

Petrova, D., Garcia-Retamero, R., Catena, A., Cokely, E., Carrasco, A. H., Moreno, A. A., & Hernandez, J. A. R. (2017). Numeracy predicts risk of pre-hospital decision delay: A retrospective study of acute coronary syndrome survival. *Annals of Behavioral Medicine*, *51*(2), 292–306.

Reyna, V. F., Nelson, W., Han, P., & Dieckmann, N. (2009). How numeracy influences risk comprehension in medical decision making. *Psychological Bulletin*, *135*, 943–73.

Rosseel, Y. (2012). Lavaan: An R package for structural equation modeling. *Journal of Statistical Software*, *48*, 1–36.

Schulz, E., Cokely, E. T., & Feltz, A. (2011). Persistent bias in expert judgments about free will and moral responsibility: A test of the expertise defense. *Consciousness and Cognition*, *20*(4), 1722–31.

Schwartz, L. M., Woloshin, S., Black, W. C., & Welch, H. G. (1997). The role of numeracy in understanding the benefit of screening mammography. *Annals of Internal Medicine*, *127*(11), 966–72.

Sinnott-Armstrong, W. (2008). Abstract + concrete = paradox? In J. Knobe & S. Nichols (Eds.), *Experimental Philosophy* (pp. 209–230). Oxford: Oxford University Press.

Steen, L. (1990). *On the Shoulders of Giants: New Approaches to Numeracy*. Washington, DC: The National Academic Press.

Steen, L. (2001). Mathematics and numeracy: Two literacies, one language. *The Mathematics Educator*, *6*, 10–16.

Stich, S., & Tobia, K. (2016). Experimental philosophy and the philosophical tradition. In J. Sytsma & W. Buckwalter (Eds.), *A Companion to Experimental Philosophy* (pp. 3–21). Malden: John Wiley & Sons.

Swain, S., Alexander, J., & Weinberg, J. (2008). The instability of philosophical intuitions: Running hot and cold on Truetemp (Keith Lehrer). *Philosophy and Phenomenological Research*, *76*(1), 138–55.

Team, R. C. (2018). R: A language and environment for statistical computing. In *R Foundation for Statistical Computing*. Vienna, Australia.

Weigel, C. (2013). Experimental evidence for free will revisionism. *Philosophical Explorations, 16*(1), 31–43.

Weinberg, J., Nichols, S., & Stich, S. P. (2001). Normativity and epistemic intuitions. *Philosophical Topics, 29*, 429–60.

Ybarra, V., Allan, J., Garcia-Retamero, R., Feltz, A., & Cokely, E. (2018). *Rethinking the Bias Blind Spot: Numerate People Are Less Biased and They Know It*. Paper presented at the Society for Judgment and Decision Making, New Orleans.

Index

abstract/abstraction 115, 176
   conditions 190, 192–6
   degree of 176
   judgments 55
   questions 104, 105
   scenario 186, 188–94
action
   and deep self 71
   effect 167–72, 174, 176, 179–82
   freedom of 92, 96, 98, 99, 106, 108, 111 n.15, 112 n.26
   and inaction 168–70, 173
   preparation 13, 15
actus reus 117
Adams, R. M. 48, 50, 51
agency 115, 116, 121, 191
aggregate responsibility scores 73, 76–8, 81, 83–5, 88
alternative possibilities 145, 148, 164 n.14, 169
ANOVA 73, 77, 81, 83, 118, 121–4
automatism 116, 119, 121, 122, 125

Bad Attitudes and Bad Affective States 50–1
beliefs 28–9
   homosexuality 57
   immoral 52
   irrational 52
   objectionable 54
Berlin Numeracy test 189
Black Sheep Effect 34
blame
   evolution of 32–3
   judgments 38, 150, 167, 181
   and moral condemnation 32–3
   step-by-step process 182
   theory of 31–2
   of victims 170–2, 182
Blame Efficiency Hypothesis 27–8, 31–7
Blame for Ignorance 53–4

blameworthy/blameworthiness 37, 46–54, 56–8, 86, 94–95, 97, 100, 106, 110, 111 n.13, 116–17, 124–6, 148–50, 153, 158, 159, 167, 168, 170–2, 174, 176, 178–82
blaming efficiently 33
bypassing 191, 195, 196
   correlations for 194
   questions 193–4
   scores 77, 78, 84

causal cognition 4, 171
causal judgments 167–70, 174, 176, 179–82
causation 99–109, 168–72, 174–6, 181, 182, 192
cognitive reflection task (CRT) 198 n.3
compatibilism/compatibilists 2–5, 14, 65, 69, 70, 86–7, 92, 94, 95, 99–103, 105–10, 126 n.3, 134, 144, 146, 147, 149, 158, 161, 163 n.8, 163 n.8, 185–91, 196, 197
compatibilist libertarianism 110 n.6
comprehension 190, 191, 193, 196
   checks 73, 76, 81, 83, 89 n.6, 94, 95, 104, 106, 111 n.12, 136
   correlations for 194
   question 188, 189, 192–3, 197, 198 n.4
concrete
   condition 190–6
   questions 104, 105
   scenarios 176, 189–92, 194, 196, 197
conditional externalism 132
conscious desire 122
control 46
   attributions of 54–6
   and blameworthiness 57
   case 67, 72–5, 77–87, 89
   condition 29, 57, 77, 78, 83, 144–7
   for moral responsibility 46–8
Control (M-/D-) condition 83

correlations 78, 84
correspondence bias 18–21
counterfactual
    questions 107, 182
    thinking 15, 169–71
counterfactual intervener (CI) 96, 97, 105
criminal law 4, 115–18, 122, 125

Deep Self 71
    Concordance model 71, 86
    Provenance hypothesis 71–4, 78, 84, 87
    scores 71, 77–9, 84, 85
derivative moral responsibility 144–6, 148
desert 72, 73, 76, 77, 81, 92, 110, 116, 126 n.1, 132, 136, 137
determinism 2, 3, 14–16, 18, 21, 65–70, 75–80, 84, 87, 89 n.3, 92, 94, 95, 99, 103, 104, 106–9, 140 n.6, 163 n.8, 185–8, 190–2, 196, 198 n.5
Deterministic (M-/D+), Good 80–1
diminished responsibility 119–20
direct manipulation arguments 66
direct moral responsibility 132, 144–50, 153, 158, 161, 164 n.16
distal mitigation 120
Don Corleone Principle, The 35
dualism 15, 16, 18
Dukakis, M. 45–6
duress 119
dyadic morality 171

emotion 21
    attributions of 58
    Dukakis and 45
    regulation 57–8
epistemic condition 145, 162 n.6
error management 35–7
event-focused moral judgments 124
Excuses, Free Will, and Responsibility 118–22
experimental philosophy
    and hard-line response 67
    and soft-line retort 67–9
expertise 187, 198 n.2
extraversion 186, 187, 196

FAD-Plus scale 190
Feltz, A. 67, 190

folk, the 38, 67, 85, 87, 105, 111 n.24, 117, 125, 126, 126 n.3, 143, 144, 146, 147, 149, 160, 161, 185, 186, 196
Frankfurt, H. G. 131, 132, 134, 138, 139 n.1, 140 n.7, 144, 146
freedom 111 n.24
    ability 96–7
    abstract questions 104
    actual sequence (AS) scenario 94, 95, 104, 106, 107
    compatibilists 92, 99, 100, 103
    counterfactual intervener (CI) scenario 96, 105–7, 109
    degrees of 97–8
    deny 104
    determination and causation 99, 102–4, 107–9
    endorse 104
    hard determinists about 92
    hypotheses 106–9
    incompatibilists 99, 101, 103
    kinds of 97–102
    and responsibility 92–4, 110 n.7, 185, 186, 197
    surveys 93–6, 103–6
freedom from 97, 98, 103
freedom from excuse 100, 111 n.14
freedom to 97, 98, 103, 111 n.17
Free Will and Determinism Scale (FAD) 14
Free Will and Determinism Scale (FWD) 14–15
free will belief 14–15, 125
    Blame Efficiency Hypothesis and 37
    correlations for 194
    and human responsibility 27
    and intention attribution 19
    manipulations 15–17, 65–6
    psychological research on 15–17
    and punishment 19–20
    and rewarding behavior 21
    and victim blaming 20–1
Free Will Inventory (FWI) 14–17
free will questions 193
Free Will Skill test 187

Goodwin, G. P. 50

Hannikainen, I. R. 94–7, 103–6, 110 n.12
hard determinism 92

hypothesized model 191, 193

Immoral, Irreligious, and Illogical Beliefs 51–2
immoral mental states 57
inaction 167–74, 176–82
incompatibilism/incompatibilists 3, 4, 14, 65, 66, 75, 85, 92, 99, 101–3, 105, 108, 109, 149, 185, 187, 191, 197
individual difference 14, 17, 21, 56, 58, 185–91, 195–7
intentionality 4, 14, 17, 20, 21, 29–32, 38, 47, 182
intention-hypothesis 17–19
internal condition 131, 132, 138
intuitive moral system 34

judgment
  on average 57, 186
  blame 38, 150, 167, 170, 181
  causal 167–70, 174, 176, 179–82
  folk 125, 186
  free will 70, 124, 125, 185, 186, 188–91, 194, 196, 197
  moral 1, 4, 5, 27–9, 32, 34–7, 48, 56, 60, 115, 116, 121, 122, 124, 125, 143, 150, 170, 171, 182

Kane, R. 198 n.5
knowingly 117, 123–5

libertarian free will 91–2, 110 n.6, 126 n.3
List, C. 110 n.6, 111 n.15, 111 n.20
locus of control 18

manipulation
  on attributions 71
  and control cases 67–8, 77–9
  Deep Self scores 85
  and indeterministic case 87
  on moral responsibility 72–4
manipulation arguments 65–6
  direct/transfer 66
  hard-line response 66, 67, 85
  indirect/explanatory 66
  soft-line response 66–9, 86
Mechanical Turk (MTurk) 119, 122, 126 n.8
mediation analysis 78, 84
Mele, A. R. 66, 69, 70, 79, 85–7

mens rea 4, 117, 118, 122, 125
mental state
  attributions of control 54–6
  blame and responsibility 46, 49–50, 54, 56–60
  challenge 48–50
  everyday blame for 50–4
  objections 59–60
meta-analysis 16, 31, 185, 186
metaphysics/science 93, 103
Modified and *Control* vignette 72
Modified manipulation case 67
Monroe, A. E. 15
moral
  condemnation 31–5, 124
  intuitionism 29–31, 145, 148
  judgments 1, 4, 5, 27–9, 32, 34–7, 48, 56, 58, 60, 115, 116, 122, 124, 125, 144, 150, 170, 171, 182
moral responsibility 3–5, 35, 132–3
  ability and responsibility ratings 152–6
  attribute 34, 58, 85, 87, 148
  Bad to Good 135–9
  and blameworthiness 37
  control and 46–8, 144
  Delivery 147, 149, 151–7, 163–4 n.14, 163 n.11
  determinism and 66
  Evaluation 146–9, 151–7, 163–4 n.14, 163 n.11
  Good to Bad 134–7, 139
  judgments of 121
  likelihood ratings 154, 157
  manipulation on 72–4
  mental state blame and 56–9
  motivated attributions of 29, 36–7
  normative/moral issue 93
  One Good Day 133–4
  Pre-manipulation Chuck 133
  ratings 73
  Sweet Jane 133

Nadelhoffer, T. 5 n.2, 15
Nahmias, E. 5 n.2, 17, 70
natural compatibilism 2–5, 144, 147, 149
negligence 117, 122–4, 164 n.16
no distal and no proximal excuses 120
normal case 83–4

No Self-Induced Inability condition 151–60
numeracy 185, 187–91, 194–6, 198 n.3

Original Long condition 151–60
Otto, M. C. 1–2
ought-implies-can principle 146
overdetermination 174, 181

partial compatibilism 92–3, 95, 96, 103
people attribute 4, 29, 31, 36, 50, 54, 58, 149, 169
Pereboom, D. 66–8, 89 n.5, 132, 138, 145
Pereboom's Four Cases arguments (Mele) 66, 67
personality trait extraversion 186
person-focused moral judgments 124
philosophers 1, 2, 4, 5, 5 n.2, 13, 14, 46, 48, 50, 51, 54, 56, 58–60, 91, 96, 111 n.24, 115, 126 n.1, 139 n.5, 144, 145, 160
philosophical question 45, 46, 58
philosophical relevant 148
praiseworthy 170
Principle of Alternative Possibilities (PAP) 143–50, 154, 157–61, 162 n.2, 163 n.8, 163 n.11, 163 n.13
psychological question 45, 46
psychologists 1, 4, 5, 5 n.1, 14, 15, 27, 47, 48, 51, 59, 60, 85, 133, 189
punishment 1, 2, 19–20, 32, 92
    crime and 28–32
    history of 27
    referees' 17
purposely 116, 123

radical reversal 134, 137, 139
rationalist theories 31–2
recklessness 117, 123, 124, 151, 158
reflective agnostics 86–7
reverse action effect 172, 179–82

rewarding behavior 21
Ryland case (Smith and Sher) 53

schadenfreude 50, 54
scientific determinism 190
self-serving bias 18–19
semi-compatibilism 4, 92–3, 95, 103
Sharp, F. C. 1–2
side-effect 30, 36, 37
skilled decision theory 187–91
Smith, A. 48, 50, 59, 60
Spitzley, J. 137–9, 140 n.11
Sripada, C. S. 50, 67–9, 71, 72, 89 n.2, 139

t-tests 193–4
Turri, J. 143–4, 146–53, 155, 158, 161, 163 n.8, 163 n.13

victim blaming 4, 19–21, 167, 170, 171, 176, 182
victims actions and inactions 172
    burglary vignette and perpetrator 173–4, 176–9
    causal and blameworthy 172–5
    joint-causation structure 175–6
    mean agreement 175, 177, 178, 180
    reverse action effect 179–81
vignette method 1–2, 18, 20, 21, 68, 72, 80, 81, 120, 148–61, 168–82, 185

Willemsen, P. 168, 169

Zygote argument 69–70, 85–6
    control case 74–5
    explanation-based version 75
    indeterministic case 74–5
    intuitions 74–80
    manipulation case 74–5
    methodology 70–1
    no difference version 75

www.ingramcontent.com/pod-product-compliance
Lightning Source LLC
Chambersburg PA
CBHW062227300426
44115CB00012BA/2245